Saul Bellow Against the Grain

Penn Studies in Contemporary American Fiction

A Series Edited by Emory Elliott, University of California, Riverside

Saul Bellow Against the Grain

Ellen Pifer

upp

UNIVERSITY OF PENNSYLVANIA PRESS   Philadelphia

Copyright © 1990 by the University of Pennsylvania Press
All rights reserved
Printed in the United States of America

Library of Congress Cataloging-in-Publication Data

Pifer, Ellen.
    Saul Bellow against the grain / Ellen Pifer.
        p. cm. — (Penn studies in contemporary American fiction)
    Includes bibliographical references.
    ISBN 0-8122-8203-5
    1. Bellow, Saul—Criticism and interpretation. I. Title. II. Series.
PS3503.E4488Z818 1990
813'.52—dc20   89-22596
                                                              CIP

To the memory of my mother
and with blessings for my daughter

"There is a fine Jewish proverb: Man thinks, God laughs. . . . But why does God laugh at the sight of man thinking? Because man thinks and the truth escapes him. Because the more men think, the more one man's thought diverges from another's. And finally, because man is never what he thinks he is."

Milan Kundera, *The Art of the Novel*

"Were I to choose an auspicious image for the new millennium, I would choose that one: the sudden agile leap of the poet-philosopher who raises himself above the weight of the world, showing that with all his gravity he has the secret of lightness, and that what many consider to be the vitality of the times—noisy, aggressive, revving and roaring—belongs to the realm of death."

Italo Calvino, *Six Memos for the Next Millennium*

Contents

Chapter 9
A Contemporary Fall: *More Die of Heartbreak*

Chapter 10
From Head Culture to Lead Culture: *The Dean's December*

Afterword: *A Theft* and Beyond

Notes

Index

Acknowledgments

Among the scholars and editors who have encouraged me in this project, Robert Alter, William Scheick, Blake Nevius, Gloria Cronin and Daniel Walden have been particularly kind and helpful. At the University of Delaware, many colleagues, students and friends extended their advice, support and good cheer. I am especially grateful to Carl Dawson, Steven Helmling (who generously lent me a number of valuable books from his library), Jerry Beasley and Patricia Hock (who drew my attention to several important references in *Henderson the Rain King*). To Drury Pifer, my husband and best critic, I owe the greatest debt of gratitude.

I wish to thank both the Delaware Humanities Forum and the University of Delaware for their financial support during the period in which this manuscript was written. In 1987–88, I held a Delaware Humanities Forum Research Fellowship; in 1986, a General University Research Grant. In addition, I am grateful to the University of Delaware for a College of Arts and Science Grant-in-Aid, which made it possible for me to participate in the First International Saul Bellow Conference, held at Haifa University, Haifa, Israel, in April 1987.

An earlier version of Chapter One of this study originally appeared in *Mosaic*, 18/2 (Spring 1985): 17–32. Chapter Six originally appeared, in slightly different form, in the *Saul Bellow Journal*. Portions of my essay, "Bellow's New World Babylon," *Humanities* (Sept./Oct. 1988), have been incorporated, with permission of the editors, in Chapters Four and Ten.

The excerpt from *Six Memos for the Next Millennium* by Italo Calvino has been reprinted by permission of Harvard University Press. Copyright © 1988 by the President and Fellows of Harvard College. The excerpt from *The Art of the Novel* by Milan Kundera has been reprinted by permission of Grove Press. Copyright © 1986 by Milan Kundera. English translation copyright © 1988 by Grove Press, Inc.

For permission to quote from Saul Bellow's works, I am indebted as follows. To Vanguard Press, a division of Random House, Inc.: Excerpts from *Dangling Man* by Saul Bellow. Copyright © 1944. Reprinted by permission of

Texts Used

Citations from Bellow's fiction are to the following editions:

Dangling Man. New York: Vanguard Press, 1944.
The Victim. New York: Vanguard Press, 1947.
The Adventures of Augie March. New York: Viking Press, 1953.
Seize the Day. New York: Viking Press, 1956.
Henderson the Rain King. New York: Viking Press, 1959.
Herzog. New York: Viking Press, 1964.
Mosby's Memoirs And Other Stories. New York: Viking Press, 1968.
Mr. Sammler's Planet. New York: Viking Press, 1970.
Humboldt's Gift. New York: Viking Press, 1975.
The Dean's December. New York: Harper & Row, 1982.
Him with His Foot in His Mouth and Other Stories. New York: Harper & Row,
    1984.
More Die of Heartbreak. New York: William Morrow, 1987.
A Theft. New York: Penguin, 1989.

Introduction

From his first novel, *Dangling Man* (1944), to his latest fiction, Saul Bellow has created a virtually unbroken series of protagonists doing mental battle with the world around them. Lone contemplatives in a society bristling with activity—an America dedicated to the glories of matter and motion—Bellow's heroes are acutely conscious of their failure to warm to this world of practical affairs and palpable profits. Still, they are defiantly protective of their right to ponder existence and plumb its mystery. Riddled with contrary emotions, Bellow's protagonists, it is often observed, waver uneasily between alternate commitments—to action, fellowship and worldly self-assertion on the one hand and to stillness, contemplation and solitude on the other.

Yet these symptoms of fracture and stress may be traced, I shall argue, to a deeper rift within the psyche; each of Bellow's protagonists is divided against himself. Joseph, the protagonist of Bellow's first novel, *Dangling Man*, suffers such intense inner strife that the perils of physical combat promise diversion as well as relief. Thus, at the end of the novel, Bellow's Dangling Man enlists in the Army, to fight in World War II. Joseph's conflict, and that of subsequent protagonists, stems from his polarized consciousness. Like Artur Sammler, fifty years older than Joseph and the protagonist of a novel Bellow wrote a quarter-century after *Dangling Man*, Joseph is unable to reconcile two distinct modes of comprehending reality: he is torn between the alternate claims of reason and faith. By delineating this rift in thought, feeling and perception, I do not mean to suggest that a conflict inevitably exists between the tenets of reason and religion *per se*. Philosophers and theologians throughout Western history have been able not only to reconcile reason and faith but to enrich our understanding of the one by acknowledging the validity of the other. The conflict that arises in Bellow's characters stems, rather, from the tendency, so prevalent in a culture enamored of scientific rationalism, to confuse reasoned analysis with metaphysical truth—and to uphold analytic methods as proof against the exigencies of spirit.

As Bellow's lifelong enterprise as a novelist has developed and deepened, so has his commitment to articulating these exigencies. More and more frequently do his readers find, embedded in the urban context and contemporary setting of each novel, those seemingly arcane terms that have, for millennia, designated the realities of spirit: words such as *mystery*, *grace*, *beatitude*, *blessedness*. Going against the grain of contemporary culture and its secular pieties, Bellow's fiction is *radical* in a profound sense; at the very source or *root* of his work, accepted notions of reality are challenged, undermined, overturned. Noting the singular nature of Bellow's vision, John Updike has recently said, "Bellow believes in the soul; this is one of his links with the ancients, with the great books." Paradoxically, I would add, it is this link with "the ancients" that clarifies the radical nature of Bellow's vision—revealing his novels to be more provocative, more daring, than has been allowed. Bellow "is one of the rare writers," Updike continues, who take "mimesis a layer or two deeper than it has gone before."[1] The degree to which Bellow's mimesis penetrates the layers of appearance is governed, as I intend to show, by his growing belief in the soul. By clarifying what is most fundamental to this novelist's vision of reality, we shall gain fresh appreciation of the boldness of his art.

Viewed in this light, moreover, Bellow's novels assume a different relationship to traditional realism, the genre with which his fiction is customarily identified. In novels from *Dangling Man* to *The Dean's December*, from *Seize the Day* to *More Die of Heartbreak*, Bellow defines, in rich and graphic detail, the individual's relationship to his environment. For these effects, and for the traditional narrative techniques he employs to achieve them, he has been alternately praised—especially by those who expect novelists to fulfill their traditional obligations to "reality"—and dismissed as old-fashioned. What has generally been ignored in Bellow's work, however, is the extraordinary way that this massive accumulation of material fact and concrete detail tends to undermine itself—subverting the realist's traditional faith in material circumstance and the world of appearance.

In his recent study of postmodern literature, *The Post-Modern Aura*, Charles Newman adopts the by now familiar stance of critics who regard Bellow's fiction as old-fashioned and, as Newman says, "aesthetically timid." The novelist's style, approach and "implicit value system" hark back, Newman contends, to the "bourgeois realism" of a bygone era. Bellow's literary enterprise represents a retrograde, ultimately futile effort to restore "the centrality of the [nineteenth-century] realist writer in an integrated and properly honorific culture." Although Newman perceptively notes the process of divestment suffered by Bellow's protagonists—the process by which, as he says, "the self" is "gained by *shedding* intellectual baggage"—he defines this Bellovian "self" historically, as the "lost content" of traditional "culture."[2] As Bellow's novels amply demonstrate, however, what the novelist strives to redeem in his fiction cannot be identified with the dead past or a dead culture. Rather, he seeks to discover and reveal the self transcending "culture" and its temporal authority. Contrary to Newman's assumption, that Bellow vainly attempts to bolster his position as a writer with the authority bestowed by a "properly honorific culture," his fiction increasingly challenges the authority of culture itself. In defiance of his "modern university education," as Bellow puts it, the novelist has come to trust more and more "the things that I really [feel] in my soul most deeply." This deepening faith in the inmost self or "soul" is, then, what fosters Bellow's vision of life, and ultimately of literary creation, as a "religious enterprise."

In Bellow's novels the densely woven background of historical and social fact, of physical event and psychological crisis, does not play back the old vision of "bourgeois realism" or shelter in its cultural authority. Rather, this dense mimetic fabric constitutes the background against which a character discovers an entirely different order of fact: the "internal fact" of revelation. Critics have had at least an inkling of this development in Bellow's literary career for some time now. Like others, M. A. Klug notes the "growing importance of the religious sense in Bellow's work." The "heroes of [Bellow's] later novels all experience what Sammler calls 'God Adumbrations,' " Klug points out. "Since *Seize the Day*, the force and significance of these 'adumbrations' have increased with each subsequent novel."[3] Having remarked this apparent development, most critics do not bother to explore the matter further. Thus while repeated allusions to Bellow's longing for "transcendence" sound throughout studies of his fiction, no one, to my knowledge, has addressed more than glancingly "the importance of the religious sense in Bellow's work." Nor has anyone traced the origin of this development to Bellow's first novel, *Dangling Man*, published over a decade before *Seize the Day*.

"A few critics have mentioned Bellow's religious concern in passing," Keith Opdahl astutely observed in 1967, "and some have explicitly denied that it exists." More than twenty years later, the situation diagnosed by Opdahl remains remarkably unchanged.[4] The constraint or indifference with which Bellow's "religious concern" has been treated is noteworthy—underscoring, as it does, the novelist's outspoken views on the intellectual constraints operating in contemporary "head culture." The latter term, which crops up in essays, interviews and fiction published by Bellow since the mid-1970s, describes a culture that "has developed a tedious sort of rationality by ruling that certain kinds of knowledge are illegitimate."[5] In an interview with Robert Boyers in 1975, Bellow distinguishes between the declared "skepticism" of Western "head culture" and the unvoiced "internal beliefs" that the individual silently keeps to himself. "You can depend," he says, "upon educated people to tell you that of course they are agnostic rationalists, but what they really are is their own very well kept secret. And the reason is that there's really no language for these secrets at the moment, and very few people whom you can take into your confidence. . . . If you ask people what they think they tell you what they learned in college."[6]

In a more recent interview with Jo Brans, Bellow testifies to his own troubling experience of this rift in consciousness and to his resolve to overcome it.

> I've become aware of a conflict between the modern university education I received and those things that I really felt in my soul most deeply. I've trusted those more and more.—You see, I'm not even supposed to have a soul. . . . The soul is out of bounds if you have the sort of education I had [in anthropology, Marx, Russell, the logical positivists, Freud, Adler, and so on]. . . . And I know how a modern man is supposed to think. The hero of my last book [*Humboldt's Gift*] says, "If you put a test before me I can get a high mark, but it's only head culture."

Because "there's no room" for "the soul" in "the new mental world that we've constructed," Bellow finds this world becoming "more and more a prison." As a writer whose business, and life, is to articulate what he knows, he must object to the public silencing of this "inner voice"—to the repression of "some unacknowledged information that we have."[7]

The predominant respectability of "rationalistic talk" in modern society was noted, early in this century, by the American pragmatic philosopher, William James. In *The Varieties of Religious Experience*, James observed that pre-rational beliefs and values—about which people in a secular age grow increasingly silent—paradoxically remain the premises upon which they conduct their lives:

> If [says James] we look on man's whole mental life as it exists, on the life of men that lies in them apart from their learning and science, and that they inwardly and privately follow, we have to confess that the part of it of which rationalism can give an account is relatively superficial. It is the part that has the *prestige* undoubtedly, for it has the loquacity, it can challenge you for proofs, and chop logic, and put you down with words. But it will fail to convince or convert you all the same, if your dumb intuitions are opposed to its conclusions.[8]

The central impetus of Bellow's fiction, I believe, is the search for a language and a literary form by which these "dumb intuitions" can be voiced and heard over the volubility of "rationalistic talk."[9] Before Bellow's characters can discover this "secret" language or inner "speech," however, they experience monumental forms of resistance, both internal and external. As Bellow's novels consistently demonstrate, the "loquacity" of rationalist thought and its assumptions—and especially of its offspring, scientific materialism—resounds not only in the public world of contemporary "head culture" but in the solitary head of each troubled protagonist.

The "God Adumbrations" gleaned by Bellow's characters are by no means the product of complacency. Punctuated by lacerating self-doubt and recurrent bouts of despair, their revelations are not the reward of obedience— of pious subjection to authority, orthodoxy or dogma. Rather, Bellow's characters must undergo the terrors of personal and cultural loss: that divestment required, as Lionel Trilling eloquently pointed out, of all modern heroes. In *Sincerity and Authenticity*, Trilling convincingly argues that authenticity is the crucial value and generative force of modern literature, if not of modern culture itself. Striving to achieve "authenticity," says Trilling, the modern Hegelian "Spirit" must divest itself of all cultural supports and descend in a "downward movement through all the cultural superstructures to some place where all movement ends, and begins." Abandoning itself to the unknown, "disintegrated consciousness" must forsake all manner of received wisdom, all established conventions of conduct, all inherited systems of ethics and beliefs: the whole world, in short, of "material and social establishment and what it is presumed to assure in the way of order, peace, honour, and beauty as emblems of the spiritual life." [10]

The modern quest for authenticity, as Trilling himself remarks, is not without its ironies. Driven to express negation rather than affirmation, the modern representatives of "Spirit" assume the role of "children of light" but seek their illumination in darkness. When, as Trilling says, "the moral life [is] in process of revising itself," the pursuit of authenticity may begin to constitute its own peculiar version of orthodoxy—nihilism becoming a covert sort of creed. [11] It is this unspoken creed that Bellow has come increasingly to suspect and to challenge in his fiction. Remarking Bellow's challenge to the "prevailing" view in *Herzog*, Trilling perceives "a gifted novelist" trying, "through his Moses Herzog, to question the prevailing [modern] negation of the old vision and to assert the value of the achieved and successful life." Because, however, the quest for authenticity has consigned "the old vision" to disrepute, Bellow's efforts, says Trilling, produce a certain "discomfort and embarrassment" in his readers. Though we may sympathize with Bellow's attempt to rescue the possibility of affirmation, the novelist has laid himself "open to the terrible charge of philistinism, of being a defector from the ranks of the children of light, a traitor to Spirit."

A wise and canny critic, Trilling overlooks, all the same, an essential feature of Bellow's literary enterprise. It is true, of course, that the novelist has long and repeatedly challenged the modernist tendency to embrace "the void," to assume that the Conradian "heart of darkness" is the only source of authentic being. Nevertheless, I shall argue, the dread of inauthenticity is as dominant a feature of Bellow's fiction as it is of Conrad's, Hemingway's, Lawrence's or Woolf's. The radical conflict operating in the psyche of Bellow's characters arises, I would suggest, from this potent dread of the inauthentic: the fear of surrendering to false pieties or, as Albert Corde says in *The Dean's December*, to "false consciousness." Yet as Bellow has shown with increasing urgency in his fiction, contemporary "head culture" may be charged with the propagation of some potent pieties of its own.

When, furthermore, Trilling speaks of the modern "disintegrated, alienated and distraught consciousness," he is aptly describing the consciousness of Bellow's own troubled protagonists. Suffering internal fracture and a profound sense of estrangement, continually riddled with self-doubt, Bellow's characters set out in search of an authentic self—hoping to discover the freedom of real being. Such is the arduous and agonizing process—hardly a simple endorsement of "the old vision" and its comforting assurances—that Herzog, contrary to Trilling's view, painfully undergoes in his quest. Only after he has delved through "all the cultural superstructures," sifted through and discarded them one by one, may the Bellovian hero awaken, as Henderson says, from "unreality" to reality and discover his authentic bond with creation.

Such affirmation, when it arrives, must overcome the fiercest opposition: the aggressive disclaimers of the protagonist's own, highly skeptical mind. The author, a rigorous thinker as well as a conscientious writer, gives full rein to the objections that his own reason, as well as the rationalist premises of contemporary culture, mounts against the acceptance of religious intuition and faith. Only by asserting the reality of these "God Adumbrations" in the midst of resounding analytical opposition can Bellow, like Dostoevsky before him, articulate his persistent apprehension of these rationally inaccessible truths.

The derivation of the word "religion" may at this point help to clarify the nature and context of the "religious sense" operating in Bellow's fiction, especially as I intend to explore it. "According to one of the traditional etymologies," says the historian Leon Roth, "the Latin 'religio' means 'binding,' and it is generally said that the Romans, a practical people, 'bound' their gods. They made bargains with them and expected the bargains to be kept." This concept of religion is, Roth points out, "hardly distinguishable from magic"; but with the foundation of the Judeo-Christian tradition, a more complex understanding of religious "binding" arises—founded on moral law rather than magical power. Thus, in the Hebrew Bible, the covenant between God and humanity rests upon "a binding of ourselves to God" and a desire to "walk in his ways." For the "tradition of Judaism," Roth adds, "moral action and religion, although not identical, are indissociable."[12]

This recognition of being "bound" to God or "the divine" further suggests, to William James, a working definition of a "personal religion"—which he distinguishes from "the fully organized system of feeling, thought and institution" recognized as organized religion: it comprises "*the feelings, acts, and experiences of individual men in their solitude so far as they apprehend themselves to stand in relation to whatever they may consider the divine*" (James's italics).[13] The Latin etymology of the word "religion"—at once more specific and more universal than the dogma and rituals of a particular creed—is thus most helpful in assessing the religious nature of Bellow's vision and the way it manifests itself in the style and shape of his fiction. In the social, moral, psychological and philosophical activities of his characters, Bellow repeatedly demonstrates that an individual's *attachment* to life, to other people, to his immediate surroundings and to the planet itself is fundamentally rooted in "religion": in the knowledge he has, or discovers, of being "bound to God."

In treating his characters' own, often reluctant, recognition of their "binding," Bellow cares little to enumerate the significant differences among the various creeds, denominations and dogmas belonging to the Judeo-Christian tradition. Kierkegaard, Dostoevsky and the Church Fathers have as much to say to Bellow's characters as the Old Testament or Martin Buber. And though their author may draw from the history and literature of both Judaism and Christianity, he never invokes the authority of dogma. Textual references and allusions serve, rather, to clarify the nature of his characters' conflict and to lend it universal perspective. While drawing on his rich heritage as a Jew and depicting many aspects of Jewish culture in his fiction, Bellow can also make the following radical declaration: "In *Herzog* and *Henderson the Rain King* I was kidding my way to Jesus, but here [in *Mr. Sammler's Planet*] I'm baring myself nakedly."[14] Bellow's reference to the comic highjinks of *Henderson*— "I was kidding my way to Jesus"—reiterates, moreover, a statement found in a much earlier novel, *The Adventures of Augie March*: "Even the man who wants to believe," Augie observes in his colloquial fashion, "you sometimes note kidding his way to Jesus" (302).

Distinctions between literary modes—between the "kidding" of comedy and the high seriousness of direct confession—should not, Bellow implies, obscure the gravity of the spiritual quest any more than traditional boundaries between religious denominations should obstruct it. Sammler, the high-minded Jew, and Henderson, the comic Gentile, both dramatize their author's self-declared spiritual quest: his "way to Jesus." What Jesus signifies to Bellow is explicitly stated, furthermore, in remarks he delivered, several years after the publication of *Mr. Sammler's Planet*, to a classroom of students:

> You read the New Testament and the assumption Jesus makes continually is that people know the difference immediately between good and evil. . . . And that is, in part, what faith means. It doesn't even require discussion. It means that there is an implicit knowledge—very ancient, if not eternal—which human beings really share and that if they based their relationships on that knowledge, existence could be transformed. So it's by no means a new idea. It's older than the hills.

What Bellow says of Artur Sammler's "religious outlook" aptly describes the author's own deepening sense of life as "some kind of religious enterprise": "I think a person finally emerges . . . when he becomes aware that his life has a much larger meaning he has been ignoring—a transcendent meaning. And that his life is, at its most serious, some kind of religious enterprise."[15]

The degree to which Bellow's fiction manifests the vision of life as a "religious enterprise" varies from one fiction to another and, particularly, from the early to the later novels. What is boldly or "nakedly" treated in, say, *Humboldt's Gift* is only faintly or obliquely developed in *Dangling Man* and *The Victim*. Such variations are in keeping with a writer who has, during half a century of literary production, delighted in producing such different kinds and forms of novels—from the sprawling picaresque canvas of *Augie March* to the narrative constrictions of *Seize the Day* and the epistolary hijinks of *Herzog*. Yet as Irvin Stock has remarked, the differences among Bellow's novels serve to highlight their essential identity; they offer "a kind of model of organic growth, . . . like a human being getting older."[16] "Bellow's consistency of vision," Stock further points out, "makes his first novel grow more interesting as its successors pile up."[17]

It is this "consistency of vision"—revealed, paradoxically, in the conflict dividing each protagonist—that I intend to trace throughout Bellow's fiction. By exposing the skeletal frame, or thematic backbone, upon which so many contrasting details and telling variations depend, I do not mean to reduce to a single system, or false unity, the discordances and differences that constitute, in fiction as in existence, vital signs of life. To the contrary, these very differences in form, shape and appearance testify, as Stock suggests, to a "model of organic growth." Moreover, by viewing this "organic" process from the perspective of maturity—by, that is, examining Bellow's early novels from the perspective of the later ones—something more than increased interest or attention is generated on the reader's part. A dynamic shift in perception also takes place. What was only faintly apprehended by the reader approaching an early Bellow novel for the first time emerges in striking clarity—or is even dramatically transformed—after the reader has experienced the later works.

For the sake of this potential gain in clarity and perspective, I have chosen to introduce my study of Bellow's novels with a detailed examination of his seventh novel, *Mr. Sammler's Planet*. Barring this marked departure from chronological sequence—and one subsequent, but slight, reversal explained to the reader in Chapter Nine—the remainder of this study traces the "organic growth" of Bellow's *oeuvre*, up to and including his latest work of fiction, the novella *A Theft*. Following Chapter One, then, each successive section will be devoted to a subsequent novel by Bellow, as each in turn was completed by the author and duly published. In Chapter Four, for reasons there set forth, I shall consider his third and shortest novel, *Seize the Day*, in the clarifying light of "Mosby's Memoirs," the title story of his first published collection. Although considerations of space and organization prevent me from focusing attention on other short stories from Bellow's two published collections, the author's "consistency of vision" allows me to point out, from time to time, thematic affinities between his short stories and his novels.

Mr. Sammler's Planet occupies a unique place in Bellow's literary career. As the novelist himself has pointed out, *Sammler* marks a turning point in his spiritual progress—the point at which he was ready to "bare himself nakedly" and to discover, in the process, that the business of life is an essentially "religious enterprise."[18] While the discovery is made by much earlier protagonists—Wilhelm Adler in *Seize the Day*, and even Leventhal in *The Victim*—it is in *Sammler* that the Bellovian conflict between two modes of viewing reality becomes a conscious matter for the protagonist as well as his author. As Bellow once remarked of his character Sammler, "Well, he's a person in a very agitated and almost mad state who is resisting everything, including his own intellectual life. . . . As I was writing the book, I began to understand what I was doing."[19]

In *Sammler*, Bellow seems to have gained insight into what he "was doing" not only in his seventh novel but in the previous ones as well. Here, at any rate, the author delineates most directly the profound conflict between head and heart, mind and body, reason and faith that fosters a rift in the consciousness of his earlier protagonists. The culmination of a long line of development, and of the author's unique quest for authenticity, *Mr. Sammler's Planet* also prefigures the more radical departures of Bellow's latest fiction. The fact is, the publication of his seventh novel met with some of the same perplexity and critical consternation that have, more recently, greeted *The Dean's December* and *More Die of Heartbreak*. While many of *Sammler's* reviewers felt that Bellow had "betrayed" his project as a writer, forsaking liberal ideology and sixties' liberation for the "reactionary" stance of a resentful septuagenarian, their consternation—especially in the light of the bafflement expressed at Bellow's more recent fiction—may be traced to a less obvious source. For in *Sammler*, as I have already suggested, Bellow "bares himself nakedly" in ways that are both startling and discomfiting to a modern audience. If, for Bellow, the business of life is an essentially "religious enterprise," this "religious outlook," although present at least intermittently in the earliest novels, can easily be overlooked or disregarded there. In the almost two decades since *Sammler* was published, however, the unsettling nature of Bellow's vision has become more pronounced—if it is still perplexing—to most of his readers and critics.

Before concluding these introductory remarks, I should like to say a few words about the way in which the present study took shape. It began, as many books do, with the sheer pleasure and immediate interest of reading, thinking about, teaching and finally writing on a novelist's fiction. Only gradually did the "thesis" or argument advanced in these pages emerge. One effect of contemporary theories of reading is to have shattered any unself-conscious pretensions to "objectivity" that critics might bring to the texts they write about. Like most practicing critics, I am aware of the inherent subjectivity of my own, as well as anyone else's, arguments. I am also aware that the critic who admires, studies and writes on Bellow is likely to share or to be influenced by the sense, permeating his literary enterprise, of working against the grain of current cultural assumptions.

Still, I believe that I came to Bellow's fiction without any pre-existing notions of what I might discover. Nor was I then familiar with the ideas, values and philosophical context now set forth. Certainly I knew little or next to nothing about the premises of religious faith and the way that they differ from rationalist epistemology. The pleasure this study has given me derives, in part, from the insight I have gained into such matters—not only from Bellow but from a host of other writers, many of whom are cited in these pages. By approaching Bellow's fiction from the neglected vantage of his religious vision, I do not presume to have "the last word" on his rich and varied works of fiction. That ultimate sense or effect is achieved by the writer's own language: a language that cannot be equaled or displaced, but at best only served, by critical explanation.

Chapter 1
"Two Different Speeches": Mystery and Knowledge in *Mr. Sammler's Planet*

Suffering the psychic rift that afflicts virtually all of Bellow's main characters, the protagonist of *Mr. Sammler's Planet* (1970) is deeply divided in his perceptions, thoughts, attitudes and feelings. In him we discern, as clearly as in any character the novelist has created, the operation of "two different speeches" that, in Bellow's view, are symptomatic of contemporary "intellectual man" and his divided consciousness. "Of course there are two different speeches" operating in contemporary "head culture," Bellow candidly tells Robert Boyers. "There are the things you say, civilly, in polite society; and there are the things you say to yourself before you fall asleep. There are the people you bless and there are the prayers that you say to yourself which you wouldn't say to anyone else."[1]

Surprisingly, most critics find Sammler unmarked by psychological conflict. They even admonish Bellow for creating a static or "dead" character, who, as Alfred Kazin remarks, "has to be right all the time."[2] Sammler's obsession with knowing, laments John Clayton, is symptomatic of a man who has "buried his passionate, modern, conflicted self."[3] The critics' failure to detect vital signs of life, or conflict, in Bellow's protagonist proceeds, I would suggest, from a tendency to regard Sammler's active inner life—and even his passion for thinking—as solely or narrowly intellectual. Yet the ceaseless dialectic of Sammler's consciousness, the urgent unfolding of his internal self-argument, is profoundly psychological in the root sense of the term. It is his psyche, not just his mind, that is divided. The issues that divide Sammler are not just matters of speculation; their nature is personal and urgently pressing. The rift in Sammler's psyche is dramatically manifested in his emotional relationships with others, in the things that happen to him and in the actions he takes. As I intend to show, Sammler's passion for thinking does not render him superfluous or irrelevant to the concerns of contemporary humanity. Superannuated, world-weary and aloof as he appears, Sammler nonetheless embodies the epitome of the "passionate, modern, conflicted self."

The rift in Sammler's psyche may be initially identified as the polarization of two modes of consciousness, the analytic and intuitive. Psychically alternating between these poles, Sammler perceives reality in radically opposing terms. Through analysis, moreover, he attempts psychologically to disengage himself from the world—and from the claims he *intuitively* knows it has upon him. The impetus of the novel's unfolding action succeeds, however, in drawing him more and more deeply into its dynamic. The conditions of mortal existence, as Bellow demonstrates, demand more from the individual than analytic solutions. As Sammler comes to recognize, he himself is part of the existential "problem." He must appropriate (in the Kierkegaardian sense) and be reconciled to the very reality he seeks to analyze and explain. For Bellow as for Kierkegaard, reconciliation to existence springs from acknowledging the source of mystery in human life. That is why Kierkegaard and other religious philosophers, such as Étienne Gilson and Gabriel Marcel, help to elucidate both the conflict and the mystery operating at the heart of Bellow's novel.

Rallying Christian thinkers to illuminate the fiction of a Jewish novelist writing about Jewish characters might startle some readers, especially if they were unaware of Bellow's own statements, cited in the Introduction, about "kidding his way to Jesus" in *Henderson* and *Herzog*, while "baring himself nakedly" in *Mr. Sammler's Planet*. Certainly Sammler, a Polish survivor of the Holocaust, shares with his author a strong ethnic and cultural identity as a Jew. Yet as Sammler avidly studies the medieval German mystic Meister Eckhart, and ponders the meaning of Kierkegaard's "Knight of Faith," he evinces a powerful attraction to the Christian mysteries.[4] To such mystery Bellow directly alludes, moreover, when discussing the authenticity of his character's revelation. Questioned about Sammler's credibility when, at the novel's close, he "speaks of what each man knows in his heart," Bellow responds: "You're to believe in it as much as you can believe in the New Testament. . . . Look, you meet someone on the street and he says, give all you have and follow me—on what does he base his injunction? He bases it on the assumption that the truth is known."[5]

Such bold statements on the author's part suggest that critics have been rather too conservative in their assessment of the dichotomies underlying Bellow's fiction. Drawing on Western rationalist traditions, most commentators discern the conflict operating in Bellow's novels as one between the self and the world, between the individual's needs and society's demands. Or, pressing a little further, they point to the novelist's occasionally "Platonic" suggestion of a world of truth and value persisting beyond the ephemeral reality of appearances.[6] Bellow's own argument appears, more radically, to be

with reason itself—or at least with the current hegemony of scientific rationalism that has driven religious modes of knowledge underground. Because the
individual's "internal beliefs" have been virtually banished from the "polite
society" of "received opinions" and educated exchange, Bellow finds, as he
tells Boyers, that "there's really no language" at the present moment in which
to articulate the "secrets" of the spirit. The volubility of "rationalistic talk" has
publicly drowned out, if not privately silenced, this ancient form of human
utterance.

Because Artur Sammler is one of the most private of Bellow's protagonists, because he is a man who speaks largely and continually to himself,
Bellow's distinction between private and public "speech" may be understood
in its deeper implications. In Sammler's consciousness there is a rift not only
between received opinions and "internal beliefs" but between two fundamental operations of the psyche as it engages or confronts the world. Employing
a distinction Pascal made centuries ago in his *Pensées*, one may say that
two modes or processes of reflection, the analytic and the intuitive, draw
Sammler's mind in opposing directions, toward meanings that contradict and
conflict. Because the principles of intuitive understanding "are felt rather than
seen," said Pascal, "there is the greatest difficulty in making them felt by those
who do not of themselves perceive them."[7] In a more acutely analytic age than
Pascal's, the "difficulty" may arise not only from a "mathematical" or logical
mind confronting an intuitive one but from the oppositions arising within a
single, "conflicted" psyche. Sammler's formidable powers of ratiocination
and analysis make him doubt the validity of his own "felt" knowledge and
internal beliefs.[8]

The shifting modes of Sammler's perception unfold a continuous dialectic
between the "two different speeches" of his consciousness. Two different
modes of reading as well as speaking—of receiving as well as articulating
reality—may be said to characterize his internal discourse. The special urgency with which Sammler takes in reality dates from his crucial experiences
during the Second World War. A fugitive first from the Germans and then from
anti-Semitic Poles, Sammler spends several months hiding out in a mausoleum. There, cut off from human society and the sweep of current events, he
turns his attention to local phenomena, finding "curious ciphers and portents"
in the tiny movements of an insect or a drop of water. In the mausoleum he
finds "symbols everywhere, and metaphysical messages" (89–90). For a Jew
hiding out, the disturbance of a straw or the movement of a sparrow is a
minute, but by no means trivial, bit of empirical data that may spell the
difference between survival and disaster, security and exposure.

It is not simply personal survival, however, that spurs Sammler to deci-
pher the messages relayed by phenomena. For him they also bring pressing
news concerning the fate of Western civilization and, possibly, the human race
itself. Not only the German nation but "all of civilized society" seems caught

up in a "state of madness." From that summer in the mausoleum, when he finds portents of disaster in the webs traced by solitary spiders, Mr. Sammler continues to read, with prophetic intuition, history's apocalyptic message: its "bad news for humankind, bad information about the very essence of being" (89–90). Probing the mystery of human fate in this way, Sammler implicitly acknowledges his own participatory role in the symbolic drama being enacted: "It was the Sammlers," he thinks, "who kept on vainly trying to perform some kind of symbolic task. The main result of which was unrest, exposure to trouble. Mr. Sammler had a symbolic character. He, personally, was a symbol. . . . And of what was he a symbol? He didn't even know" (91). What the diviner or seer does know, however, is that his own life is subject to whatever "symbolic" truth or meaning he unveils.

While engaged in this essentially intuitive mode of registering reality, Mr. Sammler is also an avid "reader" of a markedly different order. As a representative of modern "intellectual man," he seeks to know in ways and according to principles that are more widely practiced and respected. Through the "strain of unrelenting analytical effort," vast accumulations of data and facts are formulated into laws and theories that explain, rather than embody, reality (21). In the novel's opening paragraph, Mr. Sammler is already tackling these "superstructures of explanation." Awaking "shortly before dawn" in his West Side bedroom, he immediately resumes the inner dialogue that fills his waking hours: "Intellectual man had become an explaining creature. Fathers to children, wives to husbands, lecturers to listeners, experts to laymen, . . . man to his own soul, explained. The roots of this, the causes of the other, . . . the history, the structure, the reasons why. For the most part, in one ear out the other. The soul wanted what it wanted. It had its own natural knowledge. It sat unhappily on superstructures of explanation, poor bird, not knowing which way to fly."

Uneasy and unhappy, the soul perches, "poor bird," on comfortless "superstructures" that are satisfactory only to the intellect. As the world of "objective" facts and public events grows daily more accessible to him, contemporary "intellectual man" is ever more caught up in the endless relay and exchange of information, opinion and idea. He must analyze and explain the voluminous data at hand in order to understand how it affects and alters the body of information which previous analyses and explanations have erected. "All will explain everything to all, until the next, the new common version is ready," thinks Sammler (19). But meanwhile that inner world of truth and value—revealed to the soul and forming its own "natural knowledge"—tends to be swept aside by the tide of technical data and media "input."

By "natural knowledge," Bellow is not, of course, referring to biological instinct but to innate faculties of intuitive understanding.[9] In the cited passage, he suggests that where the authority of "natural knowledge," and the source of an individual's humanity, was once located, there now appears only a void.

Because human beings cannot arrive at moral values by determining and analyzing a set of facts, knowledge of these values has come to be doubted, devalued or debunked. The point is implicitly illustrated by one of the novel's critics, who challenges Sammler's affirmation of knowledge at the end of the novel because "it is not exercised by specific phenomena, by the accumulation of sensible experience."[10] I shall argue later in this chapter that Sammler does indeed undergo crucial, "sensible experience"; yet the critic's real objection may be that the basis of Sammler's knowledge remains, as Pascal says, "felt rather than seen." Not phenomena but the *mode* in which they are apprehended, or intuited, is the only real basis for such understanding. (To the scientific observer, this point will, of course, seem merely tautological.)

Challenging the tenets of scientific rationalism, Bellow invokes, in the novel's opening paragraph, the ancient truths of the soul, possessed of its own needs—"wanting what it wanted"—and "its own natural knowledge." In Western thought, says the French philosopher, Étienne Gilson, the soul has traditionally been regarded as "a spiritual principle substantially united to a body"; "mind," on the other hand, has been regarded ever since Descartes as "a thinking substance distinct from, and exclusive of, the body." As Gilson demonstrates, the Cartesian separation of mind from matter led inevitably to the disintegration of the concept of man's "substantial unity." Faced with questions concerning human existence or, for that matter, the existence of the world, the Cartesian mind—having effected its separation from the body—set itself the task of proving (or disproving) a reality that, says Gilson, "could not be proved, not because it is not true, but on the contrary, because it is evident . . . to a soul, not to a mind."[11] Things evident to a soul, in other words, are not necessarily evident to a mind. Although such brief remarks cannot possibly rehearse the argument in sufficient detail, they should serve to recall the philosophical context from which arise Bellow's own assertions concerning the "two different speeches" of divided modern consciousness: the socially acceptable discourse of the "educated," or Cartesian, mind and the persistent murmurings of the more ancient soul—once "substantially united" to the body, of both humankind and the world, but currently in hiding.

"Bellow sees the body as essential to the functioning of the soul," Sarah Cohen correctly maintains, "since only through it can the soul exercise its powers."[12] Yet Sammler, and perhaps Bellow himself, has inherited from Descartes's mathematical account of reality the modern habit of severing mind from matter, the operations of "pure" intellect from the soul's "natural knowledge." Bellow provides an objective correlative for this rift in Sammler's vision by drawing attention to his impaired eyesight. Blind in one eye, the old man sees only "partially," his left eye having been damaged during the war by a Nazi guard's rifle-butt (184). In the Holocaust Sammler "lost his wife, lost an eye" and lost the underlying sense, as well, of being grounded in human existence. He tends to regard his "onetime human, onetime precious, life" as having been "burnt away" by this century's conflagrations (15–16, 224). In his view, he is "human, in some altered way. The human being at the point where he attempted to obtain his release from being human" (251). Sammler's sense of personal devastation, loss and detachment thus dramatizes in extreme terms the rift dividing modern consciousness and issuing in its "two different speeches." Bellow draws attention to the disjunctive operations of Sammler's psyche, engaged in reading reality, by noting the distinctive appearance, and separate functions, of his character's "two different-looking eyes" (72).[13]

It is from the "blind side" of Sammler's skull that certain "inward" and "uncommunicative" processes tellingly originate (18, 259). In that blindness, as though shunning the "things met with in this world," Sammler's distressed and hampered soul seeks liberation from the "prison" formed by his "perceptions in space and time" (57). Sammler's intellect, on the other hand, remains alert and attentive to the phenomena registered by his operative right eye and the impressions transmitted to his brain by the "sightful side" of his skull (86). A passage describing Sammler in the act of reading a book highlights this point: "Careful to guard his eyesight, he passed pages rapidly back and forth before his [right] eye, the large forehead registering the stimulus to his mind. The damaged left eye seemed to turn in another direction, to be preoccupied separately with different matters" (31).

From this disjunction in perception there arises, furthermore, a dichotomy in the way Sammler responds not only to the "things met with in this world" but also to other people. It accounts for the "look of rebuke as well as the look of receptivity" that registers in Sammler's response to the claims of existence (72). His "receptivity," I would suggest, is largely mental; that is, he freely opens his mind, or analytic faculties, to stimuli from which he ultimately tries to remain detached. As a "thinking substance distinct from the body," to repeat Gilson, Sammler can glory in the operations of sight: "To see was delicious. Oh, of course! An extreme pleasure!" At the same time, "the vividness of everything" to which his right eye is exposed "also dismayed him" (298). With this sense of dismay at the human condition, he "rebukes" the world, turning his blind eye "in another direction." He would deny the bond uniting his weary spirit to the world's—and his own—body. In "contraction from life," therefore, Sammler's "dead eye" blindly seeks guidance from those who counsel divestment of worldly distractions (137–38).

Here Sammler's most prominent guide is Meister Eckhart, the medieval German mystic who preached detachment from earthly and human matters as the means to finding God: "See to it that you are stripped of all creatures, of all consolation from creatures. For certainly as long as creatures comfort and are able to comfort you, you will never find true comfort. But if nothing can comfort you save God, truly God will console you." Having read this passage from Eckhart, "Mr. Sammler could not say that he literally believed what he was reading. He could, however, say that he cared to read nothing but this" (253–54). Sammler's affinity for Eckhart would appear to be further evidence of his alleged hostility to life and other people—"his attempt to turn the world into thought in order to stay aloof and safe."[14] What tends to go unnoticed, however, is that Bellow arranges things in the novel so that Sammler, who becomes increasingly entangled in worldly affairs and in the lives of others, ultimately recognizes that such earthly divestment is both impossible for him and, in any case, a humanly insufficient alternative. As the novel develops, Sammler gradually acknowledges the bonds—indissoluble for the mortal duration—that unite soul and body and bind him to quotidian existence.

The detachment with which Sammler endeavors to view reality, the estrangement of mind from body, may account for the void he himself contemplates at the novel's opening—the void yawning between the soul's "natural knowledge" and the inadequate but elaborate "superstructures" of "intellectual man." Yet he also senses "that the way he saw things could not be right," that "life was not and could not be what he was seeing" (110). The clue to his error lies in the very formulation of this sentence, because to human beings real "life" is not merely an object to be "seen" from outside. Nor can it truly be understood without the participation of the would-be observer in its processes. Although he intermittently registers this awareness, it takes the duration of the novel for Sammler to accept, over the reluctance of extreme age and fatigue, his full initiation into the mysteries of the living.

The awareness of mystery permeates Bellow's vision of reality. To apprehend mystery is, in the novelist's own words, to ascribe to "what we don't know" a "metaphysical character," not a naturalistic one.[15] Gabriel Marcel, in his *Metaphysical Journal*, draws a similar distinction between empirical and spiritual apprehension of the unknown: "What is unknown and does not know is merely ignored. What knows and does not wish to be known, and proceeds in such a way as not to be known, is mysterious (there is also the category of that which is powerless to make itself known—this, too, belongs to the order of the ignored). The idea of mystery thus implies the idea of power and it is bound up with the very idea of God."[16] The paradox, from a strictly logical viewpoint, of all religious belief stems from the fact that spiritual knowledge, unlike scientific knowledge, is grounded in this essential mystery. While the laws of a divinity may be revealed to human beings, the nature of that divinity remains hidden. Knowledge based upon acceptance of mystery implies the discovery not of physical laws governing nature but of moral imperatives governing human life. Despite his self-consciously modern "wish that it did not persist," Sammler acknowledges his intuition of mystery and of moral imperatives (236). He affirms that "life is sacred" and murder absolute evil—despite all the practical evidence, accumulated with such ferocious intensity during this century, that human nature is destructive and even murderous. "Everybody," he says, "knows what murder is. That is very old human knowledge. The best and purest human beings, from the beginning of time, have understood that life is sacred" (18).

The belief that "life is sacred" is rooted in a fertile mystery, whether theologically formulated or not, which precedes or transcends the ability to explain and verify "facts." It is not a problem human beings are capable of solving but a condition in which they exist. A problem, by contrast, holds out the promise of solution if the proper data and methods of analysis are applied. As Marcel points out, "a genuine problem is subject to an appropriate technique by the exercise of which it is defined; whereas a mystery, by definition, transcends every conceivable technique. It is, no doubt, always possible (logically and psychologically) to degrade a mystery so as to turn it into a problem."[17] The existence of evil may serve as a case in point. From time immemorial, human beings have sought to "degrade" the mystery of evil into a problem. By objectifying evil, that is, the observer seeks to locate it outside himself, in a source or cause rather than a condition in which he participates.[18] To exempt oneself from the conditions of either evil or existence may prove, in Marcel's words, "a fundamentally vicious proceeding, whose springs might perhaps be discovered in a kind of corruption of the intelligence."[19]

In this century such "corruption of the intelligence" has proliferated in countless forms, most especially in the virulent formulations of ideologues. Bellow's Sammler, witness of two world wars and survivor of the Holocaust, has experienced firsthand the wholesale devastation that can ensue from such "corruption of the intelligence": he has been the victim of would-be ideological "supermen" who, exempting themselves from moral law, attempted to treat "the problem of evil" by locating its source outside themselves. Yet Sammler, in no way an ideologue, is also attracted to final solutions. As an intellectual and "explainer," he critically analyzes the "problem" of existence and of evil. That he mentally seeks solutions to such problems while he simultaneously seeks refuge from the demands of actual existence is both ironic and revealing. Perhaps that is the temptation, always, for the Cartesian mind grappling with the insoluble "mysteries of inhuman power" (26). There is heady freedom in thinking one has found a solution to the problem, as though the thinker were extricating himself from the binding and at times unbearable conditions of earthly existence. The acrobatic mind would soar free of telluric conditions and the tyranny of gravity, to which matter is subject.

The intellectual's attempt to treat existence "as a problem with a ready answer" has been openly dismissed by Bellow in a playful but astute metaphor. Discussing the rationalists' compulsion to debate, explain, justify or deny the value of life, he says: "The mystery is too great. So when they knock at the door of mystery with the knuckles of cognition it is quite right that the door should open and some mysterious power should squirt them in the eye."[20] In *Mr. Sammler's Planet*, the power of mystery similarly exposes the absurdity of Sammler's efforts to detach himself from the conditions of mortal existence—to think of himself as "a visiting consciousness which happened to reside in a West Side bedroom" (73).

Paradoxically, it is Sammler's habit of minute observation that draws him into the vortex of human actions from which he tries to detach himself. His good right eye, "full of observation," inevitably provokes or stimulates those "inward processes" he would rather hold aloof from the world. At the novel's opening, Sammler has already been observing for some time a pickpocket deftly plying his trade on a New York City bus (4). Rapt with attention, he watches the thief unclasp his victim's pocketbook like a doctor lightly touching a patient's belly. To Sammler, this dark action, like all "horror, crime, murder," seems to "vivify all the phenomena, the most ordinary details of experience. In evil as in art there was illumination." Thus the world is suddenly and "wickedly lighted up. Wicked because the clear light made all objects so explicit, and this explicitness taunted Mr. Minutely-Observant Artur Sammler. All metaphysicians please note. Here is how it is. You will never see more clearly. And what do you make of it?" Something about "the essence of being" is revealed to Sammler; he has "received from the crime the benefit of an enlarged vision" (11–12). Yet this illumination does not, like the rays of a microscope, light up phenomena that can be objectively measured. Sammler believes he "will never see more clearly," and yet he is left with the still unanswered question: "And what do you make of it?"

The question unanswered, the "problem" unsolved, Sammler nevertheless craves a repetition of the experience, a revelation of its essential mystery. "Four fascinating times" he watches the skillful performance repeated, until the pickpocket, inadvertently alerted, quietly follows Sammler back to his apartment (10). There, in the empty lobby, he delivers a wordless message, a sure sign of warning, to the startled old man. The thief unzips his fly and boldly exposes himself to Sammler: "The man's expression was not directly menacing but oddly, serenely masterful. The thing was shown with mystifying certitude. Lordliness. Then it was returned to the trousers. *Quod erat demonstrandum.* Sammler was released. The fly was closed" (49–50). Like a philosophical proof—*quod erat demonstrandum*—the authority of power is graphically demonstrated.

Later in the novel, the pickpocket again serves as a catalyst for illumination. Although occurring under very different circumstances, the scene again focuses on Sammler's intent absorption of visual details—bringing revelation in a rather exact sense of the term, as visually *revealed* truth. As he stands on the sidewalk, watching the pickpocket and Lionel Feffer struggle for possession of a camera, Sammler becomes acutely aware of his role as observer. Shifting his attention to the assembled onlookers and "staring hard," he examines their "faces, passing from face to face among the people along the curb. . . . Then it struck him that what united everybody was a beatitude of presence. As if it were—yes—blessed are the present" (288–89). Then, however, a dreadful feeling steals over Sammler, the suspicion that he is no longer a member of this "blessed" human community. "And suddenly he saw himself not so much standing as strangely leaning, as reclining, and peculiarly in profile, and as a *past* person" (289–90).

The reclining figure of a corpse, here graphically rendered, literally signifies the detachment from life Sammler has been seeking. Now, with this sudden vision of himself as a corpse, he perceives that he has elevated death over life and recognizes that, although physically weak, he is still very much alive, here and now, on this planet. Standing in the midst of chaos, cruelty and violence, Artur Sammler tacitly affirms life by rejecting that shadowy "past person": "That was not himself. It was someone—and this struck him—poor in spirit. Someone between the human and not-human states, between content and emptiness, between full and void, meaning and not-meaning, between this world and no world. Flying, freed from gravitation, light with release and dread, doubting his destination, fearing there was nothing to receive him" (290).

Spurred by this sudden recognition, Sammler rushes to engage with existence, attempting to break up the fight; his efforts to halt the struggle backfire, however. His son-in-law, Eisen, whose help he has sought, viciously attacks the black man. In response to Sammler's horrified protests, Eisen reminds the old man that he has known violence before: "You know. We both fought in the war. You were a partisan. You had a gun" (291). This association between Eisen's murderousness and Sammler's wartime experience is highly significant, and Bellow has carefully prepared for its development in the novel. In an earlier scene, Sammler recalls how, in the dead of winter and on the verge of starvation, he had ambushed a German soldier in the Zamosht Forest. Forced to disarm and surrender his clothes and supplies, the German, standing naked in the snow, had pleaded with Sammler not to shoot. "Don't kill me. Take the things," he had said, "I have children." Sammler had answered by pulling the trigger (138–39).

Recalling that perverse pleasure, Sammler asks himself: "Was it only pleasure? It was more. It was joy. You would call it a dark action? On the contrary, it was also a bright one. . . . When he fired his gun, Sammler, himself nearly a corpse, burst into life. . . . When he shot again it was less to make sure of the man than to try again for that bliss. To drink more flames" (140–41). Here is another illumination from evil, the world "wickedly lighted up" as it is by the pickpocket on the bus. From both illuminations, the "mystery" of evil emerges in a "clear light," vivifying "the most ordinary details of experience."

After the pickpocket exposes himself to Sammler in the lobby, Sammler regards the black man's member as a "symbol of superlegitimacy or sovereignty. It was a mystery. It was unanswerable" (55). In this "mystery," however unlikely it may seem, the old man is now shown to participate. In the Zamosht Forest Sammler had wielded the cruel sovereignty of brute force. He had released the trigger not to save his own life but to give vent to his power, to experience the animal ecstasy of conquest. Although Sammler initially perceives the pickpocket's "assertion of power" as a sign of Western culture's general "madness," the black man's ultimate function is to illuminate the *specific* existence of Mr. Sammler (55). Through this encounter with his apparent opposite, Sammler is led to confront, unexpectedly, himself: a part of the very "problem" he is attempting to analyze.

Most often described as a symbol of evil, urban violence or Sammler's own repressed sexuality, the pickpocket's function as a catalyst for Sammler's revelation appears thus far to have been overlooked.[21] Unlikely as the comparison between this "African prince or great black beast" and the aged European intellectual might at first seem, the pickpocket clearly serves to implicate Sammler in his condition (14). That Sammler acts to save the thief's life after having been mortally threatened by him is itself highly suggestive.[22] Bellow draws the reader's attention to the doubling theme in more apparent ways as well: both men, for example, gaze at the world through tinted glasses. While the pickpocket sports fashionable "gentian violet" glasses expensively ringed with "Dior gold," Sammler wears plainer "colored specs" to hide his disfigured left eye (50, 87). His most dominant features are, in fact, those "pale-tufted eyes shaded by tinted glasses" (16).

Sammler's spectacles are clearly linked to his role and identity as observer. But when, on the bus, Sammler suddenly realizes that the pickpocket has spotted *him* watching the thief's dark actions, the old man has an uncanny sense of their roles being reversed, as in a mirror: "Mr. Sammler in his goggles was troubled in focusing. Too much adrenalin was passing. . . . It was at this moment that, in a quick turn of the head, [the pickpocket] saw Mr. Sammler. Mr. Sammler seen seeing was still in rapid currents with his heart" (46–47). The observer, "seen seeing," abruptly becomes the object of observation— and the initial object, the pickpocket, now assumes the role of observer. Later, when the pickpocket proceeds with his graphic "lesson" in the lobby, he begins, significantly, by removing Sammler's (the observer's) spectacles. Delivering his "message," the black man will not allow Sammler to maintain his detached vantage: "Then the smoked glasses were removed from Sammler's face and dropped on the table. He was directed, silently, to look downward." At the lesson's conclusion, the black man "picked up Sammler's dark glasses and returned them to his nose. He then unfolded and mounted his own, circular, . . . gently banded with the lovely Dior gold" (48–49). Still later, when Sammler recalls their strange and wordless encounter, their "two pairs of dark glasses" form twinned images in his memory (65).

At this point in the novel Sammler already makes a telling, though indirect, comparison between the black man's "creatureliness" and his own: "In the past, Mr. Sammler had thought that in this same biological respect he was comely enough, in his own Jewish way" (66). Although such biological "comeliness" matters little to Sammler "now, in [his] seventies," he implicitly regards the pickpocket's exposed member as a dark reflection of his own. Sammler's "descent" into recognized creatureliness appears to be an essential aspect of his gradual and acknowledged reappropriation of earthly existence.

Indeed, when Sammler first involuntarily recognizes the thief, as the pick-pocket corners yet another victim on another bus, Sammler has the intense sensation of an "immediate descent," both physical and emotional: that of "a stone falling" and "his heart sinking" (45). This sudden assertion, by the forces of gravity, of "a law of nature" already foreshadows Sammler's ultimate return, emotionally and spiritually, to his "planet"—the earth.

Later in the novel Sammler comments on the effects of his encounter with the pickpocket: "Objectively I have little use for such experiences, but there is such an absurd craving for actions that connect with other actions, for co-herency, for forms, for mysteries or fables. I may have thought that I had no more ordinary human curiosity left, but I was surprisingly wrong" (120). Sammler makes a telling distinction here between the "objective" vantage he customarily adopts as a detached observer and his "ordinary human curiosity." Attachment to life, recognition of one's participation in the world, is identified in Sammler's mind with a kind of knowledge more "human" than that which his own "objective" analysis yields. "The objective tendency," as Kierke-gaard says, "proposes to make everyone an observer, and in its maximum to transform him into so objective an observer that he becomes almost a ghost."[23] Where matters of human existence are concerned, the objective vantage may not be assumed, as in science, to be superior to subjective forms of knowledge. That is why Sammler, in his ultimate encounter with the pickpocket, perceives detachment as the condition of one "poor in spirit"—a "past person" caught "between the human and not-human states." This is the ghostly existence Sammler rejects; it is false, "not himself."

The analogy between Sammler's and Kierkegaard's ghostly metaphors is hardly accidental. Underlying Sammler's ceaseless internal argument is the tension between perceived categories of subjective and objective knowledge, categories to which Kierkegaard devoted hundreds of pages in his *Concluding Unscientific Postscript*. In acquiring objective knowledge—of mathematical or physical laws, for example—one does not have to become subjectively involved. Their acquisition, as Gilson says, "is wholly unrelated to [one's] own *Ego*."[24] Objective knowledge of love or of God, on the other hand, is impossible, because the "object" to be known—God or the beloved—affects and is actively appropriated by the knowing subject.

Just as Sammler's powers of minute and exacting observation paradox-ically implicate him, through his encounter with the criminal, in both the "creatureliness" and the "murderousness" of his species—and in the mystery of evil—so does his propensity for "moon-visions" paradoxically draw him deeper into the labyrinth of human relationships. He learns, for example, that his daughter Shula has actually stolen Professor Lal's scientific treatise on future moon-colonies in order to show it to her father. Horrified by Shula's misguided enthusiasm, Sammler awakens to a renewed sense of responsibility not only to Lal but also to his own flesh-and-blood. He immediately becomes involved in a complicated series of events that strengthens his bond with others. He discovers, moreover, that his nephew, Elya Gruner, on whom he has been financially dependent for years, had received payment from the Mafia for illicit medical "favors." Through Gruner, he is further implicated in the flawed existence of imperfect humanity. There is nothing "pure," in the Cartesian sense, about the mixed conditions of creaturely existence. Sammler inwardly avows, however, that for all his human imperfections, Elya Gruner, who dies at the novel's end, was not only a good man but a better person than Sammler himself: "At his best this man was much kinder than at my very best I have ever been or could ever be" (313). In life Elya Gruner was able "to do what was required of him"; by the end of the novel Sammler knows that, until his own release from the "bondage" of the finite, he too must carry out the terms of the "contract" binding him, like every other human being, to existence.

At every turn in this novel, try as he may to remain a detached observer, Sammler is caught up in the web of existence; he can no more break the bonds that tie him to others than he can defy gravity itself. For Sammler is bound to humankind not just by nature or by evil, but by love. His exasperation with his crazy daughter, Shula, may be profound, but his love for her is far more profound: "He cared too much for her. He cherished her. And really, his only contribution to the continuation of the species!" (116). If one is not yet a "past person," objective analysis of the terms of existence will take second place to that subjective process by which the lover, of God or of other human beings, actively appropriates what he knows. Not until he has endured yet another mortal loss, the death of Elya Gruner, does Sammler fully embrace the "mystery of dying" and of life itself (273). Only at the novel's close does he remove the tinted glasses shielding his "two different-looking eyes." In a "level" gaze that unites the operative right eye with the left one's "sightless bubble," Sammler's divided vision appears, for the first time, to become whole (311–12).

Bellow's affinity with Kierkegaard should by now be obvious. Not only do relevant passages from Kierkegaard's writings illuminate Sammler's situation but Sammler is also shown to be conscious of such analogies: "Able to carry the jewel of faith, making the motions of the infinite, and as a result needing nothing but the finite and the usual"—this is Sammler's understanding of Kierkegaard's "Knight of Faith," as he recalls to himself a passage from *Fear and Trembling*. To arrive at a true sense of the eternal within existence is, Sammler perceives, the task of "the real prodigy" of contemporary culture (62). Rather than seek release from the bondage of the finite, this modern champion would evince his faith by participating fully in the most mundane duties and tasks. Sammler's spiritual re-entry into his "planet" at the end of the novel, his renewed recognition of the earthly obligations assumed through such a "homecoming," suggest that he may have fulfilled a quest comparable, in some ways, at least, to that of Kierkegaard's Knight.[25] In the philosopher's words, Sammler has been "reconciled with existence" while having ignored none of its cruelty and pain.[26]

That essential forms of knowledge are both subjective and rooted in the everyday is the Kierkegaardian paradox underlying Sammler's gradual reconciliation to existence. As a *speculative* possibility, this celebration of the ordinary occurs to him rather early in the novel. "What if," he thinks, "some genius were to do with 'common life' what Einstein did with 'matter'? Finding its energetics, uncovering its radiance" (147). The source of radiance in the common life of human beings is not, of course, physical light traveling at measurable speed through the universe but the soul's illumination of truth. This light does not emanate from external quanta but from the psyche engaged with phenomena and irradiated by understanding. Because, as I have tried to show, the "light" of Sammler's own understanding tends to fluctuate between the poles of analysis and intuition, or between modes of subjective (or "natural") and objective knowing, phenomena take on, in his vision, contrary shades of meaning. For Sammler, the same phenomena that evince the disorder and "madness" sweeping Western culture also yield, when seen in another "light," evidence of humanity's extraordinary and consistent "regard for order":

> But wait—Sammler [thought] cautioning himself. Even this madness is also to a considerable extent a matter of performance, of enactment. Underneath there persists, powerfully too, a thick sense of what is normal for human life. Duties are observed. Attachments are preserved. There is work. People show up for jobs. It is extraordinary. . . . For such a volatile and restless animal, such a high-strung, curious animal, an ape subject to so many diseases, to anguish, boredom, such discipline, such drill, such strength for regularity, such assumption of responsibility, such regard for order (even in disorder) is a great mystery, too. Oh, it is a mystery. (146–47)

Within the compass of this passage, Sammler moves from contemplation of the human being as problem to the mystery of being. The biological factors invoked by the analyst to account for the limited nature of man—this volatile, restless and disease-ridden ape—also testify, when beheld in a different light, to the mysterious power of the human being to transcend those limits outlined, and apparently verified, by the data.

In passages such as this one, Bellow traces the movement of a soul not turning away from reality but engaged with it, articulating what it knows. To heed that inner speech, that "different speech" affirming the soul's "natural knowledge," one does not reject concrete phenomena or the claims of existence, as Meister Eckhart counsels. Rather, by participating in the ordinary and the finite one may discover—beneath the confusing surface and overlapping "superstructures of explanation"—life's radiant source. These "energetics" cannot be uncovered by an Einstein, however; rapping with the "knuckles of cognition" will not open the door. A mystery that draws the observer into its reality, the "radiance" of common life may be penetrated only from within. The knowledge Sammler has sought in detachment he discovers, instead, through his love for others and his acknowledged participation in the conditions of mortality. This is the knowledge of which Sammler speaks, in a "mental whisper," at the end of the novel.

In the novel's closing lines, Sammler commends to God "the soul of Elya Gruner," his nephew who has just died. "Through all the confusion and degraded clowning of this life," Sammler avows, Elya knew "that he must meet, and he did meet . . . the terms of his contract. The terms which, in his inmost heart, each man knows." In these lines, as Edward Alexander points out, Bellow celebrates "the ancient idea that . . . between man and God there exists a reciprocal agreement," a covenant or bond.[27] Other critics, however, find this passage unconvincing; some detect a note of "emotional withdrawal" or even of "self-reproach" on Sammler's part.[28] The form of Sammler's utterance, I would point out, is of paramount significance here. Contrary to Alfred Kazin's assumption, for example, that the closing lines reiterate Sammler's "Jewish passion" for "ratiocination as the only passion that doesn't wear out," the mode of Sammler's address appeals neither to reason nor to scientific objectivity.[29] He speaks, after all, in a medium that is the soul's acknowledged mode of discourse—the language of prayer itself: "For that is the truth of it—that we all know, God, that we know, that we know, we know, we know" (313).

The knowledge affirmed at the end of *Mr. Sammler's Planet* is, as Gilson says, "evident to a soul, not to a mind." Uttered in the ancient cadences of prayer, Sammler's affirmation is embedded in the contemporary language and structure of the novel that it concludes. With unflagging energy Bellow has traced the disjunction between the "two different speeches" of Sammler's divided psyche. Giving full rein to the "modern, conflicted self" and his internal debate, the novelist arrives at that self's most buried "secrets" and gives voice to his "dumb intuitions." Thus Bellow's language retrieves, in some measure at least, that ancient knowledge of which modern "intellectual man" has all but dispossessed himself.

Chapter 2
Between Free Fall and Faith:
Dangling Man

Bellow's early protagonists are even more reluctant than Mr. Sammler to heed the "secret" promptings of "the soul." The narrator of Bellow's first novel, *Dangling Man* (1944), is acutely aware of the inner conflict, and the contradictions, created by polarized consciousness—a condition he knows he shares with other members of his generation:

> Great pressure is brought to bear to make us undervalue ourselves. On the other hand, civilization teaches that each of us is an inestimable prize. . . . Therefore, we value and are ashamed to value ourselves, are hard-boiled. We are schooled in quietness and, if one of us takes his measure occasionally, he does so coolly, as if he were examining his fingernails, not his soul, frowning at the imperfections he finds as one would at a chip or a bit of dirt. (119)

Here, at the very outset of his career, Bellow describes the tendency of modern "intellectual man" to devalue his inner life by subjecting himself to detached analysis. Straining to assume an "objective" attitude toward his deepest "internal beliefs," the avatar of "head culture" takes "his measure" as though he were examining "not his soul" but "his fingernails."

Comprising a journal or "record" of the protagonist's "inward transactions," *Dangling Man* is an attempt, on the narrator's part, to break free of the strictures of cultural authority. As Joseph, the Dangling Man, self-consciously avows, "to keep a journal nowadays is considered a kind of self-indulgence, a weakness, and in poor taste. For this is an era of hardboiled-dom." The secular creed of a nation of pragmatists, "hardboiled-dom" exalts action, toughness, efficiency and material success at the expense of the "inner life," its needs and values. One of the code's central "commandments," Joseph adds, is the repressive mandate of silence: "Do you have an inner life? It is nobody's business but your own. Do you have emotions? Strangle them. . . . If you have difficulties, grapple with them silently" (9).

The role that "hardboiled-dom" plays both in Bellow's depiction of America in the forties and in his protagonist's conflicted inner life can hardly be overemphasized. By focusing, moreover, on Joseph's *writing* as the definitive act of resistance against "hardboiled-dom"—with its code of silence, action and indifference to the "inner life"—Bellow underscores the implicit challenge mounted by his authorship. The composition of Joseph's journal and, by inference, the creation of this highly introspective novel, implicates the writer in deliberate acts of literary impropriety. And in this overt challenge to cultural attitudes and assumptions Bellow also implicates his readers. He invites us to recognize that this novel, *Dangling Man*, is conceived against the grain of conventional wisdom and current idols. Accordingly, on the very first page Joseph makes several pointed allusions to a famous celebrity-author, Ernest Hemingway. For the generation of the forties, Bellow suggests, Hemingway exemplifies the only acceptable version of the writer—as literary man of action. Both Hemingway and the generation that lionizes him are, in Joseph's words, boldly "unpracticed in introspection"; they are "badly equipped to deal with opponents whom they cannot shoot like big game or outdo in daring." Emphasizing the contrast between current cultural heroes and his unheroic self, Joseph adds, "they fly planes or fight bulls or catch tarpon, whereas I rarely leave my room" (10).

So many of Bellow's protagonists—Sammler, Herzog, Citrine, Corde—share Joseph's reluctance to leave his room that the observation is by now a commonplace. Even when Bellow's characters light out, like Henderson, for new and exotic territory, their adventure takes the form of a journey into the interior—not so much the heart of a continent as the inmost recesses of the self. A detailed account of Joseph's journey into the interior, *Dangling Man* records, as well, the diarist's own resistance to his quest. While, that is, Joseph struggles against society's current devaluation of the "inner life," the journal he creates in defiance of "hardboiled-dom" reveals its "inhibitory effect" upon his inmost feelings and perceptions. The pervasive effect of such internal constraints is to thwart or repress, at moments of "truest candor," the spontaneous expression of Joseph's "internal beliefs." His vigilant skepticism toward the life of "his soul," and his concomitant failure to find meaning or purpose in existence through rational analysis, erects a psychic wall that seals him off from any lasting illumination. Intermittently, however, Joseph is graced by what he calls "consummating glimpses" of life's underlying mystery—and of the faith or "necessary trust" by which a human being could make "sense" of it. Recognizing at such moments the "element of treason to common sense in the very objects of common sense," he experiences "revelation" of the non-rational premises underlying human life: the ground from which the life of reason itself springs (190).

The intermittent moments of revelation at which Joseph arrives tend, as I shall demonstrate, to reappear with increased intensity and clarity in the lives of Bellow's subsequent protagonists. The context that Bellow creates for them here, in his first novel, will help us to trace their development in the later fictions. Yet as earlier suggested, viewing Bellow's first novel from the rich vantage of its successors also provides a more immediate advantage. While Joseph's inner conflict is left unresolved at the end, its nature and significance are vividly highlighted by the perspective lent by *Mr. Sammler's Planet*—most particularly, by our awareness of the "two different speeches" contending in Sammler's divided consciousness. To gain fresh appreciation of Joseph's plight as a "dangling man," we must examine, as *Sammler* helps us to do, the tensions operating in Joseph's similarly polarized, and to some extent paralyzed, consciousness.

Joseph, it has often been observed, is a "dangling man" because he is helpless to affect, or effect, his own destiny. Summoned for induction into the Army, he resigns from his job only to find his draft-call delayed by a bureaucratic entanglement. His journal covers the last months of a prolonged period of waiting, one that has spanned nearly a year. Unable during this period to gain back his former job, he passes his time in Chicago with "nothing to do but wait, or dangle, and grow more and more dispirited." As he himself says, however, this protracted period of waiting is "only one of the sources of my harassment," only "the backdrop against which I can be seen swinging" (12). Joseph, in other words, astutely perceives that his "dangling" condition is symptomatic of a deeper malaise. He is as troubled, if not more troubled, by being spiritually unmoored as he is by the protracted agony of waiting. On the one hand, he desires to be "cut down," released from inactivity by a summons from the Army. On the other, he is already adrift in a moral free fall that takes him further and further away from any sense of purpose or commitment, either to himself or to others The aimlessness of his present condition notwithstanding, he also has fleeting "glimpses"—at moments of "truest candor"—of being somehow attached to a higher, more purposeful reality. These occasional intimations, emanating from a center of non-rational understanding, keep Joseph "dangling" in a positive sense: lacking this sense of attachment, he might well be cut loose ontologically, plunging into the abyss of nihilistic despair.

Prior to his present condition of stasis, Joseph had been convinced of the power of reason to guide human destiny. Making a study of "the philosophers of the Enlightenment," he had researched a paper on one of its greatest proponents, Diderot, who edited the *Encyclopédie* (11). Emulating these eighteenth-century thinkers, Joseph had sought what Ernst Cassirer, in his discussion of the foundation of Enlightenment thought, calls the "rationalistic solution to the problem of man." From his present, "dangling" condition Joseph thus describes his former or "older self" as an acolyte of reason: "a sworn upholder," as he puts it, "of *tout comprendre c'est tout pardonner*." Just as the Enlightenment thinkers believed that, as Cassirer says, "mathematical reason is the key to a true understanding of the cosmic and moral order," so Joseph, trusting in reason to solve all human dilemmas, had "worked everything out in accordance with a general plan. Into this plan had gone his friends, his family, and his wife" (29).[1] Like the other elements of this "plan," however, Joseph's wife Iva persists in remaining "as far as ever from what I once desired to make her" (152).

As the "sworn upholder" of rationalistic solutions, a veritable "creature of plans," Joseph had sought to create among his fellows "a colony of the spirit"—a community whose "covenants forbade spite, bloodiness, and cruelty." Not through the ancient "covenants" of Mosaic law, but through laws based on mathematical reason and logic, he endeavored to redeem society, or at least his immediate circle of friends. The turning point for Joseph, the point at which he gave up his rationalistic "plan" and abandoned his project on Diderot, occurred at a party held at the home of his two friends, Minna and Harry Servatius. Recounting the events of that night in his journal, Joseph describes how "shocked" he was by the spectacle of cruelty, meanness, deceit and petty vengeance that unfolded.

Joseph describes with particular emphasis an event that occurred near the end of the evening, when one of his "oldest and best friends," Morris Abt, agreed to hypnotize his hostess (44). What begins as a last-ditch effort to rescue the partygoers from boredom quickly grows into a sordid demonstration of petty vengeance and "corruptness." As Minna Servatius submits to Abt's mesmeric devices and gradually falls into a trance, she becomes the victim of his cruel whims. Abt humiliates Minna by ordering her to count, in front of all the guests, the number of drinks she has imbibed during the evening. Everyone watching Abt's little game knows, as does Joseph, that prior to being hypnotized Minna had been quite drunk; they know, moreover, that her heavy drinking was caused by her husband's embarrassing attentions to one of the female guests. Abt's command is so humiliating for Minna that, in her emotional distress, the trance is actually shattered, releasing her from his sadistic manipulations.

Highly intelligent and ambitious, Morris Abt was Joseph's roommate at college as well as a fellow student of the Enlightenment. In the past, Joseph tells us, Abt dreamt of becoming "another Locke." Although repulsed by Abt's cruelty to Minna at the party, Joseph clearly shares with his "oldest friend" some telling psychological traits. The fascination of both young men with intellectual power, for example, leads each in his own way to seek dominion over reality. Just as Abt toys with Minna's sense of reality by hypnotizing her—first persuading her that she is suffering from extreme cold and then convincing her that she feels no pain where he had pinched and twisted her flesh—so Joseph perversely delights in mentally imposing arbitrary conditions upon reality. In Joseph's case, however, he is his own victim. "I have," he says, "been able to persuade myself, despite the surrounding ice, that the month was July, not February. Similarly I have reversed the summer and made myself shiver in the heat. And so, also, with the time of day." Such mental "tricks," he admits, "can be carried too far," can "damage the sense of reality" (13).

Citing a passage from Goethe's *Poetry and Life*, Joseph, perhaps unwittingly, reveals the peril that threatens him. "All comfort in life," says the German poet, "is based upon a regular occurrence of external phenomena," including the cyclical return "of the seasons." To ignore these "mainsprings of our earthly life," Goethe adds, leads to "the sorest evil, the heaviest disease— we regard life as a loathesome burden" (18). Ignoring Goethe's counsel, willfully alienating himself from the "mainsprings of earthly life," Joseph grows perilously indifferent to whatever lies outside the dominion of his own feverish brain. As he mentally toys with inverting the order of the seasons, he effectively dislodges himself from any felt connection with the universe, any bond with creation. Exploiting the tendency of the Cartesian mind to detach itself from what it observes, Joseph gradually becomes unhinged.

Compelled to seek intellectual "satisfaction" even from those around him, Joseph at times seems to parody the methods of rational inquiry in which he once trusted—forcing them to serve in impossible situations. Thus, in "a state of mind that required directness for its satisfaction," Joseph bluntly queries his father-in-law, asking Mr. Almstadt how on earth he manages to put up with such a prattling wife (21). At other times Joseph admits that he cannot address the complexities of human life with such narrow logic; human relationships have, he admits, "a quality that eluded me." There is "a difference between things and persons" that severely limits the usefulness of rational inquiry in comprehending the range of human experience (25). People themselves are rarely reasonable or logically explicable. Joseph's neighbor, Mr. Vanaker, is a case in point. When Joseph discovers that Vanaker has stolen a pair of his socks, he tries to find a possible explanation for Vanaker's strange behavior. Knowing that Vanaker "has a good job in a garage" and that he leaves for church on Sunday mornings "well dressed," Joseph asks himself: "What can have inspired this theft of my worn socks?" (126).

Critics have attempted to answer Joseph's question by positing a symbolic relationship between the two men, whose alienation is mutual. Vanaker literally puts "himself in Joseph's socks" because, as M. Gilbert Porter says, he is Joseph's "alter ego, a Conradian secret sharer."[2] Whether we refer to the doubles of Conrad and Dostoevsky or to those of Poe and Hoffman, they elicit a sense of the contradictory, ambivalent and enigmatic aspects of human nature. The bonds that emerge between apparent opposites tend to undermine the logical distinctions we make between disparate individuals. Dostoevsky, whose influence on Bellow's fiction is pervasive, created his *Doppelgänger* effects to suggest the irrational configurations not only between disparate individuals but between opposing aspects of the self. Torn by contrary impulses of good and evil, love and hate, admiration and jealousy, power and fear, the soul is a force-field of conflicting desires unfathomable to plain reason or common sense. Hence Dostoevsky's well known contempt for his rationalistic contemporaries—bedazzled, in his view, by the false lucidity of a "Crystal Palace."

Dostoevsky's influence on Bellow has long been noted by critics, especially with regard to the double motif. More than one passage in *Dangling Man*, Daniel Fuchs points out, may be read as a "low-keyed recasting" of Dostoevsky's melodramatic encounters between a protagonist and his double.[3] The structural and thematic parallels between Dostoevsky's and Bellow's fiction obviously demonstrate more than a formal interest, on Bellow's part, in the Russian master. Perhaps more than anything else, it is Dostoevsky's prophetic insight into, and criticism of, the modern zeal for "rationalistic solutions" that has influenced Bellow's own development as a writer. In *Crime and Punishment*, Fuchs reminds us, a silly minor character, Lebeziatnikov, tells Raskolnikov that "in Paris they have been conducting serious experiments as to the possibility of curing the insane, simply by logical argument." Here, comments Fuchs, "we have a delicious reduction of the excessive faith in rationalism which Dostoevsky condemns as western."[4] In *Dangling Man*, Mr. Fanzel, the tailor, displays a marked affinity with another minor character from *Crime and Punishment*, Mr. Luzhin, the miserly suitor of Raskolnikov's sister, Dunya.

Both Luzhin and Fanzel are grasping and selfish men who justify their complacency toward the suffering of others by invoking the concept of rational self-interest. In Dostoevsky's era this concept was popularized by such utilitarian philosophers as Jeremy Bentham and his circle, whom Joseph recalls as "the English economists" (112). Mr. Fanzel's views on moral conduct are also a self-serving version of enlightened self-interest; they are ironically summed up by Joseph in the following motto: "Look out for yourself and the world will be best served" (109). Fanzel, like the miserly Luzhin, has indeed looked out for himself—and with great success, too. When Joseph goes to Fanzel's tailorshop to have a button sewn on his jacket, he finds that the tailor's fee has tripled since the outbreak of war. The social and political upheavals wrought by war have served to upgrade Fanzel's clientele and to double his profits. For him, as for many more wealthy and powerful, World War II has proved terrific for business.

That the world is "best served" by such zealous dedication to self-interest strikes Joseph as highly dubious. Reminded by Fanzel of a passage in Dostoevsky's novel, in which Luzhin lectures Raskolnikov on the foolish irrationality of Christian charity, Joseph rehearses Luzhin's argument: " 'If I were to tear my coat in half,' [Luzhin] says, 'in order to share it with some wretch, no one would be benefited. Both of us would shiver in the cold.' " Dryly remarking the utter "reasonableness" of Luzhin's view, Joseph adds: "And why should both shiver? Is it not better that one should be warm? An unimpeachable conclusion. If I were to tell this to Mr. Fanzel . . . , he would certainly agree. . . . The wretched must suffer" (112).

Clearly Joseph is no Luzhin or Fanzel. His conscience is outraged by the flimsy "reasons" garnered to justify blind selfishness. Yet Joseph's own, more sophisticated line of reasoning has also failed to arrive at any key to moral understanding. Reason alone yields no answer to the overriding moral question that preoccupies him, as it preoccupies Bellow throughout his fiction: "How should a good man live; what might he do?" (39). It is the apparent insolubility of the question, left unanswered by the abject failure of his rationalistic "plan," that brings Joseph to his present impasse. Comparing his plight to the situation of an artist-friend living in New York, Joseph momentarily admits that the truth and purpose he seeks cannot be discovered as long as he remains locked within himself, confined to the "six-sided box" of his solitary room.

While Joseph avows that he is "only too anxious to find a reason" to leave his cell, he admits that he is "poor at finding reasons" to do so. Locked in his circular logic, he "seldom go[es] out," keeping, instead, to his jail (14). Having estranged himself from nature, other people and his own inner knowledge, Joseph fruitlessly consults his reason for reasons to carry on with life. In a grotesque parody of Descartes's famous dictum, *cogito ergo sum*, Joseph plays at creating reality by mental fiat: "Re-entering waking life" after having been asleep, he declares, "I admit the world." But this lordly assumption, of being able to shut out or "admit the world" at will, is immediately contradicted by the confused and unstable nature of Joseph's mental operations. Awaking to the certainty that he is hungry, he goes straight to a restaurant, only to "discover that I am not hungry at all." Later, when attempting to read a book, a sense of mental vacancy overwhelms him. Joseph "cannot key [his] mind to the sentences on the page," even though his "mind redoubles its efforts" to concentrate: "thoughts of doubtful relevance," he says, "keep straggling in and out." When, from this mental strain, Joseph's mind finally "shut[s] off," he switches on the radio in an effort to fill the void. From its presumed authority and control, his mind descends to abject powerlessness: "It is as vacant as the street" (15).

A persistent sense of vacancy, of carrying out hollow rituals and empty gestures while sunk in "craters of the spirit," haunts Joseph throughout the novel (66). Seeking to fill the void, he sometimes turns for solace to art. Listening to the music of Haydn, he is humbled by the expression of human suffering and his attendant recognition of his own failings. Joseph then asks himself how he is to become "a whole man": "in what quarter" might he seek "for help, where was the power? Grace by what law, under what order, by whom required? Personal, human, or universal, was it? The music named only one source, the universal one, God" (67–68). Yet Joseph instantly recoils from this religious perception, thinking "what a miserable surrender" such belief implies. Faith, which by definition exceeds the test of reason, does not yield "satisfaction" to Joseph's interrogating mind. "Is there no way to attain" an answer to the dilemma of existence, he asks, "except to sacrifice the mind that sought to be satisfied?" Composed by "a religious man," Haydn's music announces "a belief in God" that, Joseph admits, "went so easily to the least penetrable part of me, the seldom-disturbed thickets around the heart." But despite this penetration of the barriers that reason has erected "around the heart," Joseph refuses to accept any answer that is not of reason's "own deriving": "Out of my own strength," he says, "it was necessary for me to return the verdict for reason . . . and against the advantages of its surrender" (68).

Joseph's near-"surrender" to the emotive power of Haydn's music sets the stage for one of the most telling scenes in the novel: his angry confrontation with his fifteen-year-old niece, Etta. Joseph introduces his account of this scene by describing how his wealthy older brother, Etta's father, attempts to give him money. Refusing to cash the checks Amos sends him, Joseph is charged by his brother not to "be so proud and stiff-necked" (60). The word "stiff-necked" alludes, of course, to the biblical description of the children of Israel, who, in their stubborn pride, resisted God's law. In a subsequent passage Joseph recounts his visit to Amos's home. Describing his brother's wife and daughter, he reiterates the biblical allusion but transfers Amos's charge to his own daughter, Joseph's "stiff-necked" niece. The charge begins as a compliment; like her mother, Dolly, says Joseph, Etta has a "very graceful neck." He adds, "I can well understand why it provoked the prophet Isaiah to utter the words: 'Because the daughters of Zion are haughty, and walk with stretched forth necks and wanton eyes, . . . therefore the Lord will smite with a scab the crown of the head of the daughters of Zion, and the Lord will discover their secret parts.'" Etta, Joseph proceeds to observe, is "a vain girl":

> I am sure she spends a great many hours before the mirror. I am sure, also, that she must be aware of the resemblance she bears to me. It goes beyond the obvious similarities pointed out by the family. Our eyes are exactly alike, and so are our mouths and even the shape of our ears, sharp and small—Dolly's are altogether different. And there are other similarities, less easily definable, which she cannot help recognizing. (60–62)

Despite the "long-standing antagonism" that exists between him and his niece, Joseph is explicitly aware of their resemblance; the mirror in which "vain" Etta admires herself reflects his own likeness. Significantly, the one concrete detail rendered by Joseph's description of their likeness, the "sharp and small" ears, draws attention not to a physical trait so much as an underlying psychological one—of impishness or even of perversity—that Etta shares with her uncle.

Still more suggestive of their psychological likeness is the fact that Etta herself interrupts Joseph in the process of "surrendering" to Haydn's music. By insisting on playing some pop records on the phonograph, Etta incites Joseph's anger. The clash of wills quickly ignites into verbal, then physical combat. Describing the ensuing fight with his niece, Joseph says, "I snapped her head back"; in the process of trying to spank her, he adds, "I press down her neck." Amos and Dolly quickly arrive on the scene, to find Etta stretched across Joseph's lap, "her thighs bare." (In ironic fulfillment of Isaiah's prophecy, one might say, Etta's "secret parts" are exposed.)

At this point Joseph tellingly wonders whether Amos and Dolly "were capable of observing how exactly alike [he and Etta] looked at that moment" (68–71). To Joseph, this "similarity of faces must mean a similarity of nature and presumably of fate." He "assume[s] that [their] physical resemblance was the basis for an affinity of another kind" (74). The fact that Etta, a reflection in female guise of Joseph's own "stiff-necked" pride, distracts him from Haydn's religiously inspired music is, I think, especially telling. As soon as she enters the room where Joseph is seated, listening to the music that penetrates "the seldom-disturbed thickets around the heart," he finds himself distracted by "that fresher and somewhat harder . . . version of my own face. I *now scarcely heard the music. I was already braced for a struggle*" (68–69, italics added). A "harder" version of her uncle, Etta arouses Joseph's combative responses and severs his contact with the source of his deepest feeling. Putting a finishing touch to this thematic development, Bellow draws the scene to a close by having Joseph reiterate, to his brother's face, Amos's previous charge. Facetiously defending his behavior toward Etta, Joseph reminds Amos that he, Joseph, is "rash and stiff-necked" (73).

Through this intricate pattern of allusions Bellow creates a biblical context for Joseph's demonstrations of "stiff-necked" pride. Earlier in the novel, we learned of his discarded "plan" to establish a "colony of the spirit," whose members would be bound together in loyalty to certain laws or "covenants." The implicit reference to Mosaic law and Israel's covenant with God is then more explicitly introduced in the passage citing Isaiah. The *presence* of these and other references to biblical history and vision serves to heighten the oppressive sense of *absence* permeating Joseph's mind, which is left "as vacant as the street." As background, or foil, to Joseph's attempts at finding rationalistic solutions to moral dilemmas, these images and allusions attest, like Haydn's music, to a mystery inaccessible to reason.

Even the party at Minna Servatius' home, which causes Joseph to abandon his "plan," is introduced in a passage constructed on this antiphonal pattern. Just before entering the party, Joseph is visited by a sudden revelation: "And it came to me all at once," he says, momentarily abandoning the rhetoric of reason for prophetic figuration, "that the human purpose of these occasions had always been to free the charge of feeling in the pent heart." Like our remote ancestors, Joseph adds, "we, too, flew together at this need as we had at Eleusis, with rites and dances, and at other high festivals and corroborees to witness pains and tortures. . . . Only we did these things without grace or mystery, lacking the forms for them and, relying on drunkenness, assassinated the Gods in one another and shrieked in vengefulness and hurt" (46). Soon enough, the spectacle of human "vengefulness and hurt" vividly emerges at the party, where "drunkenness" fails to provide adequate release for "the pent heart."

Like his biblical namesake, Joseph has, furthermore, a prophetic dream that articulates from the depths of his psyche symbolic truths inaccessible to the reasoning mind. In this dream, one of a series of "ominous" and "fearful" portents, Joseph finds himself on a mission to reclaim the victim of a massacre in some unidentified East European country. Although the dream culls details from reported events of the war currently raging abroad, its context expands to contain biblical references: a "Gehenna" of "the damned" and the slaughter of innocents, who have "childlike bodies with pierced hands and limbs." That such martyrdom, recalling Christ's, is inherent at birth, in the very condition of mortality, is vividly suggested by the slaughtered—who look "remarkably infantile," lying in "rows of large cribs or wicker bassinets." Transfiguring immediate history, the events of World War II, into symbolic time, Joseph envisions the infant's cradle as a coffin: the sentence of mortal life is death. Yet even in his dreams he attempts, in a maneuver characteristic of his waking mind, to remain "an outsider." To his dream "guide" he declares his "neutrality," hoping to detach himself from these horrifying conditions (120–21). But the terrifying metaphysical landscape looms inescapable: human beings, with their first breath, receive the inexplicable sentence of death. Implicated in the mystery of life and death, Joseph can hardly hope to remain a neutral "outsider."

Recounting this dream in his journal, Joseph recognizes its "guide" to be the "ancient figure" of death, "*the* murderer"—who "one day," with a stranger's greeting, "will drop the smile of courtesy or custom to show you the weapon in his hand, the means of your death" (122, Bellow's italics). The war and Joseph's imminent draft-call are, of course, immediate cause for his growing apprehension of death. From its opening pages, however, the novel reveals the omnipresence of death in the everyday world, under the most ordinary conditions—thus interweaving the prophetic message of the dream with Joseph's waking life. Early on Joseph reports, for example, that his elderly landlady, Mrs. Kiefer, "has been bedridden for more than three months. The old woman is not expected to live long" (16). Glimpsed from time to time behind the curtains of the room where she lies, the old invalid is slowly dying throughout the novel; her funeral is described at its close (186).

In the course of his infrequent excursions from his room, Joseph encounters other reminders of mortality and death, down to "a half-cleaned chicken" lying next to the sink in his mother-in-law's kitchen. With "its head bent as though to examine its entrails which . . . splattered the enamel with blood," the chicken appears stunned by death (24). Joseph's father-in-law makes his initial appearance in the novel as a sick man confined to his bed: "He was lying with his knees drawn up and his shoulders raised, so that his head seemed joined without a neck directly to his body. Through an opening in his pajamas his flesh showed white and fatty under graying hair" (20). Here Mr. Almstadt's loose flesh and helpless posture bear a distinct resemblance to the personified image of the chicken, stunned by death.

Not surprisingly, fragments from Joseph's waking existence are woven into the nightmarish landscape of the dream-massacre. The dream's deathly "guide," with his ominously "pointed face," recalls the actual face of a policeman Joseph encounters on one of his rare outings. The incident takes place after Joseph emerges from the "Randolph and Wabash" station of the El train one day. Suddenly he sees "a man sprawl out in front" of him. The stranger has apparently suffered a stroke or seizure. Rushing to relieve the man by unbuttoning his collar, Joseph gazes down at the stranger's stricken face, seeing in it a startling "prevision" of his own death. Lying in the street with his hat "crushed under his large bald head," the "fallen man," as Joseph refers to him, triggers Joseph's realization that his "beliefs are inadequate" to this mystery. His reasoning mind cannot answer or "guard" against the terrifying insolubility of mortal existence. Soon joined by a mounted policeman on duty, Joseph turns his attention "to the policeman's face. It was as long and as narrow as a boot." The uniformed policeman, leaning over "the fallen man's" body, appears like an emissary of that crushing power which grinds all beneath it—until, as Joseph says, "we lie, a great weight on our faces, straining toward the last breath which comes like the gritting of gravel under a heavy tread" (114–16).

As Joseph gazes at this representative of fallen humanity, he is reminded of the death of his mother, which has marked him, literally and symbolically, for life. Joseph's forehead bears a scar, recalling the mark of Cain, where his grief-maddened Aunt Dina had clawed him as he tried to drag her away from his mother's dead body (115). Later, reviewing the nightmare of the massacre and recognizing the policeman's face, "narrow as a boot," in death's "pointed face," Joseph is impelled to ask himself questions for which, he knows, no logical answer exists. "What is this [life] for?" he queries; "what am I for?" Confronting the apparent "chaos" of life and death, he is stymied. His attempt to make a "reckoning or inventory" leaves his mind "flapping like a rag on a clothesline in cold wind."

Not for the first time, however, this revelation of *absence*—the inadequacy of reason to confront the ultimate nature of existence—gives rise to a fleeting vision of underlying meaning that reason, by itself, cannot comprehend. Gazing through his window at the sunset beyond, Joseph perceives, in the sky's "apocalyptic reds and purples," bruises "such as must have appeared on the punished bodies of great saints, blues heavy and rich" (123–24). Here the physical landscape of setting sun and purple sky seems to point to ultimate revelation—not of human suffering alone but of its significance within the order of things. Otherwise Joseph would not recall the "great saints" who endured suffering, even the torments of bruised and "punished bodies," with resignation rather than despair.

At such moments of heightened awareness, Joseph, who has formerly lamented the absence of "grace or mystery" in contemporary life, appears to be visited by a form of grace. Suddenly, without logical forewarning, he makes contact with Goethe's "mainsprings of earthly life" and finds in "the regular occurrence of external phenomena" patterns of sustaining significance. One of these "consummating glimpses" occurs while he is watching the maid, Marie, wash the windows of his rented room. The pleasure Marie takes in the activity of cleaning brings to Joseph's attention "its importance as a notion of center, of balance, of order." "A woman," he thinks, first practices such rites "in the kitchens of her childhood, and it branches out from sinks, windows, table tops, to the faces and hands of children, and then it may become, as it does for some women, part of the nature of God" (113). Now, in a rare instance of expanded vision, he perceives an undercurrent of "grace or mystery" where before was only meaninglessness. In the performance of the most mundane tasks, devotion to others is enacted and faith in life's purpose affirmed. By acknowledging the "godly" significance of such humble rites, Joseph validates a religious principle that controverts his "dangling" condition—for he recognizes a profound connection between gesture and meaning, ritual and purpose, appearance and reality.

Joseph's inner conflict lies here, then, between his intellectual reliance on "the verdict" in favor of reason and his heartfelt longing for revelation. The distinction between the realms of reason and revelation goes back to the Middle Ages, and it may be helpful at this point to recall, briefly, what medieval philosophy had to say on the subject. As Cassirer points out in *The Philosophy of the Enlightenment*, the realm of reason comprised "everything whose understanding and confirmation require no other aid than the natural forces of knowledge," by which are meant those forces that "spring from human reason alone." Such knowledge "is communicated to us through sense perception and its supplementary processes of logical judgment and inference, of the discursive use of the understanding; the other [realm] is accessible only through the power of revelation. There need be no opposition," Cassirer adds, "between belief and knowledge, between revelation and reason. . . . The realm of grace does not negate the realm of nature."[5] But while medieval philosophers could accept reason as "the servant of revelation," the opposite obviously obtains for Joseph, living many centuries later in "the era of hardboiled-dom." Scientific rationalism, as Bellow points out, has all but *dis*graced any belief in grace among the educated members of advanced Western societies. For Joseph, the conflict between dual modes of perception is never really resolved. The extraordinary thing, however, is that Joseph is persistently compelled, time after time, to give voice to the "secret" knowledge he intermittently gleans but cannot accept as authentic.

Near the end of the novel, Joseph goes, as Daniel Fuchs puts it, "as far" as he "will go towards religion." Here he envisions the condition of "pure freedom" in spiritual rather than existential terms—as the freedom "to seek grace": "We are all drawn," Joseph says, "toward the same craters of the spirit—to know what we are and what we are for, to know our purpose, to seek grace" (154). Because he espouses the search for "pure freedom," critics have tended to identify Joseph's outlook with that of the French existentialists. M. Gilbert Porter even calls on Sartre's well-known phrase, "condemned to freedom," to describe Joseph's perception of his condition.[6] In contrast, however, to Sartre's vision of an absurd universe, Joseph's understanding of "pure freedom" is teleological—the freedom "to know what we are for." It is freedom defined, as Fuchs observes, "in Dostoevskian fashion, not simply as free will but as will defining itself as spirit."[7] Implicit in Joseph's perception of freedom, in other words, is the religious concept of "binding." Only through *attachment* to a higher purpose, a transcendent or divine principle, does the human being discover the "pure freedom" that is identical with "purity of the heart": the ability, as Joseph puts it, "to stop living so exclusively and vainly for our own sake, impure and unknowing, turning inward and self-fastened" (154).[8]

Despite this avowal on Joseph's part, as he is led to contemplate the non-rational premises on which human existence, meaning and "pure freedom" are based, he does not find release from his "impure and unknowing" condition. The Dangling Man's journal breaks off rather than concludes—and the novel's final two entries, dated April 8 and 9, respectively, create a suitably antiphonal ending to Joseph's unresolved dilemma.

In the journal entry dated April 8, Joseph describes a visit he makes to his parents' home and to the bedroom he occupied for twelve years during his boyhood. "It was suddenly given me," he says, "to experience one of those consummating glimpses that come to all of us periodically." As he gazes at the familiar objects in his old room, he suddenly perceives "an element of treason to common sense in the very objects of common sense." The term "common sense" here suggests the rudimentary operation of reason, as earlier defined by Cassirer: knowledge "communicated to us through sense perception and its supplementary processes of logical judgment and inference." Yet the objects of Joseph's sense-perception now strike him as betraying the very "sense" or logic by which they are known. In this "consummating glimpse," the room and its objects suddenly dwindle before Joseph's eyes—becoming "a tiny square, swiftly drawn back, myself and all the objects in it growing smaller. This was not a mere visual trick," he adds, but "a revelation of the ephemeral agreements by which we live and pace ourselves" (190).

Joseph's expanded awareness transcends the immediate dimensions of time and space. Thirty years earlier, he thinks, this room and these objects were not even here: "Birds flew through this space. It may be gone fifty years hence. Such reality, I thought, is actually very dangerous, very treacherous." The world of appearances, of objects of sense-perception or "common sense," is not solid and incontrovertible; it constitutes a set of "ephemeral agreements" and relationships. The premises by which we live, the very foundation of our most obvious and common "sense" of things, depend not on any permanent, objective reality but on a "necessary trust, auxiliary to all sanity": trust in a stable order underlying the sheer flux of phenomena. Thus Joseph affirms an "anterior" meaning and order—patently *not* of reason's "own deriving"—which is, in the conduct of daily life, taken on trust. Such an act of faith, primary and necessary, he now perceives as the very ground of sense, reason, "sanity" (190).

On April 8, having experienced this "consummating glimpse" of the non-rational premises of existence, Joseph cannot support the "verdict for reason." He hopes, instead, that by enlisting in the Army and participating in the war, he may "sound creation through other means." At this point Joseph's readiness to fight and die appears in a surprisingly affirmative light. "Perhaps the war could teach me, by violence, what I had been unable to learn during those months in the room," he declares. The violence of war and the threat of imminent death suggest, paradoxically, a potentially *creative* force powerful enough to break through the "inhibitory effect" of Joseph's own doubt, dread and skepticism. The next day, however, in his subsequent and final journal entry, Joseph's affirmation and hope are nullified by a characteristic resurgence of "hardboiled" skepticism. Contradicting his previous assertion, Joseph now cheers, in a tone of bitter self-mockery, the soldierly life as an escape *from* freedom. Having decided to enlist, he rejoices at being "relieved of self-determination, freedom canceled." He greets the prospect of "regular hours" like a man eager to exchange the dilemmas of "the spirit" for a form of "supervision" that is really repression. "Long live regimentation!" he cheers in the novel's closing line. Taking his place among the ranks of the "hardboiled," Joseph ends his record of prolonged introspection by celebrating the glories of action—and the power it has to supplant thought.[9]

Joseph's temporary freedom from routine obligations and commitments has proved a false freedom—merely "a void," as Tony Tanner says, "in which he hangs, unable to reach any solid reality."[10] The lack of attachment is the antithesis of Joseph's expressed longing for "pure freedom," the discovery of purpose, commitment, belief: "to know what we are and what we are for, to know our purpose, to seek grace." The freedom "to seek grace" implies, in the Judeo-Christian vision from which Joseph's language springs, a recognition of being both "fallen" from and bound to God. Unable, however, to accept that he is "fallen," Joseph keeps on drifting—suspended, morally and metaphysically, between free fall and faith.

Chapter 3
Hot Stars and Cold Hearts:
The Victim

Ungainly, indecisive, unsure of himself, Asa Leventhal appears at first glance the very antithesis of the "hard-boiled" hero, Hemingway's man of action. Lacking confidence and courage, the protagonist of *The Victim* (1947) is both self-conscious and defensive in his behavior. Yet this very defensiveness—most particularly, Leventhal's internal resistance to "certain kinds of feeling"—recalls Joseph's observations, in *Dangling Man*, regarding the "inhibitory effects" of "hardboiled-dom." With studied "impassivity" Leventhal represses his own intuitions and insights, in order to avert his gaze from disturbing realities. Even the incurious stare of Leventhal's eyes discloses "an intelligence not greatly interested in its own powers, as if preferring not to be bothered by them, indifferent; and this indifference appeared to be extended to others. He did not look sullen but rather unaccommodating, impassive" (98, 13).

At the heart of Leventhal's "indifference" lies his fear of the unknown: his dread of the uncontrollable, "accidental and haphazard" forces underlying existence and creating peril on every side. Convinced that he has barely skirted the abyss of failure—personal, social and professional—he warily navigates through life, fearing to be sucked into its fathomless depths and seeking to "hid[e] his fear in impassivity" (234).[1] Just as, in Joseph's view, the code of "hardboiled-dom" represses the "inner life," so Leventhal finds introspection dangerous (DM 9).[2] By plumbing those internal depths he might unsettle the precarious balance he has struggled to maintain in a turbulent and threatening world. Oppressed, furthermore, by the knowledge that his mother died in an insane asylum, Leventhal fears the world's madness and, potentially, his own (13, 53). By remaining aloof—and by closing his eyes to human suffering, passion, despair—he hopes to spare himself and avert disaster.

Sometimes, in rare moments of tranquility and confidence, Leventhal glimpses the absurdity of his efforts to seal himself off from the frightening "depth[s] of life" (277). Mortality is, after all, a condition of incipient risk and exposure:

> We were all the time taking care of ourselves [thinks Leventhal], laying up, storing up, watching out on this side and that side, and at the same time running, running desperately, running as if in an egg race with the egg in a spoon. . . . Man is weak and breakable, . . . hides money in his mattress, spares his feelings whenever he can, and takes pains and precautions. That, you might say, was for the sake of the egg. Dying is spoiling, then? (99)

In the race to win material comfort, success and safety, the anxious competitors dash forward in pursuit of victory. At the same time, they strain to shield their precious "eggs" or egos from the forces of disaster—forces set in motion by the race itself. Yet the effort to win is doomed, from the start, by the conditions of mortality: one "wins" this race only by dying. With sudden clarity Leventhal recognizes that even if the "egg" were carried safely through to the finish line, shell intact, its ultimate end is to spoil, or die. Even "hard-boiling" the egg—as Leventhal has sought to develop a protective shell of indifference—will not preserve one from ultimate extinction.

To the reductive view of life's journey as an "egg race" Bellow opposes a more authentic vision of reality: the existential journey shared by all human beings. As Leventhal moves through the thronged streets of New York City or crosses the bay to Staten Island, where he visits his brother's wife and her ailing son, he takes his place among this vast "crowd of souls, each concentrating on its destination" (64). Even though Leventhal feels he does "not have a conscious destination"—even though he exists "under the dread of being the only person in the city without one"—Bellow counters his character's dread with images evoking the reality of universal interconnection (136). The author's description of the ferry crossings, as critics have noted, evokes the ancient myth of Charon, rowing his passengers across the waters of the river Styx to their final destination. While each soul on the ferry concentrates uniquely "upon its immediate destination," each is linked to the others by a shared fate (64). To a sense of this shared destination, this interconnectedness, Leventhal gradually, in the course of the novel, awakes.

From the vantage of this metaphysical journey, moreover, Leventhal's concerted efforts to ignore his own "powers" of insight prove more *humanly* dangerous than the acknowledged perils of existence. Attempting to stave off threatening reality with a "hard-boiled" shell of indifference, Leventhal seals himself off not only from other people but from the "mainsprings" of his inner life. According to Marcus Schlossberg, a secondary character whom Stanley Trachtenberg identifies as the novel's "spokesman for reality," each individual must act upon knowledge that springs from the inmost self.[3] In Shlossberg's view—which, as I shall demonstrate, further develops Bellow's challenge of rationalistic solutions—only the "secret" life of the spirit yields the trust or affirmation necessary to the conduct of an "exactly human" life. By cutting himself off from the source of his own deepest "powers," Leventhal endangers his own humanity.

During the course of the novel, Leventhal gradually senses that his efforts to repress his own powers of insight betray a serious flaw: "He had used every means, and principally indifference and neglect, to avoid acknowledging [his fault] and still he did not know what it was. But that was owing to the way he had arranged not to know. He had done a great deal to make things easier for himself, toning down, softening, looking aside. But the more he tried to subdue whatever it was that he resisted, the more it raged" (158). Out of fear and insecurity Leventhal determines "not to know" himself; yet spiritual "indifference and neglect" serve only to magnify the unknown source of his terror.

Told by his wife, Mary, that he is "unsure" of himself, Leventhal thinks, "my God, how could anyone say that he was sure? How could he know all that he needed to know in order to say it?" (53–54). Insisting that he would have to "know all"—as though self-knowledge were a matter of accumulating sufficient data—Leventhal justifies his stance of knowing *nothing*. Before reaching the "verdict," one has to have all of the facts; but Leventhal despairs, quite understandably, of securing a complete set of data. His approach to the matter of self-knowledge reveals an obvious misconception. The "facts" of an individual's life are never complete; he can never "know all" there is to know about himself or his potential reactions to unforeseen circumstances. The only way to gain confidence in one's sanity is to consolidate those "powers" of insight that Leventhal, in his fear, has shunned.

The knowledge Leventhal rejects is not the objective knowledge derived from empirical research and its methods of inquiry. Such procedures, in which the observer attempts to distance himself from the objects of analysis, pose no threat to Leventhal's studied impassivity. Systems of classification, schematic tables, scientific nomenclature—all suggest, by their logical order and completeness, that the fathomless "depths of life" can be safely charted. "Many of the things that terrified people," Leventhal observes, "lost their horror when a doctor explained them" (53). The medical term "hypochondria," which his wife has applied to Leventhal's apprehensions about his sanity, proves "helpful," therefore, in alleviating his deepest fears—until "he had better evidence" (54). Similarly, when Leventhal's nephew Mickey falls ill with a rare disease, his fears for the boy's welfare are—mistakenly—assuaged by the doctor's medical diagnosis. Classifying the disease as "a bronchial infection of a rare kind," the doctor "named it two or three times." To Leventhal, this ritual of naming appears magical; the medical scientist, omnipotent. Leventhal's confusion of science with magic, of *naming* with ultimate knowledge and power, is ironically commented upon by the doctor's appearance at this moment: "The thin discs of the doctor's spectacles were turned to the sky, both illumined in the same degree by the bulb over his head" (64). In this mock-illumination, the glare of reflected light conveniently shields the doctor from Leventhal's gaze and from answering further questions about Mickey's ailment.

Contrary to the things that Leventhal arranges "not to know," objective "facts" and scientific explanations both attract and reassure him. Yet such assurances are often misleading—especially in the case of Mickey, who eventually refutes the validity of the doctor's "sensible advice" by dying. The knowledge Leventhal shuns but ultimately cannot ignore is that which derives from *connection* rather than detachment: what is "learned," as he later admits, by the "heart, rather than [the] eye" (277). Intimacy, not distance, informs the knowing heart; in the course of the novel, Leventhal's own heart is opened to this discovery. By accepting his shared intimacy with others, even his worst enemies, he is substantially, though not completely, liberated from the yoke of dread.

Endeavoring, throughout most of the novel, not to confront and identify—much less to express—the source of his dread, Leventhal is still drawn, perhaps unconsciously, to those who would articulate the knowledge he shuns. Thus he listens to an eloquent speech by an old man, the previously mentioned Mr. Schlossberg, whose name in German means "castle-mountain," suggesting loftiness and nobility. "Illumination in the Jewish tradition," Sarah Cohen reminds us, "is often received on a mountain."[4] Prefiguring Mr. Sammler's affirmation at the end of Bellow's seventh novel, Mr. Schlossberg declares the authenticity of the heart's knowledge. From truths known to each of us, he says, spring the values and premises by which we live. In a cafeteria on Fourteenth Street, Schlossberg presides over a gathering of younger men whom Leventhal joins one Sunday afternoon. The conversation begins with shop-talk; the men are discussing an actress whom one of their group, a talent scout named Shifcart, apparently discovered some years before. Schlossberg quickly expands the topic of conversation to address the question of good acting. He declares that in a recent movie, a leading Hollywood starlet acted like "wood"; she failed utterly "to show in her face" any of the emotions— "fear, hate, a hard heart, cruelness, fascination"—intrinsic to the dramatic situation she was attempting to render (125).

Schlossberg then proceeds to draw a connection between *being* and *acting*, one that takes on special significance within the novel: "She is not an actress," he says, "because she is not a woman, and she is not a woman because a man doesn't mean anything to her" (126). Later he adds, "Good acting is what is exactly human" (133).[5] Schlossberg's insistence on being open to life and other people offers a marked contrast to Leventhal's reserve and impassivity. Even Schlossberg's "wide, worn face" provides an oblique comment on Leventhal's habitually "expressionless" one (123, 5). Through his own "wooden" impassivity, Leventhal has tried to shield himself from experience. Expressionlessness has become his mask, his poor method of *acting* and, therefore, of *being*. When stirred to respond to Schlossberg's remarks, Leventhal even notes that his uttered opinions "sound queer to him"; "he had never before expressed them" (129).[6]

Insisting upon the capacity of human beings to know truth and to act upon their knowledge, Schlossberg implicitly challenges the premise of Leventhal's earlier self-query: "How could anyone know all that he needed to know in order to say he was sure?" To those who credit only what they see with the eye or through a "microscope," Schlossberg insists that subjectively known values, such as "greatness and beauty," are no less real: "What do you know? No, tell me, what do you know? You shut one eye and look at a thing, and it is one way to you. You shut the other one and it is different. I am as sure about greatness and beauty as you are about black and white. If a human life is a great thing to me, it *is* a great thing. Do you know better?" (134, Bellow's italics). Emphasizing the intuitive knowledge upon which moral, aesthetic and spiritual values are based, Schlossberg suggests that contemporary culture has grown overly dependent on what Pascal called mathematical knowledge, the product of analysis and logic. "And really," Schlossberg says, "we study people so much now that after we look and look at human nature—I write science articles myself—after you look at it and weigh it and turn it over and put it under a microscope, you might say, 'What is all the shouting about? A man is nothing, his life is nothing' " (134).

Such nothingness, Schlossberg suggests, may be *nothing more* than a product of the analytic method—of an instrument like the microscope, which focuses upon smaller and smaller units of reality until the whole disappears from view. If, on the other hand, human life is perceived, by the "heart rather than the eye," as "a great thing"—then "it *is* a great thing." From the affirmation of value—the belief in "greatness and beauty," for example—human truth is created. "Choose dignity," says Schlossberg. If we do not believe in ourselves, know ourselves capable of greatness, we cannot achieve it. To believe that human life is nothing is to make nothing of it. At the end of Schlossberg's eloquent address, one of the younger men stridently cheers and Shifcart laughingly pronounces, "Amen and amen" (134–35, Bellow's italics). Though his response is ironic, a characteristically "hard-boiled" reaction to the expression of deep feeling and belief, Shifcart's mocking "amen" may be more appropriate to the occasion than he recognizes. For Schlossberg's affirmation of "greatness and beauty" originates in the same source of knowledge affirmed by prayer itself. *Mr. Sammler's Planet*, we recall, ends with just such a prayer: Sammler, echoing Schlossberg, affirms the knowledge "which, in his inmost heart, each man knows. As I know mine. As all know."

Faith in what a human being may be said *to know* is precisely what Leventhal fails, throughout most of the novel, to accept and to act upon. Viewed in the context of Schlossberg's statements—and of subsequent developments in the novel, to which we shall now turn—Leventhal's "fault" or failure suggests a spiritual disorder as well as a psychological flaw. It is not the wise Schlossberg, however, who manages to break through the "hard-boiled" shell of Leventhal's spiritual indifference—shattering his obdurate blindness to the suffering as well as the "promise" of life. It is Kirby Allbee, a former colleague of Leventhal's, who suddenly appears on the scene to enact the role of scourge. Having lost his job and later his wife, Allbee has fallen on hard times and accuses Leventhal of being responsible for his suffering: Leventhal has committed specific wrongs against Allbee and, more generally, he is guilty because he is a Jew.

Goaded by Allbee's anti-Semitic jibes and personal affronts, Leventhal tries to meet them with a mask of indifference. But impassivity quickly gives way to inner turmoil, to spells of "confusion and despair." Unable to "clarify his thoughts or bring them into focus," Leventhal nevertheless finds himself, at odd moments, feeling strangely reassured: "He drew a deep, irregular breath and raised his hands from his lap in a gesture of exorcism against the spell of confusion and despair. 'God will help me out,' passed through his mind, and he did not stop to ask himself exactly what he meant by this" (229). Instinctively relying on faith or spiritual knowledge to "help" him through a trying time, Leventhal is yet indifferent to the implications faith has for the way he perceives reality or his place within it. If belief in God implies belief in a supreme power or mystery that binds human beings together in recognition of their shared, and "fallen," plight—then without a doubt Leventhal is "helped out," sustained in his humanity, by this faith. The mystery surrounding his initial encounter with Kirby Allbee gradually develops into the mystery of Leventhal's affection for a man who insults, repels and nearly destroys him.

Each aspect of this mystery partakes of what Leventhal, in the novel's closing chapter, finally acknowledges to be his own "very mysterious conviction" that "at the start of life, and perhaps even before, a promise had been made" (286). Recognition of this "promise," which implies an ulterior purpose and meaning to existence, ultimately sets Leventhal apart from Joseph, in *Dangling Man*. At the end of *The Victim*, Leventhal, unlike Joseph, has at least begun to discover the "freedom to seek grace." He is able, albeit tentatively, to free himself from seeking, in Cassirer's phrase, a "rationalistic solution to the problem of man." Leventhal no longer despairs of knowing "all that he needed to know"—all, that is, that his reason demands to know—in order to be "sure" that his life has meaning or that he is sane.

The catalyst for Leventhal's eventual release from wooden impassivity, Allbee unsettles him from the moment they meet—even before Leventhal understands the nature of Allbee's charges against him. At their first encounter, the anger in Allbee's "deeply ringed eyes" is enough to make Leventhal read there an accusation of his own "effrontery and bad acting." Here Leventhal's response appears to anticipate Schlossberg's discourse, which occurs later in the novel, on the nature of good and bad acting. At any rate, Leventhal's reaction is characteristically defensive, for he immediately turns the detected accusation against Allbee rather than himself: " 'Just like a bad actor to accuse everyone of bad acting,' thought Leventhal, but he was troubled nevertheless" (28). Both Allbee and Leventhal, it becomes clear, are "bad actors" who, shunning knowledge of their own complicity in the human condition, project their fears upon others by blaming and accusing them. In Leventhal's case, it is only by *acknowledging*—by accepting his inmost *knowledge* of—the bond that ties him to his adversary that he is released from indifference and able to recognize Allbee's "fallen" condition as his own.

When the two men meet for the first time in years and Allbee accuses Leventhal of wanting to run away—now that he has "found out that I [Allbee] exist"—Leventhal characteristically attempts "not to know" what the other man means. He strains to appear detached and indifferent, hiding fear and defensiveness beneath a show of logic: "Why should I doubt that you exist? . . . Is there any *reason* why you shouldn't?" (28, italics added) Leventhal's query is both facetious and revealing, betraying his inept attempt at detachment. The rationalistic assumption underlying his query—that there is a "reason why" one should or should not exist—parodically suggests the limitations of reason to sound the meaning of existence.

Like his many subsequent attempts to treat Allbee with detachment, Leventhal's rhetorical question obliquely points to the mystery of their relationship. Anxious at first to discover Allbee's motive for invading his privacy, Leventhal eventually perceives that no logical explanation exists. What Allbee "had hoped for in the first place remained a mystery" (274). Paradoxically, it is Leventhal's unwillingness to face what he inwardly "knows" that drives him to search for the "reason why" Allbee has disrupted his life. "[Allbee] had been spying on him, and the mystery was why! How long had he been keeping watch on him and for what reason—what grotesque reason?" Fear of persecution quickly unsettles Leventhal's speculations, and he "suddenly felt that he had been singled out to be the object of some freakish, insane process, and for an instant he was filled with dread. Then he recovered and told himself there was nothing to be afraid of." He quells his terror by invoking the logical distance separating Allbee, a "bum and a drunk," from his own respectable station in society. "There must be reasons" for a drunkard's behavior, Leventhal tells himself, "but they were beyond anybody's ability to find out— smoky, cloudy, alcoholic" (31).

Later, when Allbee brings hitherto unsuspected facts to Leventhal's attention, facts implicating him in Allbee's misfortune, it appears that a reasonable solution to their dilemma has been found. Certainly Leventhal clings to this hope, telling Allbee at one point, "if that's the reason I may be to blame in a way, indirectly" (33). At first it even seems that, as Allbee says, they are "making headway" in clarifying the causal relationship between past actions and present consequences. Yet the more intently Leventhal seeks "a good reason" to account for Allbee's predicament and his own contribution to it, the greater the mystery enfolding the two men appears to grow (35). The disturbing "intimation of a shared secret" between them, a secret at which Allbee continually hints, gradually becomes an acknowledged reality.

The ambiguous nature of Leventhal's "knowledge," his fear of knowing and of being known, receives significant emphasis in the passage of the novel that describes his initial encounter with Allbee. Walking to the nearby park, he notices a stranger who, "scrutinizing him," "seems to know" Leventhal. Perceiving the stranger to be "one of those guys who want you to think they can see to the bottom of your soul," Leventhal is instantly on his guard (26). When the stranger utters his name, Leventhal asks in a loud voice, "What, do you know me?" Then, in the next few sentences, four additional references to the theme of knowledge and acknowledgment occur. Allbee says to Leventhal, "Why shouldn't I know you. I thought you might not recognize me, though." In response, Leventhal pronounces Allbee's name "with gradual recognition," and Allbee in turn comments: "So you recognize me?" Leventhal reluctantly affirms that he knows who Allbee is; yet he does so "rather indifferently," casting a "sidewise" glance at his old acquaintance. In the next moment he "walk[s] off." Despite this demonstration of indifference, Leventhal is puzzled and disturbed by the fact that he has "recognized [Allbee] instantaneously. What a box, the mind," he exclaims to himself—characteristically attempting to distance his inmost self from the apparently autonomous operations of this mechanical "box" (27). He would prefer not to think that Allbee, whom he has "never liked," has any claim on his attention or memory. Confronted by this disturbing reality, Leventhal typically "arrange[s] not to know."

While Leventhal tries to belittle the significance of his spontaneous recognition, or acknowledgment, of a man he has not seen for years, Bellow instills the atmosphere of their encounter with a sense of mysterious significance. Based on the plot of Dostoevsky's short novel, *The Eternal Husband*, *The Victim* also employs many of the Russian master's characteristic effects.[7] In the Dostoevskian manner, Bellow deliberately refrains from supplying a logical explanation for the coincidence of his characters' initial encounter or for Leventhal's uncanny perceptions. Leventhal is shown, instead, to be mysteriously drawn to the park where, unbeknownst to him, Allbee is waiting. (A letter from Allbee, inviting Leventhal to meet him in the park, lies unopened in Leventhal's mailbox, to be discovered only *after* he returns home from this encounter.) Bellow employs, moreover, Dostoevsky's characteristic device for heightening the sense of mystery: he deliberately blurs the boundary between his character's waking and dreaming states of consciousness.

Just before going to the park, Leventhal awakens from apparent sleep; confused as to whether he has really slept, he is not sure, either, that he is now awake. The passage describing Leventhal's apparent transition from sleep to waking is deliberately ambiguous: "[Leventhal] thought he would doze off. But a little later he found himself standing at the window, holding the curtains with both hands. He was under the impression that he had slept. It was only eight-thirty by the whirring electric clock on the night table, however. Only five minutes had passed" (23). With the boundary between sleep and waking blurred, Leventhal "finds himself standing at the window" but does not know how he got there.

In this ambiguous condition he "set[s] off for the park," entering a landscape strangely resonant of human intimacy, an atmosphere thickened by a sense of shared secrets and mutual recognition: by everything, in short, against which Leventhal has tried, with a hard shell of indifference, to shield himself. "Eyes seemed softer than by day, and larger, and gazed at one longer, as though in the dark heat some interspace of reserve had been crossed and strangers might approach one another with a kind of recognition." Precisely at this moment Leventhal "suddenly had a feeling that he was not merely looked at but watched" by the "stranger" who turns out to be Allbee (25–26). Later, when he tells Allbee that he did not receive the letter inviting him to come to the park, Allbee assumes Leventhal is lying; for, he says, "if you didn't get it, this [encounter] would be quite a coincidence" (29). In this way Bellow draws attention to Leventhal's eery premonition of his "recognition" and hints, like Dostoevsky, at a powerful though hidden reality beneath appearances, one largely inaccessible to reason.

While Leventhal is a man who "arranges not to know," his author has arranged for the opposite to occur. Literally and symbolically, Allbee's haunting presence forces Leventhal to look and to learn. Described early in the novel as a man "who could not study," Leventhal no sooner meets this troubling emanation from his past than he finds himself "study[ing] Allbee more closely" (14, 28). "When you didn't want to take trouble with people, you found the means to turn them aside," Leventhal reflects (98). Unable to dismiss Allbee from his mind, he "takes the trouble" not only to think about him but even to envision the conditions under which Allbee has lived and suffered. "Of course, [he has known] suffering, Leventhal told himself gravely: down and out, living in a moldy hotel somewhere, hanging out in bars, sleeping whole days, picked up off the streets by the paddywagon or the ambulance, haunted in his mind by the wrongs or faults of his own which he turned into wrongs against himself; and that stirring around of the thoughts and feelings, that churning—everybody experienced it, but for a man like that it must be ugly, terrible, those thoughts wheeling around" (38).

What here spurs Leventhal's understanding of Albee is his internal recognition of those reflexes by which he, too, turns his own "wrongs or faults" into perceived "wrongs against himself." Opposites in every obvious respect—social position, ethnic background and general upbringing—the Jew and the anti-Semite are shown, at a deeper level, to partake of a common identity, the "shared secret" Leventhal would deny. Allbee, for his part, insists on treating Leventhal according to his idea of the stereotypical Jew and goads him with anti-Semitic barbs; yet he betrays fears and anxieties similar to those of the Jew he pretends to scorn. The scion of a distinguished New England family, Allbee manifests the same metaphysical insecurity that haunts Leventhal in a specifically Jewish form: the dread of persecution. Both men have tried to erect, against the uncertainty of a chance-ridden universe, a system of psychological defenses based on suspicion and the conviction that they have been singled out for mistreatment. At various points in the novel, each man betrays his fear of being victimized—either by the random forces of a chaotic universe or by a conspiracy that has singled him out for punishment. Thus, Allbee says, "it's all blind movement, vast movement, and the individual is shuttled back and forth." Success or failure is only a matter of "luck"; people "have a destiny forced on them" and "that's all the destiny they get, so they'd better not assume they're running their own show" (70–71). Haunted by a similar sense of impermanence, waiting for his own "good luck" to be "canceled" and "all favors melted away," Leventhal also laments that he, "like everybody else, was carried on currents, this way and that"—the helpless victim of random forces (91).

Leventhal and Allbee, each in his own way, erect a network of blame and suspicion that keeps them—in lieu of any affirmation or faith—from sliding into the abyss. Whenever Leventhal is bewildered by failure, therefore, or feels helpless to affect events, he counters despair with the suspicion of being persecuted; he reverts to the notion that "a black list" somewhere exists upon which his name is written (46–47, 142). To be condemned by human intention seems more bearable than to be crushed by random forces. Allbee, in his much more flagrant and grandiose manner, is similarly convinced that the Jews, having mysteriously allied themselves with those who "run things," are in some way responsible for present social ills and his own lack of success. To the anti-Semite's immediate charge, that Leventhal deliberately sought to have Allbee fired from his job, Leventhal responds by saying that his role in Allbee's downfall was, "at worst, an accident, unintentional" (96). Such an argument carries little weight with Allbee, however; for, as Bellow indicates, Allbee's anti-Semitism is itself a tenuous defense, desperate and degrading, against the engulfing chaos of accidental reality.

Allbee's loss of faith in a Christian vision of the world—"a world created for man," in which each human "life is necessary"—leads him to despair of a universe that is either completely arbitrary or tyrannized by malignant forces. In a way that suggestively prefigures the quandary of Pynchon's Oedipa Maas, in *The Crying of Lot 49*, Allbee alternately perceives the world as consisting of "hot stars and cold hearts" *or* as dominated by "evil" that "is as real as sunshine" (195, 146). In the first case, the universe is a dynamo charged by random explosions of "hot stars." In such a humanly indifferent world, where entropy is the only discernible law, hearts have already suffered heat-death and grown "cold." In Allbee's alternate vision, evil appears to be the morally negative counterpart of a "hot star," or exploding sun, charging the earth with its energy. Yielding to the blackness of this Manichean vision, Allbee tells Leventhal that the present is "a sort of Egyptian darkness": "You know, Moses punished the Egyptians with darkness" (144). To the anti-Semite, the God of Moses emblemizes the supreme power now "running things," elevating the Jews to social and professional prominence. Charging Leventhal with being "right at home" in the hellish conditions of "modern life," Allbee compares the Jew to "those what-do-you-call-'ems that live in the flames—salamanders" (141).

Allbee is, of course, mistaken in assuming that Leventhal is "at home" among the quandaries of "modern life"—just as his suggestion that the Jews worship the Devil is demented. Far from being "at home" in the world, Leventhal is as much in exile as any of his Jewish forebears. Dogged by a sense of the "queerness of existence" and his own tenuous place within it, Leventhal feels he might sink, at any moment, among "the lost, the outcast, the overcome, the effaced, the ruined" (288, 20). Allbee, on the other hand, insists that New York is "a very Jewish city"; there are "so many Jewish dishes in the cafeterias," so "many Jewish comedians and jokes, and stores, . . . and Jews in public life" (73). Amazed as well as horrified by Allbee's contention that Jews are "at home" in the harsh "conditions" of "modern life," Leventhal exclaims in agony: "That's just talk. Millions of us have been killed. What about that?" (141, 147). Yet as the arguments between the two men intensify, so does their sense of a "shared secret" and a mutual identity. Leventhal finds himself "singularly drawn with a kind of affection" to Allbee. "It oppressed him, it was repellent. He did not know what to make of it. Still he welcomed it, too" (224). Meanwhile Allbee's remarks betray an increasing fascination with the Jew. He says, for example, that the wiry thickness of Leventhal's hair "amazes me. Whenever I see you, I have to study it. . . . I've often tried to imagine how it would be to have hair like that" (224). Standing up to touch the Jew's hair, Allbee teasingly, but with a tinge of real admiration, "fingered Leventhal's hair, and Leventhal found himself caught under his touch and felt incapable of doing anything" (225).

Strangely enough, it is Allbee, the anti-Semite, who late in in the novel offers an alternate vision both to his paranoid perception of conspiratorial forces and to the random, accidental universe of contemporary science. Recalling the teachings of the Christian faith into which he was born, Allbee unwittingly reaffirms the knowledge that Schlossberg, a Jew, has identified as the foundation of an "exactly human" life. Recalling "John the Baptist coming out of the desert," Allbee says that John's message to mankind was, "Change yourself." Allbee wrongly assumes, however, that only "the Christian idea" of repentance attests to the intrinsic human knowledge of which Sammler, like Schlossberg, speaks. "Everybody knows but nobody wants to admit [what they know]," declares Allbee. "*I* know. Everybody knows." The "way we keep our eyes shut is a stunt," he adds, "because they're made to be open" (227, Bellow's italics). While Allbee cannot be said to act upon the knowledge he avows here, Leventhal *is* significantly changed by his confrontation with Allbee and the suffering he can no longer ignore, deny or "turn into wrongs against himself." In the end it is Leventhal's "large eyes" that begin to "stare as though he were trying to force open an inward blindness with the sharp edge of something actual" (207).

Invading, and finally shattering, Leventhal's "inward blindness" is the goading presence of Allbee himself—whose "intimate nearness" alternately "oppressed and intoxicated" him (160, 107). And though Allbee's taunting "intimation of a shared secret . . . aroused and vexed Leventhal, and sickened him," he ultimately experiences a "closeness" to Allbee that weighs upon him like a burden and a promise at the same time (30). He has "the strange feeling that there was not a single part of him on which the whole world did not press with full weight"; yet he perceives in this burden, "despite the pain it was causing him," a "disguised opportunity to discover something of great importance" (257–58). While the nature of this discovery is never logically explicated in the novel, the breakdown of Leventhal's "wooden" impassivity and his felt "closeness" to Allbee offer a strong suggestion of its source and significance. It is to Bellow's "actual" rendering of Leventhal and Allbee's developing relationship, and to Leventhal's gradual discovery of their bond, that we must, therefore, now turn.

Leventhal begins, we recall, by envisioning the degraded conditions to which Allbee has been subjected. Then, as though aroused by his own understanding of the other man's fears, he imagines his own life taking place in the awful surroundings he has pictured. From envisioning "hideous cardboard cubicles painted to resemble wood" and the "flophouse sheets and filthy pillows," Leventhal progresses to more intimate sensations of smell and touch, as his own buried recollections of abject failure and poverty begin to surface. Now recalling the "smell" of "the carbolic disinfectant" permeating the misery of society's rejects, Leventhal feels as though "it were *his* flesh on those sheets, *his* lips drinking that coffee, . . . *his* eyes looking at the boards of the floor" (69–70). But it is not just memories of the sordid past that Allbee awakens in Leventhal; by physically insinuating himself into Leventhal's solitude (Leventhal's wife, Mary, is out of town, visiting her mother), Allbee drags in the sordidness with him. Tracking Leventhal through the streets of New York City, showing up at his place of work, Allbee ends by penetrating the inner sanctum of Leventhal's apartment and even his bed. Meanwhile

Leventhal's heightened consciousness of Allbee's "closeness" works a profound psychological change in him, breaking down his "hard-boiled" defenses from within.

As Allbee weighs on his consciousness, Leventhal grows so aware of the other man's being that at times he seems to occupy Allbee's skin. He is so "conscious of Allbee" that he is "able to see himself as if through a strange pair of eyes: the side of his face, the palpitation in his throat." He is "changed in this way into his own observer" (107). Though burdened by his awareness "that Allbee hated him," Leventhal cannot escape the "curious emotion of closeness—for it was an emotion"—that he experiences with Allbee (160–61). It is this emotion of intimacy, this sympathetic recognition from within of another human being's plight, that obviates Leventhal's attempts to distance himself from his supposed "persecutor." "You keep your spirit under lock and key," Allbee accuses him at one point. But just as he manages to gain entry into Leventhal's private domain—even to obtain a spare "key" to his apartment—so Allbee breaks through the wall of Leventhal's defenses. Into the hidden chamber of Leventhal's locked "spirit," as well as the privacy of his home, Allbee drags all the reality of suffering, passion, shame and disorder that Leventhal dreads to confront.

Allbee even violates the sanctity of Leventhal's marriage bed. One day, to his horror, Leventhal arrives home to discover Allbee there with a naked woman. Enraged at Allbee for "bring[ing] this woman into my bed," Leventhal receives from him the following rebuke: "Where else, if not in bed. . . . What do you do? Maybe you have some other way, more refined, different?" (272). Though he vigorously airs out the apartment after Allbee and the woman leave, the "smell of [her] comb," which he finds on the carpet, continues to plague Leventhal (272, 275). This lingering odor, like the "smell of carbolic disinfectant" permeating his recollection of the flophouse, violates Leventhal's indifference from within. Penetrating the inmost recesses of consciousness, the woman's scent disturbingly implicates him, through his own undeniable knowledge of what has transpired, in Allbee's lust.

Just as Sammler must acknowledge his bond of "creatureliness" with the black pickpocket, whose member is a "double" of Sammler's own, so Leventhal is implicated in, as well as outraged by, Allbee's sexual conduct. As Allbee's insinuating comments tellingly suggest, the intercourse he has enjoyed with the naked woman is, physically speaking, a replica of those acts performed on the same bed by its rightful owners.[8] The "smell of the comb" returns to remind Leventhal of this actuality throughout the night, "coming over him with some fragment of what had occurred that evening in its wake, like a qualm," and implicating him in its reality (275). Against this "feeling of intimate nearness" all of Leventhal's concerted efforts "not to know" prove fruitless. And just as Leventhal's "close consciousness" of Allbee has created an empathic awareness of the other man's plight, so the woman's lingering scent rouses him to similar awareness of her distinct being: "It must have been frightening, sickening for her to hear the crash of the door and then to run out of bed—still another bed," he thinks to himself. Shifting his perspective to her point of view, he is once again changed "into his own observer." Leventhal perceives that "he ought not to leave himself out of the [recollected] picture, glaring at them both." Like Mr. Sammler "seen seeing," Leventhal proves more than a detached observer; he is an actor. He has played his own role in this "low" and "painful," but intensely "funny," scene from the human comedy.

As Leventhal recollects this scene with both amusement and dismay, he is, significantly, divested of his customary impassivity. The novel's narrator describes how, "when he was done laughing and coughing, [Leventhal's] face remained unusually expressive" (276). Allbee, by violating Leventhal's psychological as well as physical isolation, has served as the catalyst for this change. When he later attempts the ultimate violation—by trying to kill himself with the gas from Leventhal's oven and, because Leventhal is asleep in the apartment at the time, nearly destroying them both—the full flood of Leventhal's dammed emotions bursts through "like a cold fluid, like brine." He feels "released by the breaking open of something within him" (282). Under the pressing threat of death, the bulwark of his defenses gives way— opening the floodgates of feeling. Immediate danger galvanizes Leventhal to act, freeing him from paralyzing dread of the unknown. Fighting for his immediate survival, he is "sure," for once, of what he must do. He runs to the kitchen, grabs Allbee away from the open door of the oven, hurls him out of the apartment and turns off the gas. Then, as he proceeds once more to air out the apartment, he becomes strangely calm. "In spite of the struggle, . . . he did not seem greatly disturbed. He looked impassive." Fatigued beyond care, Leventhal is drained of both feeling and fear: "He would sleep undisturbed; he cared about nothing else" (283–84).

Although a touch of his old defensiveness is perceptible, Leventhal's "impassive" face here signals exhaustion from experience rather than a further attempt to ward it off. Marking the end of the story proper, this sinking into sleep also suggests that some permanent chink has been opened in the "hardboiled" shell of his defenses. In the novel's closing chapter, which serves as an epilogue to the foregoing events, Leventhal's suggested transformation is confirmed. "The consciousness of an unremitting daily fight, though still present, was fainter and less troubling. . . . Something recalcitrant seemed to have left him; he was not exactly affable, but his obstinately unrevealing expression had softened" (285).

Through recognition of his "closeness" to Allbee, Leventhal has confronted not only disturbing realities but death itself. Indeed, the "destination" of Leventhal's journey throughout the novel—despite his earlier mentioned "dread of being the only person in the city without one"—is confrontation with death. Like Allbee's attempted suicide that almost kills them both, the death of Leventhal's nephew Mickey brings him face to face with the conditions of shared human existence. Earlier in the novel, an old woman, Mrs. Harkavy, had tried, in absurd fashion, to deny the mystery of death. Like Dostoevsky's Lebeziatnikov—who, we recall, assures Raskolnikov that experiments in Paris will lead to curing the insane "simply by logical argument"—Mrs. Harkavy invokes a rationalistic solution to the problem of death: " 'Someday science will conquer death,' she said. 'Last Sunday there was a symposium in the *Times* about it' " (245–46). In the next moment, however, the old woman drops the logical pretense that "there are brains enough [to solve] everything"; her eyes meet Leventhal's "own with a familiar, instantaneous significance" (246). In this flash of mutual recognition, each acknowledges the mysterious origin as well as the common "destination" of all.

Confrontation with death is only the most dramatic reminder, however, of the metaphysical voyage implicating Leventhal in universal human experience. Just as Mickey's illness draws him into the center of his brother Max's family, providing Leventhal the opportunity to discover a renewed "closeness" with Max, so Allbee's much stranger intrusion on Leventhal's life leads to his acknowledged "closeness" with others. The park where Leventhal first encounters Allbee provides a suggestive setting for this discovery, hinted at by the mandala-like pattern of the benches, which form "a dense, double human wheel":

> There was an overwhelming human closeness and thickness, and Leventhal was penetrated by a sense not merely of the crowd in this park but of innumerable millions, crossing, touching, pressing. What was that story he had once read about Hell cracking open on account of the rage of the god of the sea, and all the souls, crammed together, looking out? But these were alive. (183–84)

Although critics usually cite this passage for its rendering of the urban landscape as a kind of hell, I find that these images, evoking a mythical underworld, have a more positive effect. Linked to earlier images, already discussed, of Charon's ferry transporting souls across the river, those in the passage cited above suggest the shadowy nature of temporal reality and the ultimate mystery shimmering beneath its surface. Poking through the fabric of appearances—like the souls of the dead, "crammed together, looking out" at those who are "alive"—the mystery of human destiny links the living to the dead, as it links each one of the living to all others.

The attentiveness with which the imagined dead "look out" at the living belies the indifference Leventhal has sought to erect against the world and other people. "Alienation," Joseph points out in *Dangling Man*, is "a fool's plea": "you can't banish the world by decree if it's in you" (DM 91). In a sense

Leventhal has tried to do just that, banishing from his insight and concern a great deal of the world to which Bellow shows him inextricably bound. Leventhal has, for example, tried to dismiss Allbee's claims on him with an outsider's logic, telling him: "You don't owe me anything. I don't owe you anything, either." Because Allbee will "not accept this," Leventhal is first annoyed, then disturbed and finally shocked into recognizing his complicity both in Allbee's misfortune and in the turbulent reality of which he is a part (164). Despite the enmity between them, Leventhal comes to recognize in Allbee his spiritual "double," thereby validating through personal experience his discovery of a general truth: "Everybody committed errors and offenses," he realizes midway through the novel, "but it was supremely plain to him that everything, everything without exception, took place as if within a single soul or person."[9] Significantly, Leventhal associates Allbee with the discovery of this truth: "He had a particularly vivid recollection of the explicit recognition in Allbee's eyes which he could not doubt was the double of something in his own. Where did it come from? 'Speak of black and white,' he mused. Black and white were Schlossberg's words, to which he frequently returned. Either the truth was simple or we had to accept the fact that we could not know it, and if we could not know it there was nothing to go by" (169).

When, several years after Allbee's failed suicide attempt, the two men meet again, Leventhal's intuition that life is not an "egg race" is confirmed. As he discovers in the course of the novel's epilogue, the "promise" of life has nothing to do with "tickets to desirable and undesirable places." Leventhal bumps into Allbee, appropriately enough, at the theater. While Allbee, prosperous-looking and in the company of a celebrated actress, appears to be "sitting in a box," Leventhal and Mary are seated downstairs (290). Nevertheless, neither Allbee's elevated position at the theater nor his look of prosperity prevents Leventhal from detecting the "decay of something" in the other man's appearance. "There was very little play in the deepened wrinkles around his eyes. They had a fabric quality, crumpled and blank. A smell of whiskey came from him" (292). Displaying obvious improvement in his physical appearance and social station, Allbee has prospered materially but not spiritually. Noting Mary's pregnancy he cannot refrain, moreover, from commenting wryly on the Hebrew God's commandment to "increase and multiply." In response to this slur Leventhal's former defensiveness surfaces momentarily, then is quickly supplanted by deeper "powers" of insight. Allbee, Leventhal realizes, "had no real desire to be malicious; he was merely obedient to habit. He might have been smiling at himself and making an appeal of a sort for understanding" (292).

To this silent appeal Leventhal reacts with generous understanding. As his conversation with Allbee almost playfully repeats the patterns of the past— ironic response countering barbed accusation as the two men fence verbally— a sense of the old intimacy also persists. No longer averting his gaze, Leventhal sees that Allbee's "smile gave a touch of cynicism to the sensational, terrible look of pain that rose to his eyes. Leventhal *saw* that he could not help himself and pitied him" (293, italics added). Actively engaged in such insight, Leventhal is able to pity the suffering soul beneath the mask of mockery. Allbee, in his turn, takes this opportunity to be candid; he wants Leventhal to know that when, years before, he tried to commit suicide, he did not mean to harm Leventhal. "I know I owe you something," he adds.

To this declaration of gratitude Leventhal remains silent, even pulling his hand away from Allbee's, as though wordlessly rejecting, once again, any mention of a debt or bond between them. Yet despite this reversion to old habits, Leventhal does not walk away from Allbee as he did so often in the past; nor does he refrain from smiling as their conversation resumes. He may not be willing to acknowledge that each man "owes" the other something, but the bond is manifested by the understanding that flows between them. The anti-Semite recognizes that he has been treated by the Jew with decency, humanity, charity, even affection. Through his own irrational behavior, moreover, Allbee has managed to penetrate Leventhal's elaborate system of defenses, forcing him to recognize in the cracked mirror of Allbee's troubled existence a distorted reflection of his own. Thus Allbee has, through his own desperate need, helped Leventhal to confront and finally to honor what he knows.

"When you turn against yourself," Allbee tells Leventhal, "nobody else means anything to you either" (293). The sympathy and insight that Leventhal can bring to other people, beginning with Albee, is a direct result of the "softening" he has undergone toward himself. "Something recalcitrant seemed to have left him," the narrator comments in the epilogue (285). Leventhal's former obduracy was founded on "hard-boiled" resistance to his inmost self. Having marshalled indifference against his own deepest "powers" of insight and "extended [it] to others," Leventhal was in danger of destroying his humanity—the very self that silence and impassivity were mistakenly intended to protect. Only through relentless exposure to light and to other human beings, Bellow suggests, can the tender ego, the embryonic human spirit, flourish and grow. Shattering Leventhal's protective shell, forcing him to abandon simplistic notions of the "egg race" for a profounder vision of life's journey, Allbee inadvertently rescues Leventhal's moribund inner life as surely as Leventhal saves the suicidal Allbee from physical death.

In the theater, after the intermission and just before Allbee rushes upstairs to his appointed seat, Leventhal asks him, with a tinge of habitual anxiety, "Wait a minute, what's your idea of who runs things" (294). Mined with hidden dangers, the world is still a threatening place for Leventhal. Assuaging his dread of the unknown by reverting, at least momentarily, to the notion of a conspiracy that "runs things," he still worries about being "singled out" for disaster or punishment. But the old dread, arising from an acute sense of metaphysical uncertainty, is at least tempered by Leventhal's perception of the "shared secret" binding him to the rest of humanity—most particularly, to his unlikely "double," Kirby Allbee. Recognition of their common origin and mutual "destination" is what finally inspires Leventhal to affirm, and try to fulfill, the "promise" of life—by being, in Schlossberg's terms, "exactly human." Based on avowedly intuited knowledge, Leventhal's subjective commitment to such an ideal is what makes it true, confirms its reality. Affirmation cannot rationally refute, but may assuredly fill, the empty wastes of a universe created by "hot stars and cold hearts."

Chapter 4

A Test of Earthly Powers:
The Adventures of Augie March

For Augie March—young, vigorous, full of himself—life is charged with promise. Embarked on a series of colorful "adventures," Augie is both a modern-day picaro—restlessly and, to all appearances, aimlessly on the move—and a hero with a purpose: a young man seeking to discover "what I was meant to be" (310). Unhampered by Leventhal's paranoia and guilt, Augie is eager to embrace experience, express his feelings and attend to his "private soul" (199). Yet for all his openness and exuberance, Augie is subject to some of the same constraints that operate upon Joseph and Leventhal. In a passage occurring midway through *The Adventures of Augie March* (1953), Augie reflects, in the manner of Bellow's Dangling Man, on the cultural codes constricting one's "freedom to seek grace." Registering these "inhibitory effects" on his own vision, Augie chides himself: "Oh you chump and weak fool, you are one of a humanity that can't be numbered and not more than the dust of metals scattered in a magnetic field and clinging to the lines of force, determined by laws, eating, sleeping, employed, conveyed, obedient, and subject" (316).

Yet even while denigrating his "foolish" quest for something "of the highest," Augie's language challenges the hegemony of scientific rationalism (84). In the passage mentioned above, Augie's description of the magnetic force-field evokes a despotic regime, in which determining "laws" and "lines of force" exert authority over a population of "obedient" subjects. Similarly, each of the "Machiavellis" in the novel seeks to "recruit" others to his own particular "version of what's real" (402). Grandma Lausch, Einhorn, Augie's brother Simon, Mrs. Renling, Thea Fenchel, the fanatical positivist Bateshaw—each would gain dominion over a population, a "band of particles" rendered "obedient" by the exertion of physical, economic, intellectual or political "lines of force" (516). On a larger scale, Bellow further suggests, technological society, with its power to broadcast the authority of rationalistic assumptions and to multiply the effects of the "conditioning forces," disseminates a collective "version" of reality that holds its members spiritually in thrall.

Ultimately Augie refuses to yield to the authority of these earthly powers, wielded individually or collectively. To the the strenuous machinations of the Machiavellis—and to the "Niagara Falls torrent" of statistics, data, news and information that threatens to drown his inner life and "feelings" in a flood of facts—he opposes a biblical vision of human life and destiny (455). This ancient vision of existence is evoked, on the most obvious level, by the numerous biblical images and allusions interwoven throughout Augie's narration. By invoking the Bible's ancient wisdom—that earthly power is fleeting and trust in its authority misplaced—the allusive texture of Augie's narration consistently undermines the authenticity of each "version" of reality promoted by the Machiavellis. Beyond this effect, however, lies another, less obvious one that I intend to demonstrate as well: through the language and structure of the novel, Bellow portrays the Machiavellis' drive for earthly power as a distorted expression, or perversion, of the human being's innate longing for the divine.

From the vantage supplied by hindsight we may recognize, furthermore, that what Bellow implicitly renders in his third novel is explicitly articulated in his seventh. There, in *Mr. Sammler's Planet*, Bellow's protagonist openly identifies the "madness" of contemporary culture—its pursuit of sexual "extremes" and material excess—as a "base" expression of religious longing. It is this longing, which William James defines as the need to attach oneself to the transcendent or divine, that Sammler discerns beneath the bizarre behavior and outlandish costumes of New York City's rootless population. Having exalted "Reason" and "swept" the world clean of mystery, the "middle class," Sammler observes as he walks along Broadway, has "failed to create a spiritual life of its own." Having "invested everything in material expansion," human beings now "faced disaster," giving vent to "despair" and "terror" in "scene[s] of perversity." Such "madness," Sammler observes, is "the attempted liberty of people who feel themselves overwhelmed by giant forces of organized control. Seeking the magic of extremes. Madness is a base form of the religious life" (MSP 145–46). Beneath the crazy get-ups and the desperate behavior of Broadway's freaks and dropouts, Sammler discerns the same yearning for freedom that informs Augie's own challenge of "the conditioning forces" and the materialist view of existence. Whether manifested in perverse or profound forms of expression, the longing is, in the words of Bellow's Dangling Man, for "the freedom to seek grace."

In *The Adventures of Augie March*, Augie's perception of the Machiavellis' ambitious striving as a "base" or perverse expression of religious longing is not, as in Sammler's case, explicitly articulated. Yet the connection is implicitly developed throughout Augie's narration, as the following brief example should help to illustrate. Mrs. Renling, who tries to adopt Augie as her own son, is one of the more benign Machiavellis with whom he comes in contact during the course of his "pilgrimage" (424). The wife of a successful businessman, she is one of those "energetic people," says Augie, "who build against pains and uncertainties," hoping to create something permanent by means of their elaborate material "constructions." Like Mrs. Renling, each of the Machiavellis regards himself as a "realist" because he strives so intently to *realize* his schemes in the concrete world. Yet each of these schemes or "constructions," Augie points out, is actually based on infinite longing—on the hope that one's consuming idea or treasured "thoughts will be as substantial as the seven hills to build on" (151–52).

In describing Mrs. Renling's and the other Machiavellis' "constructions," Augie evokes the ancient legend of the founding of Rome—"the eternal city" built upon "the seven hills." The ultimate aim of these apparently pragmatic "constructions" is, his language suggests, transcendent rather than practical: the dream of constructing "an eternal city" out of "bricks and planks." In this dream, fostered by human beings since time immemorial, Augie detects mankind's age-old confusion of earthly with heavenly powers. The confusion is as old, at least, as the biblical architects of Babel, who mistook physical elevation for spiritual ascendancy, proximity to the heavens for closeness to God.

Chicago is Bellow's symbol for present-day Babel, and Babylon. A parody of the "eternal city," Chicago's imperial size and weight foster the illusion of permanence. Augie's description reveals, to the contrary, an empire on the verge of dissolution: "Around was Chicago. In its repetition it exhausted your imagination of details and units, more units than the cells of the brain and the bricks of Babel. The Ezekiel caldron of wrath, stoked with bones. In time the caldron too would melt. A mysterious tremor, dust, vapor, emanation of stupendous effort traveled with the air" (458). A "stupendous effort" of the human "brain," to whose "cells" its structural units are compared, Chicago's monstrous empire is actually composed of "the bricks of Babel": it is erected upon "so many fool amateur projects for the Tower of Babel" (304).

The inhabitants of this New World Babylon have, like their wayward ancestors, invested all trust, hope and faith in earthly powers: mistaking matter for divinity, images for ultimate reality, they have become idolaters. Bellow's vision of modern-day idolatry—which serves as a suggestive backdrop throughout *The Adventures of Augie March*—becomes, as we shall see, an increasingly explicit theme in his later novels, most particularly in *Humboldt's Gift* (1975). There, in his own quest for spiritual enlightenment, Bellow's protagonist, Charlie Citrine, will declare his need to penetrate beneath "the plastered idols of the Appearances": to free himself of the "tyranny" of the materialist vision and its "categories devoid of spirit" (HG 16–17, 363).

In *Augie March*, the Machiavellis, idolaters of earthly power, exercise a similar "tyranny" as they seek to rule over the "meek" and mild of this earth (4). Although helpless in every worldly sense, the "meek" are shown, at the same time, to be mysteriously gifted or blessed.[1] Figuring most prominently among the ranks of the meek and mild are Augie's Mama, with her simple mind and failing eyesight, and her "mind-crippled" son Georgie. Singularly incapable of any "conscious mental" maneuvers, these two feeble-minded people are shown, nevertheless, to possess some essential knowledge from which the Machiavellis are cut off. Like Henderson and Herzog in the later novels, Augie seeks to recover this knowledge, to discover what his author calls the "primordial person" within. This primordial self, Bellow tells an interviewer in 1984, exists within each of us. "He is not made by his education, nor by cultural or historical circumstances." To this "primordial person" the novelist traces the "invariable, ultimately unteachable [knowledge] native to the soul."[2] Published some thirty years before these remarks, *Augie March* already evinces the author's belief in the "primordial person." Thus Augie, noting his Mama's "original view of doom or recovery," recognizes the knowledge she possesses "without any work of mind, of which she was incapable" (54). In his idiot brother Georgie's face, he glimpses another trace of this wisdom, which he later identifies as "the oldest knowledge, older than the Euphrates, older than the Ganges" (454). As Augie studies the "subtle look that passed down [Georgie's] white lashes and cheeks," he deems it a "reflex from wisdom kept prisoner by incapacity, something full of comment on the life of all of us" (50).

The "wisdom kept prisoner" by Georgie's "incapacity" to reason is further constrained by those who mistake their own "worldly reasoning" for wisdom. Thus Grandma Lausch, an old lady who boards at the Marches' during Augie's youth, assumes control of the family by dint of her superior intelligence and will. Feared and obeyed by Augie's meek mother, who is Grandma's drudge, the old lady is, in Augie's words, "one of those Machiavellis of small street and neighborhood." Neither the March children nor their mother, long since abandoned by Augie's father, is any match for Grandma's cunning intelligence and domineering will. Yet the opposition between earthly power and spiritual freedom is highlighted by the contrast between Grandma's tireless strategies for supremacy and Mama's meekness.

With her sharp wit and "schooling temperament," Grandma Lausch "instructs" Augie and his brother Simon in strategies for gaining advantage in the world—making sure, at the same time, that no one defies her sultanic authority in the household (13, 8). She prides herself, as Augie puts it, on having "a different understanding from ours." To her, knowledge is power—earthly power—and she assumes that she "owned and supervised everything" (34). True to her Machiavellian vision, Grandma Lausch demands respect for her superior powers of "worldly reasoning" and deems love a weakness: "A child loves, a person respects," she lectures. "Respect is better than love." To the members of the March household and their immediate neighbors, Grandma is "a proper object of respect" and authority. When she decides, therefore, that Georgie must be sent to a home for the mentally indigent, Augie's mother is helpless to oppose her will:

> George sat there with one foot stepping on the other and ate the gravy in that unconscious, mind-crippled seraph's way of his by contrast to [Grandma Lausch's] worldly reasoning. Mama in her hurt, high voice tried to answer but only spoke confusion. She was anyway incapable of saying much that was clear, and when she was excited or in pain you couldn't understand her at all. Then Georgie stopped eating and began to moan. (51)

The overweening nature of Grandma Lausch's "worldly reasoning" rather precisely recalls William James's observation, discussed earlier, on the "prestige" of rationalism in modern culture: "it has the loquacity, it can challenge you for proofs, and chop logic, and put you down with words." Against Grandma Lausch's vociferous arguments for sending Georgie away, Augie's gentle mother is "incapable of saying much that was clear." Meanwhile the old lady, "getting down to cases," dispenses her "mixture of reality" with the same relentless logic she employs to "close a trap in chess" (50–51, 43).

As Augie later makes clear, the idiot-child's senseless moaning evinces something more profound than brute nature. In Georgie's "unconscious" reaction we may even detect what his author later describes, in a 1975 essay, as "traces of the soul": "Why, since the unconscious is by definition what we do not know," Bellow rhetorically asks, "should we not expect to find in it traces of the soul as well as aggression?"[3] In the mysterious ground of his characters' being—which is, as Augie says, "full of comment on the life of all of us"— Bellow discovers more than Freudian instinct or appetite. Incapable of reason and devoid of speech, Georgie is nevertheless able, in Augie's phrase, "to do with his soul" (57). While Georgie fidgets under Grandma Lausch's tyrannical rule, idiotically stepping with one foot upon the other, neither his senseless movements nor his stunned mind obscures from Augie's vision the angelic radiance of his brother's soul—gazing like "a far traveler" from the height of his "pale, mind-crippled handsomeness" (56).

If knowledge is power, then the power derived from the "oldest knowledge"—"older," as Augie says, "than the Euphrates, older than the Ganges"—does not extend itself imperially. It lies closer to what Augie calls the "power of being" and resides even in the "meek" and "mind-crippled." Augie's "oldest knowledge" summons an ideal of wisdom distinct from Socratic reason—the knowledge that persists even when, as in Mama and Georgie's case, reason is crippled. Thus Georgie's "wisdom" is "kept prisoner," but not erased, by the "incapacity" of his mind. Bellow's rendering of Georgie's beatific nature suggests that his vision of human nature may be closer to that of a religious writer, such as Flannery O'Connor, than to the nineteenth-century American realists, such as Theodore Dreiser and Sinclair Lewis, with whom he is often linked.[4] In *The Violent Bear It Away* (1960), published seven years after *Augie March*, O'Connor also depicts a "mind-crippled" boy, the idiot-son of a schoolteacher, who becomes the focus of his father's struggle against faith. In the schoolteacher, Rayber, the struggle between reason and faith becomes a fight to the death. Recalling O'Connor's stark vision of the absolute forces contending within the human soul may help to clarify the more muted features of Augie's own struggle against the Machiavellis and their rational "constructions." A cursory paragraph should suffice, for our purposes, to outline the role that the idiot-child, Bishop, plays in O'Connor's novel.

To his father, a zealous atheist, Bishop is a freak of nature, a victim of "conditioning forces" gone awry. According to Rayber's "version of what's real," as Augie might put it, Bishop is a witless and therefore pointless creature—he has no function. Tormented by the spontaneous love that he feels for his child, Rayber is determined to extinguish it altogether. For him such love is a repellent confirmation of irrational faith: a faith preached by Rayber's "prophet" father and abhorred by the son. To kill his irrational love for his idiot-child means, for Rayber, to destroy once and for all the expression of a faith his reason abhors. Eventually Rayber attempts to murder Bishop and ends by cutting himself off from all feeling—a kind of death in itself. So "savage" is O'Connor's portrait of the "rationalist," even her most sympathetic critics charge, that it falls short of "serious representation." Rayber's "rationalism" is so zealous that it yields its opposite—fanaticism.[5] Yet this is surely O'Connor's point: when the mystery of creation, the paradoxes of human existence and human love, are subjected to narrow methods of analysis and logic—Grandma Lausch's "worldly reasoning"—monstrous distortions may arise.

In the course of Augie's adventures, he will encounter some "Machiavellis" whose reasoning leads, if not to killing their own children, to some gross distortions of the human. We have only to recall, for example, Augie's bizarre encounter with a "cuckoo" scientist named Bateshaw during the war. When their ship is torpedoed off the Canary Islands, he and Bateshaw end up in the same lifeboat. Convinced by the observable "data" that they are drifting close to the Canaries, where he hopes to land and be interned for the rest of the war, Bateshaw does everything—including clobbering Augie on the head with an oar and tying him up—to prevent Augie from sending out flares to passing ships. After Augie manages to signal a British tanker that eventually picks up the two men, he discovers that they "were way past the Canaries and somewhere off the Rio de Oro." So much for "this scientist Bateshaw," he exclaims. "Why, he was cuckoo! Why, we'd both have rotted in that African sea, and the boat would have rotted, and there would have been nothing but death and mad ideas to the last. Or he'd have murdered and eaten me, still calm and utterly reasonable" (512).

With his fanatic's faith in reason and "scientific authority," Bateshaw, like the schoolteacher Rayber, vociferously denies the reality of love (507). When, before the two men are rescued, Augie asks Bateshaw whether a certain woman had been "in love" with him, Bateshaw answers by delivering a lecture on the "reality situation"—that is, the biological facts. "She had pulmonary phthisis," Bateshaw tells Augie, "and people like that are frequently highly stimulated" (499). Bateshaw does not allow, with Pascal, that "the heart has its own order; the intellect its own, which is by principle and demonstration. The heart has another." The challenge that Pascal poses to the rationalist is made especially clear in Rayber's case. Were he to accept the heart's "order" and truth, he would leave himself open to the possiblity of faith: "It is the heart," says Pascal, "which experiences God, and not the reason." Faith, he adds, "is a gift of God."[6]

In contrast to both Bateshaw and Rayber, Augie accepts the authority of love—just as he acknowledges the "ancient knowledge" possessed by Mama and Georgie in their helpless and apparently senseless existence. For Augie, love actually transforms the apparent "accidents" of circumstance into significant existence. Thus, he insists to Mimi Villars that his own conception "couldn't have been all accident. On my mother's side at least I can be sure there was love in it." Logically speaking, what Augie says here makes little sense. In order to understand how love can redeem Augie's physical conception from the sphere of random events, one has to believe that, in Augie's words, love evinces "the desire that there should be more life . . . gratitude" (254). Such "gratitude" for life, even in the most dire and chaotic circumstances, is an implicit avowal that existence cannot be measured or reckoned on a score sheet. Human life is not a function, accomplished or failed, but a gift bestowed.

Augie's belief, that human beings have "fates" rather than "functions," owes more, he knows, to the saint's knowledge than to the scientist's (516). "I don't know who the saint was," he says near the end of the novel, "who woke up, lifted his face, opened his mouth, and reported on his secret dream that blessedness covers the whole Creation but covers it thicker in some places than in others. Whoever he was, it's my great weakness to respond to such dreams. This is the *amor fati*, that's what it is, or mysterious adoration of what occurs" (526–27). The charge of "weakness" that Augie levels at himself is something of a rhetorical ploy—just as previous claims to being a "chump and weak fool" tend to disarm the modern reader in his skepticism. Augie's trust in his "purest feelings" should not, however, be dismissed as simple (or even profound) romanticism.[7] As our brief discussion of O'Connor—hardly a romantic writer by anyone's definition—serves to suggest, the intrinsic relationship between love and faith is clearly demonstrated in Rayber's compulsion to repress the former in order to deny the latter. In *Augie March*, the relationship is just as clearly suggested.

In Georgie's love for Grandma Lausch, for example, we see a direct relationship between the idiot-child's capacity to love and the saint's dream of "blessedness" that "covers the whole Creation." Unable to absorb the lessons Grandma tirelessly delivers, Georgie still persists, beatifically, in loving this unlovable old crone:

> But Georgie loved . . . Grandma, whom he would kiss on the sleeve, on the knee, taking knee or arm in both hands and putting his underlip forward, chaste, lummoxy, caressing, gentle and diligent. . . . The old lady let him embrace her and spoke to him. . . . And [then] she'd sharply push his forehead off with her old prim hand, having fired off for Simon and me, mindful always of her duty to wise us up, one more animadversion on the trustful, loving, and simple surrounded by the cunning-hearted and tough, a fighting nature of birds and worms, and a desperate mankind without feelings. Illustrated by Georgie. (9–10)

As Grandma delivers her "lessons of hardness," Augie's vivid depiction of the scene conveys an opposing vision—of her own vulnerability, which Georgie appears to understand (36). Reading "lessons off poor Georgie's head," she inadvertently illustrates the power not of "fighting nature" but of love: a lonely old lady receiving the affection of an idiot—the gift her reason scorns. Grandma's need for the love she professes to disdain is further confirmed when her sons arrive, on rare occasions, to visit their mother. Then Augie notes the way she has "of capturing their heads when they bent down to give her the kiss of duty." Such scenes leave Augie unconvinced by the "lessons of hardness" that Grandma delivers to the March brothers; "maybe," he thinks, "she sermonized us both about love because of her [neglect by] her sons" (28).

Revealed in her weakness and vulnerability, Grandma Lausch yet aspires to godlike authority. While her view of "a fighting nature of birds and worms" echoes Darwin's "survival of the fittest," her assertion of earthly power strikes Augie as having a more ancient source. To him "she is Eastern," resembling "a great lama" or the "lower trinity" of three brown monkey-figures "squatting" on "the sideboard, on the Turkestan runner," like "lesser gods" (9). Like all idols, however, she has clay feet; despite her silence on the subject of death, she cannot hold out forever against old age. Apprehensive and superstitious, Grandma introduces her own form of "kitchen religion" to ward off the forces of decay: she "burned a candle on the anniversary of Mr. Lausch's death, threw a lump of dough on the coals when she was baking, as a kind of offering, had incantations over baby teeth and stunts against the evil eye" (12).

The iron laws of Grandma's regime are belied by her evident mortality, just as her intended "lessons of hardness" betray her own vulnerability. The

ultimate subversion of Grandma's earthly power is, inevitably, her enfeeblement by age and approaching death. Athough she commandeers the March
family into sending Georgie to a home for the retarded, it is only a matter of
time before she too is sent away, by Simon, to die in a home for the aged. Even
before this final development, and immediately after she sends Georgie away,
Grandma appears to have "outsmarted herself." Without Georgie at home, the
March household experiences "a diminished family life, as though it were care
of Georgie that had been the main basis of household union." Augie's family
is Grandma Lausch's only empire; "diminished" by Georgie's departure, the
Marches' dwindling household spells the loss of her earthly power. By her own
ruthless strategies, Grandma has been "power-robbed" (58). One thinks of the
Breughel painting described by Augie later in the novel, in which a thief who
has cut the string of an unwitting old man's purse is "enclosed in a glass ball,
and on the glass ball there is a surmounting cross, and it looks like the
emperor's symbol of rule. Meaning," Augie speculates, "that it is earthly
power that steals while the ridiculous wise are in a dream about this world and
the next" (190–91).[8] In this case, however, Grandma's ruthless exercise of
earthly power leads to her own loss; exerting her power over Georgie and
Mama, "the ridiculous wise," she unwittingly robs herself. Perhaps that is the
true significance of the glass ball enclosing the thief: the worship of earthly
power is itself a trap.

After Georgie's departure, Augie points out, "the house was changed . . .
dinkier, darker, smaller; once shiny and venerated things losing their attraction
and richness and importance. Tin showed, cracks, black spots where enamel
was hit off, threadbarer [sic.], design scuffed out of the center of the rug" (58–
59). In this passage no "as if" or other explanatory phrase qualifies the absolute
nature of the household's fall from grace. Not only the inhabitants but the
house itself—the floors, objects, even the rug—suffers Georgie's loss. The
"once shiny and venerated things" have lost their "richness and importance";
once sacred, they are now flimsy and finite, no longer transformed or redeemed
from the plane of accidental existence by the power of love.

The March family's bereavement is underscored, furthermore, by the
contrast Bellow draws between past and present conditions. Before Georgie's
expulsion, the humble household is described by Augie as a temple devoted to
ritual worship and "the love of God": "Here you smelled the daily cleaning
wax, and everything was in place on a studious plan—veneer shining, doilies
spread, dime-store cut-glass, elkhorn, clock set in place—as regular as a
convent parlor or any place where the love of God is made ready for on a base
of domestic neatness" (23). Augie's description here echoes the earlier discussed passage from *Dangling Man*, in which Joseph observes that the rituals
of domestic cleaning "may become," when infused with the spirit of love,
"part of the nature of God."

Whether one takes Augie's description of the household's decline metaphorically or literally, it is clear that the strength of Grandma Lausch's earthly empire has depended on the very "weakness," the very love, she disdains. The care and devotion of Augie's Mama—"the prime example of this weakness" in Grandma's eyes—are all that sustain the old lady in her local glory. When Mrs. March's eyesight wholly fails and she can no longer care for the old woman, Grandma's reign, in the family and eventually upon earth, is doomed. When Augie later visits Grandma in a home for the aged, he is shocked by the "weakly, even infant and lunatic" cast of her eye—and of her once cunning mind.

Each of the novel's "reality instructors"—Grandma Lausch, William Einhorn, Mrs. Renling, Simon, Thea Fenchel, Manny Padilla, Clem Tambow—reiterates in his own way Grandma's belief in "hardness" and "a fighting nature." Scoffing at Augie for believing in love, Padilla tells him he is "going against history" (and, Bellow implies, against the grain of literary fashion as well). "The big investigation today," Padilla chides Augie, "is into how *bad* a guy can be, not how good he can be" (431, Bellow's italics). Another friend, Clem Tambow, diagnoses Augie as having a "nobility syndrome"; he should give up the notion of "Man, with capital M, with great stature," and "adjust to the reality situation" (434). According to the "reality principle," one is either victor or victim, predator or prey. One should "accept the data of experience"; to survive in "fighting nature" requires superior force, not virtue (436). This law of the "Machiavellis" is succinctly stated by William Einhorn, "the first superior man" of Augie's acquaintance. In "the naked form of the human jelly, one should choose or seize with force," says Einhorn, and "have the strength of voice to make other voices fall silent—the same principle for persons as for peoples, parties, states" (183).

Most of the Machiavellis Augie encounters seek dominion by exerting mind over matter. Like Grandma, they elevate their elaborate schemes, strategies and *idées fixes* to the status of "reality principles" and employ them to hold sway over others. Einhorn, the "superior man," is the definitive version of the strong-minded, strong-willed Machiavelli. Although Augie must help Einhorn, a physical cripple, to get dressed—just as he used to assist his "mind-crippled" brother, Georgie, at dressing— Einhorn's association with the weak and the helpless appears to stop here. A "weakness for complete information," not the "weakness" of love, characterizes this shrewd and crafty invalid. Like Grandma, who is also physically weak, Einhorn makes "mind the chief center of trial"—the focus of the competitive struggle for supremacy—and asserts his power "through mind" (71, 100).

In describing Einhorn to the reader, Augie places a "superior" brain at the top of the list of Einhorn's earthly powers: "He had a brain and many enterprises, real directing power, philosophical capacity" (60). It is Einhorn's formidable mind that qualifies him, in Augie's view, for a position on that "eminent list" of legendary "kings," which includes Caesar and Ulysses. To

Einhorn, dishonesty and cheating do not constitute ethical weakness but practical strength; they are, in fact, skills to be honed. Obsessed by the most trivial possibilities for cheating others, he spends hours each day practicing these skills. Einhorn's daily routine, Augie observes, includes "ordering things on approval he didn't intend to pay for—stamps, little tubes of lilac perfume, . . . and all the sort of items advertised in the back pages of the Sunday supplement. He had me write for them in my hand and give fictitious names, and he threw away the dunning letters, of course, and said all of these people calculated losses into what they charged" (69).

Rejecting any authority higher than his own "superior" powers, Einhorn is another self-styled "god" with clay feet. Like Grandma Lausch, he eventually betrays his fallen condition. The mortal fallibility of this "superior" man proves a greater "lesson" to Augie than any which Einhorn endeavors to teach. The 1929 Crash, for example, leaves Einhorn mentally as well as financially shattered. The "speed and depth of the fall" of Einhorn's earthly empire, like the spectacle of "the fallen man" in Bellow's first novel, evokes a biblical vision of earthly transitoriness. The drive for power is itself symptomatic of human weakness; dreading the "exposure and shame" of his "limp and feeble and poor" nature, the Machiavelli strives to "appear better and stronger than anyone else." All these exertions, Augie comes to realize, stem not from one's "power of being" but from powerlessness. Sensing "no real strength in himself," the "feeble" and misguided human being "cheats and gets cheated, relies on cheating, believes abnormally in the strength of the strong" (401–02).

At every turn, Augie discovers, existence yields paradoxes. Like the literal-minded builders of Babel, hopelessly confused in their search for the eternal, the strictest rationalists turn out to be martyrs-in-the-making. Augie notes, for example, the high "value" that Mimi Villars, a free-thinker who scorns the bourgeois institution of marriage, "set on the intelligence of men." Unlikely as it may seem, all the power of Mimi's "clinching will" and "hard reason" is devoted to the absolute worship of love—the all-encompassing, infinitely demanding love between a man and a woman. Eager to sacrifice herself to such an ideal, Mimi could live, Augie remarks, "in desert wilderness for the sake of it, and [eat] locusts" (209–11). The difference between Augie and the Machiavellis is that Augie seeks to devote himself to a truth or principle that transcends personal need and desire—to discover, as he says, "something greater than myself" (203–04). The Machiavellis are obsessed, on the other hand, with constructing an ideal in their own image, as if they would embody the very divinity they seek.

Human longing for the divine, Augie perceives, permeates the most godless times, even "times of of special disfigurement and world-wide Babylonishness" (76). Just as sexual "madness" can, as Sammler observes, express a "base form" of religious longing, so matter itself becomes the exalted object of idolatry. The luxury hotel where Augie's brother, Simon March, marries his rich young bride does not resemble the royal palaces of the past, whose ornate embellishments served as "the setting of [human] power." Now, in the empery of mighty Chicago, "luxury," Augie remarks, is "the power itself": "luxury without anything ulterior. Except insofar as all yearning, for no matter what, just so its scope is vast, is of one cluster of mysteries and always ulterior" (237–38). Charged with dominion over man, matter provides not the "setting" for his authority but a god for him to serve:

> But in this modern power of luxury, with its battalions of service workers and engineers, it's the things themselves, the products that are distin-guished, and the individual man isn't nearly equal to their great sum. Finally they are what becomes great—the multitude of baths with never-failing hot water, the enormous air-conditioning units and the elaborate machinery. No opposing greatness is allowed, and the disturbing person is the one who won't serve by using or denies by not wishing to enjoy. (238)

With these startling inversions Augie suggests that the contemporary blas-phemer is not the atheist, who denies the God of Abraham or Paul, but rather the "disturbing person" who "won't serve" the ostentatious god of luxury. The utilitarian "products" of advanced technology are thus seen to resemble the biblical idols of yore—wrought by human ingenuity, shaped by mortal hands, but invested, all the same, with transcendent authority. The "modern power of luxury" is idolized not in the form of golden calves but in the ingenious "products" that reward the slavish worshipper with streams of "never-failing hot water" and eternally vigilant "air conditioning units," miraculously at-tuned to the slightest shift in atmospheric conditions.

In *Augie March*, each of the Machiavellis upholds an idol "constructed" by human thought, ingenuity and skill as the embodiment of ultimate truth. Each "version" of reality travesties the mysterious source of creation, to which the truly religious seek attachment. To these idols, worshipped in their vaunted supremacy by the human beings who devise them (or by the human beings who usurp their roles), Augie himself remains in "opposition"—even when his immediate happiness, comfort or security is at stake (117).

Augie's "opposition," as we have seen, begins with Grandma Lausch. Much later in life, he journeys with Thea Fenchel to Mexico, where Grandma's "fighting nature of birds and worms" is graphically demonstrated and at the same time radically qualified.[9] Possessing exceptional beauty, conviction and intelligence, Thea Fenchel is another "superior" creature under whose spell Augie temporarily basks. Because the flawed realm of "ordinary reality" and "faulty humanity" falls disastrously short of her demands, Thea seeks a "better, nobler reality" in the stark world of "fighting nature" (316). In the Darwinian struggle for survival she perceives an absolute law of reality; in nature, moreover, she finds none of the deceit, betrayal and cringing cowardice she abhors in the human world. Embarking with Augie on a hunt in the wilds of Mexico, Thea seeks the fiercest species of "bird," a majestic bald eagle she intends to train in the ancient skills of falconry. By capturing and training her savage prey, she aims to assert her own identity as victorious hunter—a triumphant "bird" in Grandma's "fighting nature of birds and worms." Thea's favorite pastime in the wilds consists, in fact, of hunting the deadliest sort of "worms": massive, lethal snakes of every conceivable variety.

The bald eagle that Thea begins to train in Mexico is so fearsome a creature, with eyes expressing such "awful despotism," that Augie names him Caligula (335). The eagle's vicious eye, monstrous wing and savage claw initially strike Augie as a virtual "manifesto" proclaiming the savage authority of earthly power—and the insignificance of feeling. "He didn't require that I should love him," Augie says of Caligula; "meat was how you came to terms with him" (333). Ultimately, however, Caligula proves a bitter disappointment to Thea, because he turns out to have something "human" about him, after all. When, at the end of the eagle's training period, Caligula is sent out to hunt, he quickly swoops to capture an iguana in his mighty talons. But when the lowly reptile suddenly bites his captor, the eagle drops his prey and abandons the hunt. No pure, cruel instinct for conquest compels this mighty "hunter" and "chief" of birds to tear apart the "worm"; the struggle is not worth the pain. Thea cannot reconcile herself to such a display of "cowardice" on Caligula's part; it mars her pristine notion of "a fighting nature" undespoiled by "human" fears and hesitations. For Thea, Augie explains, "it was hard to take this from cruel nature, that there should be humanity mixed with it." She feels deceived by nature's evident "fraud, that [the eagle] should look such a cruel machine, so piercing, such a chief, and have another spirit under it all" (355).

The suggestion of "another spirit" underlying "fighting nature" does not alarm Augie, of course, for he intuitively rejects Thea's "version" of reality as sheer conflict and struggle for dominion. Instead, his contact with the eagle, whom he trains and feeds, brings Augie revelation of a mysterious bond linking all elements of creation. With Caligula, he says, "I got the idea of what it was to hunt, not with a weapon but with a creature, a living creature you had known how to teach because you'd inferred that all intelligences from the weakest blink to the first-magnitude stars were essentially the same. I touched him and stroked him" (360). At this moment Augie recovers an ancient vision of reality, not as discontinuous and alienating but as resplendently connected. Animated by divine "intelligence," every aspect of this universe, from "the weakest blink to the first-magnitude stars," is a link in the chain of creation binding the lowest to the highest spheres of existence

Characteristically, Augie's moment of revelation is swiftly and ironically undercut by events that immediately follow. No sooner does he experience this bond of kinship with nature than he tumbles from his horse. Because of Augie's clumsiness, the horse is also thrown to the ground—wildly kicking as he goes down. One of the animal's hooves catches Augie "square in the head" and cracks his skull (361). In similar fashion, most of Augie's revelations are rudely interrupted, as the brutal accidents of quotidian existence reassert their authority. Yet the cumulative effect of Augie's recurring insights builds and intensifies throughout the novel, as each "version" of reality promulgated by the Machiavellis fades before his radiant apprehension, persisting through all the disasters that befall him, of life's mystery. One of these insights occurs, moreover, shortly after Augie's fall from the horse—an accident that abruptly ends his career as animal trainer and hunter. (Thea, disappointed by Caligula's failure, abandons the project anyway.)

While convalescing from this accident, Augie is at leisure to observe Thea's captured snakes—for which he has, until now, felt only loathing—as they undergo a dramatic ordeal, the snakes' "casting of skins." As their giant bodies proceed to "writhe out of the epidermis" and their eyes "cloud with a dirty milk," Augie raptly witnesses the snakes' miraculous regeneration. After protracted suffering, they "would gleam out," he says, "and their freshness and jewelry would even give me pleasure, their enemy, and I would like to look at the cast skin from which they were regenerated in green or dots of red like pomegranate seeds or varnished gold crust" (369). The "pleasure" Augie gains from watching the snakes emerge from their cracked skins is akin to the sense of "gratitude" for life that wells up in him after each disappointment or disaster. Such *visible* demonstrations of recovery, regeneration and sheer beauty are immensely important to Augie; he is aware that intuitive apprehension of "another spirit" permeating creation offers no concrete evidence to the detached observer. How can inner assurances, a deeply felt "gratitude" for life, or even the enduring emotion of love measure up against the massive weight of material evidence that, like the bulk of Simon's newly amassed fortune, shores up the Machiavellis in their "versions" of reality?

At one point Augie poses the question to himself, musing about his brother Simon: "Nothing visible backed me, as it did him, to see and trust, but all was vague on my side and yet it was also very stubborn" (252). In the novel's Mexican chapters Augie plunges into the ruthless world of "fighting nature"; yet his experience with the eagle as well as the snakes yields visible evidence, to him at least, of a principle transcending the imperial logic of power. In the life of these specific "birds and worms" he discovers not just the struggle for survival but the potential, among diverse members of creation, for harmony and even sympathy.

Although swept up in the "Niagara Falls torrent of history," Augie has an abiding "curiosity about details" that tends to undermine rather than to reinforce familiar notions of reality. He notes, for example, the mysterious gradations of color unreeling in the smoke of factory chimneys, the "soft glossiness" of a character's "eye whites," or the curious "crowding" of a man's "underjaw" by the "brute charge" of animal vitality (206, 231). Such exacting

observation has the effect of rescuing resplendent particulars from the schematic "versions" of reality propagated by the Machiavellis with their "*idées
fixes.*" "Everyone," says Augie, "tries to create a world he can live in, and
what he can't use he often can't see. But the real world is already created"
(378). In deference to this "real," "already created" world—and to the hidden
source of its creation—Augie endeavors to see what others "can't see" because they have excluded from view what they "can't use" in their "versions"
of reality.

Even the apparent formlessness of Augie's narrative—the casually linked
series of adventures befalling a passive picaro who fails to exert his will on
events or other people—expresses latent "opposition" to the general schemes
and notions of the novel's Machiavellis. Augie's notorious passivity, his temporary surrender to the conflicting demands of the various people he encounters, is symptomatic of his "opposition" not only to being "recruited" to serve
but to becoming an earthly power himself. The fullest declaration of his
passive resistance occurs near the end of the novel:

> And this is what mere humanity always does. It's made up of these
> inventors or artists, millions and millions of them, each in his own way
> trying to recruit other people to play a supporting role and sustain him in
> his make-believe. The great chiefs and leaders recruit the greatest num-
> ber, and that's what their power is. There's one image that gets out in front
> to lead the rest and can impose its claim to being genuine with more force
> than others, or one voice enlarged to thunder is heard above the others.
> Then a huge invention, which is the invention maybe of the world itself,
> and of nature, becomes the actual world—with cities, factories, public
> buildings, railroads, armies, dams, prisons, and movies—becomes the
> actuality. That's the struggle of humanity, to recruit others to your version
> of what's real. Then even the flowers and the moss on the stones become
> the moss and the flowers of a version. (402)

What does Augie mean, we might ask, by suggesting that "the world itself"
and "nature" are an invention that "becomes actuality"? It may seem, at first,
that he is contradicting what he has previously said. Here he appears to say that
creation, to which he has formerly opposed the "inventions" and "images"
propagated by would-be "chiefs and leaders," is itself made-up and "make-
believe"—an invention. Yet Augie, rarely given to the "hard persuasion" of
strict logic and "hard reason," may be suggesting something else entirely. His
legerdemain with regard to the "actual world" succeeds in stylistically divest-
ing matter—all these "cities, factories, public buildings, railroads," etc.—of
its assumed permanence and authority. The world and nature have come into
being out of nothing, he reminds us, and all the weight of accomplished
creation—the "invention" that is now "actuality"—cannot disguise its myste-

rious origins. The earthly power of so many vast "armies, dams, prisons" rests, like Grandma Lausch's apparently solid authority in the March household, upon a foundation as impalpable as Mama's meek devotion and Georgie's inarticulate soul.

An important element of Bellow's style, then, is easily overlooked in the dense undergrowth of Augie's language, charged with the burden of so much observed detail: it is the recurring suggestion of a mysterious presence, or power, giving the lie to familiar notions of reality. I have already discussed, for example, the attention Augie pays to what Georgie can "do with his soul" and to the silent devotions carried out by Mama's ritual cleansing of the household. The unnamed presence of "another spirit" at work in the world, in history and in human beings, is as real, Bellow suggests, as the mysterious power enabling Winnie, Grandma Lausch's old poodle, to know "even when she became deaf before her death that she was spoken of" (50). This unseen power or "spirit" is an operative force in Bellow's universe. It is as real as the help Augie receives, during his wanderings in the Midwest, from a mysterious stranger.

The incident occurs during the Depression, when Augie, trying to hitch-hike back to Chicago, is stranded in Ohio, among throngs of the unemployed. The crowd, he observes, is a "wanderer population without any special Jerusalem or Kiev in mind, relics to kiss, or any idea of putting off sins, but only the hope their chances might be better in the next town. In this competition it was hard to get lifts" (166). When he spies a freight train moving toward Cleveland, Augie decides to try his luck: "I ran too, down from the unlucky highway, up the rocky grade where I felt the thinness of my shoes, and took hold of a ladder. I wasn't agile, so ran with the red car, unable to swing from the ground until I was helped by a boost from behind. I never saw who it was that gave it—someone among the runners who didn't want me tearing my arms from their sockets or breaking the bones of my feet" (166). The helping hand is offered casually enough, but spontaneity does not disguise the fact that this "runner" remains anonymous because he does not make it, with Augie, on board the train. In the instant available, he chooses, instead, to give Augie, a perfect stranger, a boost from behind. The apparent absence of any faith or charity in this "wanderer population" competing for survival is suggestively countered by the unseen presence of this stranger, whose charitable act assists Augie on his journey homeward.

The faint sounding of a "secret" speech or an unseen presence in Bellow's fiction helps to explain why critics so often invoke the term "visionary" to describe its style and effects. In an essay on Dostoevsky, Lev Shestov comments on the difference between the visionary writer—who apprehends what Bellow calls "traces of the soul" in reality—and the historian interested solely in events that "are visible to everyone": "Of what has been, the historian only knows as much as has been absorbed into the stream of time, and so has traces in the world which are visible to everyone. . . . But as to what has happened without leaving any trace behind, the historian knows nothing and wants to know nothing; and still less does he want to know about things which have happened, but cannot be shown to every one."[10]

The "history" narrated in a novel differs, of course, in precisely this way from the historian's. Most novelists seek to register the invisible flow of anonymous human life through history—the private impressions, unspoken thoughts and feelings, the drift of consciousness through the world of public events. Thus Augie speaks, at the end of the novel, of all the "terribly hard work" that has taken place within him during the course of the novel, while he has considered himself "going around idle": "Hard, hard work, excavation and digging, mining, moling through tunnels, heaving, pushing, moving rock, working, . . . panting, hauling, hoisting. And none of this work is seen from the outside. It's internally done" (523). Yet the unseen presence and the "traces of the soul" discoverable in *Augie March* comprise more than the merely personal, ephemeral or anonymous; they are linked to the biblical vision underlying the novel and transcend any material definition of the unseen.

The essential difference between secular and biblical history is that the latter concerns itself with the movement of invisible forces—divine or spiritual—through the visible world. Deliberately ignoring this distinction, however, Augie frequently interweaves allusions to both sacred and secular history as he recounts his experience. One overriding effect of juxtaposing spiritual and secular history is to suggest that for Augie they belong to the same plane of reality—that the spiritual is no less real, in other words, than the material. When, for example, he is released from a Detroit jail, where he has been locked up for suspicion of robbery, Augie likens his sudden deliverance to "the day the angel visited" Tobit in the Bible (175). To begin with, the biblical allusion enhances the contrast between Augie's sense of miraculous deliverance—like the miracle of the angel's appearance—and the blind indifference of those who are witness to the event: "There was a dawn smokiness and scratchiness in the station as the patrolmen off the night beat were taking a load off themselves, unstrapping guns, lifting off hats, sitting down to write out reports. Was there a station next door to Tobit, the day the angel visited, *it would have been no different*" (175, italics added).

Augie's release from jail is for him an emergence from "darkness" into light; the other men, indifferent to Augie's plight, would appear justified in their blindness. And yet something in the configuration of the passage, particularly in its final clause, suggests that this logical assessment is not quite correct—that the blind indifference of the men at the station is not quite innocent. Indifferent to Augie's release from spiritual "darkness," they may also be blind to their own. What "cannot be shown to everyone," to repeat Shestov, remains "unseen" not because it is unreal but because some see only, as Schlossberg says in *The Victim*, "with the eye"—not the heart or soul.

Augie's vision of the world, by contrast, is increasingly rendered in terms that transcend the logic of sensory perception:

Now there's a dark Westminster of a time when a multitude of objects cannot be clear; they're too dense and there's an island rain, North Sea lightlessness, the vein of the Thames. That darkness in which resolutions have to be made—it isn't merely local; it's the same darkness that exists in the fiercest clearnesses of torrid Messina. And what about the coldness of the rain? That doesn't deheat foolishness in its residence of the human face, nor take away deception nor change defects, but this rain is an emblem of the shared condition of all. It maybe means that what is needed to mitigate the foolishness or dissolve the deception is always superabundantly about and insistently offered to us—a black offer in Charing Cross. . . . With the dark, the solvent is in this way offered until the time when one thing is determined and the offers, mercies, and opportunities are finished. (201)

In this passage, rich with allusions to the work of another "visionary" novelist, Charles Dickens, Augie meditates on the "darkness" that is no product of the season or the weather. Nor is it the mere absence of physical light, for the "darkness" exists in landscapes drenched in fierce sunlight—in the "clearnesses of torrid Messina." The oxymorons in this passage suggest how Augie's vision transcends logic as well as sensory data to find clarification and illumination in darkness. Just as the dark obscures from sight the superficial appearances of an apparently solid material universe, so Augie's intuition of humanity's fallen condition, a shared darkness, dissolves like a "solvent" or "rain" the illusion of his own permanence on earth.

Even physical darkness, the black of night, reminds us of the subjugation of all finite existence to death—"when one thing is determined and the offers, mercies and opportunities are finished." How much more keenly, then, does recognition of a more profound darkness hold out a "black offer," the possibility of a "true vision of things" (76). Is it nature that "insistently offer[s]" this "gift" of true insight? Or is there an unseen presence behind the "multitude of objects" and phenomena crowding our physical perception? In any case, the "darkness" is ambivalent, illogical, contradictory. It clarifies through blackness; it illuminates by exposing the depth of our ignorance. It sheds the radiance of mystery upon the black doom of mortality.

An affinity exists, moreover, between this "black offer" of a "true vision" and that other "gift," the "gratitude" for life, that often emerges from Augie's dark experience of disaster. His near-fatal accident in Mexico—when he falls from the horse while hunting with the eagle, Caligula—brings him dark awareness of "the price of being in nature, and what the facts are about your tenure." The "social sugars dissolve" upon contact with the bitter taste of death's immediacy; and the "news" of mortality "registers with dark astonishment" in Augie's freshly opened eyes (362). Yet there is something regenerating as well as bitter in the process: "true vision" also restores to one's cluttered eyesight "the air, a light gold, thin but strong before daily influences took it away from you" (367). "Everything," Augie observes, "lives in the face of its negatives" (407).

The union of darkness and illumination, death and joy, the "black offer" and the "gift" of grace definitively links Augie's vision to that of the biblical Fall. Humankind, "that disfigured image of God," Augie notes, "falls away by its sin from Eden" but is also "inflamed by promise of grace to recover its sacredness and golden stature" (184–85). This vision of humanity's "mixed reality" is, finally, what inspires Bellow's lifelong distrust of the rationalist's tendency to explain away evil. "To a rational mind," says a foolish professor in the title story of *Him with His Foot in His Mouth* (1984), "nothing bad ever happens"; he is convinced of "the ultimate unreality of evil" (HWHF 17). Augie, meditating on the "darkness" or evil inherent in our "shared condition," recalls that other philosophers have also sought to deny, in elegant rational formulations, what the rest of humanity "very well know": "Only some Greeks and admirers of theirs, in their liquid noon, where the friendship of beauty to human things was perfect, thought they were clearly divided from this darkness. And these Greeks too were in it. But still they are the admiration of the rest of the mud-sprung, famine-knifed, street-pounding, . . . grief and cartilage mankind, . . . some inside a heaving Calcutta midnight, who very well know where they are" (175).[11]

The jumbled misery of a Chicago or a Calcutta does not foster ultimate trust in reason's clear light or the perfectibility of human existence. To Bellow, chaotic Chicago offers a truer vision of the human condition than "pert, pretty Paris." Paris, with its celebrated architecture, the "Greek Tuileries heroes" and the "overloaded Opera," is perceived by Augie as "the gaudy package of the world." The self-proclaimed "City of Man," Paris is "the capital of the hope that Man could be free without the help of gods, clear of mind, civilized, wise, pleasant." Here, in the City of Light, the elegant geometry of gardens, squares, and tree-lined boulevards celebrates the dream of reason, the Enlightenment ideal that promised to illuminate human darkness once and for all—to wipe irrational terror from the shining face of the civilized world. But the French Revolution inspired by Enlightenment ideals ended in The Terror. And the Paris in which Augie sojourns at the end of the novel has only yesterday been liberated from Nazi occupation and the terrors of a Holocaust that continue, to this day, to confound reason and defy imagination. Thus Augie wryly asks, "Which Man was [Paris] the City of?" He answers by suggesting that Paris, too, represents "Some version again. It's always some version or other" (521).

The "gaudy package" of Paris belies the terrors it has witnessed and served. In this sense it is only a more sophisticated version of the age-old practice of magic. With equally "gaudy" masks and paint did primitive man, Augie points out, try to fend off the "great terror" of existence: "The timid tribespeople, they flatten down heads or pierce lips or noses, or hack off thumbs, or make themselves masks as terrible as the terror itself, or paint or tattoo. It's all to anticipate the terror which does not welcome your being" (402–03). To the superstitious magic of primitive tribespeople and the sophisticated belief in science's "magic," Bellow opposes the biblical vision of "Man's" fallen condition—a vision that acknowledges the darkness and disfigurement of human nature but offers promise of redemption as well. The life of "each separate person" recounts both the loss and the promise entailed by Adam and Eve's Fall—implicating "everyone beginning with Eden and passing through trammels, pains, distortions, and death into the darkness out of which, it is hinted, we may hope to enter permanently into the beginning again" (84). Knowledge of the Fall, like that of original sin, can claim no rational basis; it is, as Pascal observed, "shocking to our reason." "And yet," Pascal adds, "without this most incomprehensible of all mysteries we are incomprehensible to ourselves. The kernel of our being is to be found in this abyss; so that man is even more incomprehensible without this mystery than this mystery is to man."[12]

How can the myth of lost Eden, Augie asks himself early in the novel, possibly illuminate the experience of urban humanity, with its "deep city vexation" that holds no memory of "silken, unconscious, nature-painted times." Yet as he himself goes on to demonstrate, his "first world"—while offering little resemblance to any version of the pastoral, from the Arcadia of "shepherd-Sicily" to the Hebrew *gan eydn*—was bathed in the love of Georgie and Mama (84). It is their love that, despite the harsh urban setting, recalls to Augie a prelapsarian world of innocence from which he, like Adam, is rudely expelled. When, moreover, Augie refers to his Mama's "original" vision of things, he is thinking of an "original" world not yet disfigured by the "conditioning forces" of history and the drive for earthly power. Augie's fate, at once unique and universal, is to leave this first world of "primordial" innocence and inexperience and to suffer the degenerate reality of the shared human condition. Even before he leaves home, moreover, his "first world" degenerates from this "original" condition, beginning with Grandma Lausch's "fall" and moving on to "the speed and depth of [Einhorn's] fall." In the novel's last chapter, the theme of the Fall is reiterated once again, creating a final "opposition" to the rationalistic view of existence that it undermines throughout the novel.

As the novel closes, Augie, now married and living in Europe, but still a "traveling man," recounts a recent business trip to Italy. Arriving in Florence, he goes to visit the Piazza del Duomo, where, as a hotel clerk has told him, he can find "the gold doors of the Baptistery with the sculptures of Ghiberti." Standing before the Baptistery, gazing at "the gold panels telling the entire history of humankind," Augie studies the "gold heads of our supposedly common fathers and mothers . . . while they told once and for all what they were." To his annoyance, he is approached by an old Piedmontese lady who recounts to him, in "balled up" fashion, the biblical tales represented on the panels. It is in the stricken expression of the old woman's face, however, that Augie reads the biblical legend writ large (or small): "What was the matter," he thinks to himself, "that she still was as if in the first pain of a deep fall?" (517–519). What Augie finds in the Piazza del Duomo—the Court of Man—is a fuller and deeper rendering of the human condition than any offered by Enlightenment Paris, the presumed "City of Man." Here the wrinkled visage of an old lady, with "the skin slackening and sinews getting stringy," provides a living inscription of humanity's fallen condition—making visible to Augie the unseen reality that eludes the secular historian and his empirical methods. The spiritual history of humankind is both universal and particular, recorded in millennia past but very much alive in the present. Augie's "adventures" in the modern world thus constitute his "earthly pilgrimage" through a landscape both ancient and contemporary—a New World Babylon (478). It is this aged and disfigured landscape, trod and endured by so many before, that rehearses their suffering while it promises to each something "of the highest." What is uniquely meaningful in each individual's life is, at the same time, discoverable to all: the "gift" of creation, the legacy of their shared condition. "There always is"—says Augie, implicitly affirming Bellow's "primordial person"— "a *me* it happens to" (519, Bellow's italics).

Chapter 5

The Heart and the Head:
Seize the Day and *Mosby's Memoirs*

While Augie March delights in opposing "the world's business," Wilhelm Adler, in *Seize the Day* (1956), has spent most of his forty-four years trying to succeed at it. And while Augie—young, handsome, sought after—has no trouble appearing successful, Wilhelm betrays all the characteristics of a "loser" (36, 21). Sloppy, ineffectual and inept, Wilhelm not only looks like a loser; he also seems more stupid than he is— emotion always overwhelming his attempts to think clearly. Even when he struggles to arrive at a measured decision, Wilhelm winds up acting on impulse: "And then, when he was best aware of the risks and knew a hundred reasons against going and had made himself sick with fear, he left home. And this was typical of Wilhelm. After much thought and hesitation and debate he invariably took the course he had rejected innumerable times" (23). Because Wilhelm acts so impulsively, so emotionally, failing to sustain any reasonable course of action, the reader feels ambivalent about the suffering Bellow's protagonist calls down upon himself. As one critic of the novel puts it, Wilhelm is at once a "comic slob" and a "passive sufferer": "Bellow presents Tommy Wilhelm as a clown-victim" at whom the reader "smile[s] wryly" but "look[s] with sympathy."[1]

Wilhelm's propensity to suffer has led a number of critics, drawing upon psychoanalytic theory, to describe him as a "moral masochist," a man who "luxuriates in suffering."[2] That Wilhelm views himself as a failure and often behaves self-destructively cannot be denied. So much has been made of his apparent guilt, self-hatred and need to fail, however, that this character's peculiar strength of spirit, sickened though it may be, tends to be overlooked. Although Wilhelm is subject to bouts of despair and depression, especially in his hour of crisis, his emotions reveal more than self-pity or the need to suffer. Like Augie March, Wilhelm Adler possesses a special talent, a real gift, for feeling; graced with Pascal's intuitive knowledge, Wilhelm often experiences, in Augie's phrase, "an emotion of truth" (AM 384). To feel from the heart—to feel not just intensely but generously, humanely, even selflessly—is not, as the novel's other characters attest by default, a trifling human matter. From the depths of such feeling, says Mr. Schlossberg in *The Victim*, arises our "dignity"—the "exactly human" capacity for moral and aesthetic perception.

In *Seize the Day*, Bellow provides ample evidence of the "dignity" as well as the confusion inherent in Wilhelm's compassionate nature, his "unsought" and "general love" for humanity (84). All of the elements of this novella—its language, structure and array of minor characters—serve to confirm Wilhelm's profound apprehension of human sorrow and to reveal his own suffering in a meaningful light. While Bellow never suggests that suffering is to be sought or valued for its own sake, he shows Wilhelm's suffering to have meaning and even purpose. Revealing more than a pathological disorder, Wilhelm's series of trials on this, "his day of reckoning," affirms what many of the world's religions have endeavored to teach: that suffering may provide a means to spiritual awakening and recovery (85).[3] Alerting the reader to Wilhelm's potential for renewal, Bellow calls attention to the "dignity" and refinement lurking beneath his character's dishevelled appearance. In one passage, as the viewpoint shifts from Wilhelm's fastidious father to his slovenly son, the narrator comments: "Wilhelm sat, mountainous He was not really so slovenly as his father found him to be. In some aspects he even had a certain delicacy. His mouth, though broad, had a fine outline, and his brow and his gradually incurved nose, dignity" (42).

Alert to such suggestions, the reader may even detect in Wilhelm's painful indecisiveness and baffling ineptitude signs of spiritual struggle. In him there emerges, as in Augie and other Bellovian seekers, the dilemma of a man who "has to believe that he can know why he exists." Viewed in this light, Wilhelm's true failing may be traced to the fact that, as he himself admits, he "has never seriously tried to find out why [he exists]" (39). Spiritual sloth rather than masochism, in other words, may constitute the true source of Wilhelm Adler's troubles. Too lazy or fearful to undertake the existential quest, Wilhelm has tended to pursue "the world's business" instead of the real "business of his life." Abandoning the search for a significant fate, he has consigned himself to "function" and failed to discover "what a man was for" (36, 39).

On the "day of reckoning" during which *Seize the Day* takes place, Wilhelm—who has already lost his job, home and family—is in the process of losing even "his last seven hundred dollars" (41). This day of drastic losses proves, however, a spiritual turning point in his life. In the process of losing "everything," Wilhelm is also divested of false hopes and illusions. Dimly aware that he has failed to pursue an authentic fate, he is forcibly struck by Dr. Tamkin's remarks on the distractions of the "pretender soul," which obscure the needs of one's "true soul": "It was the description of the two souls that had awed him" (72). The process by which Wilhelm discovers his "true soul"—accepting "the spirit, the peculiar burden of his existence" in all its "mysterious weight"—is excruciatingly painful; far from pathological, however, his suffering brings enlightenment as well as loss (38–39).

In order to highlight the special "dignity" concealed beneath Wilhelm's slovenly appearance and inept behavior, I shall draw not on the theories of psychoanalysis but, rather, on the concrete details of another work by Bellow: the title story of his first collection, *Mosby's Memoirs* (1968), published a decade after *Seize the Day*. Because Willis Mosby, the protagonist of "Mosby's Memoirs," is quite literally Wilhelm's opposite, countering the latter's weakness and ineptitude with his own worldly success and power, a comparative discussion of the two characters may reveal aspects of Wilhelm's character that would otherwise go unnoticed. By comparing Wilhelm—a man who is, for better or worse, *all heart*—to "Mosby the thinker," we may achieve, though somewhat arbitrarily, the broader perspective that characterizes Bellow's major novels (MM 161). The internal self-argument articulated by most of Bellow's conflicted heroes—the dialectic between modes of knowledge that, as in Sammler's case, arises from a psychic rift—is scarcely apparent in Mosby or Wilhelm. Confined, perhaps, by the limits inherent in shorter forms of narrative, each of these protagonists is almost exclusively identified with one pole of the dialectic that Bellow develops throughout his longer works of fiction. When viewed in relationship, however, each of these characters emerges as a remarkable foil to the other; each highlights, by means of contrast, aspects of the other and, by doing so, clarifies his own nature for the reader.

Barring the syllabic configuration of their names, then, Wilhelm Adler and Willis Mosby are polar opposites. Physically and mentally, Wilhelm is sloppy, clumsy and undisciplined. Mosby—a political thinker and noted author who has served as a high-ranking government official—is fastidious, agile, adroit. A "fanatic about *ideas*," Dr. Mosby is a "master" of "logical tightness, factual punctiliousness, and merciless laceration in debate" (Bellow's italics). While Wilhelm has drifted through life making mistakes, Dr. Mosby has carried out "imperative tasks" with rigorous discipline (MM 160, 176, 184). And while Wilhelm, destitute at forty-four, faces personal and professional failure, elderly Willis Mosby—who has spent his successful career in American universities and the leading circles of government—has been awarded a Guggenheim grant to write his memoirs. In conduct and appearance, Dr. Mosby is as trim, elegant and self-possessed as Wilhelm's own father, Dr. Adler, a medical "diagnostician" revered by all who know him as "a fine old scientist, clean and immaculate" (SD 12). Dr. Adler's cool disdain for his son and his relative indifference to the memory of his wife, whose year of death he cannot remember, is more than matched by Mosby's heartless treatment of his bumbling friend Lustgarten—a man whose physical, emotional and mental ineptitude bears a striking resemblance to Wilhelm's own (SD 27).

At one point in "Mosby's Memoirs," Bellow affords his reader a stark glimpse into the depths of Mosby's heartlessness; here he recounts "certain facts" strategically "omitted" from the memoirs Dr. Mosby is composing, in "the language of diplomacy" and "mandarin irony," for his audience. In the past Mosby not only conducted an affair with his friend Lustgarten's wife but also "arranged" that she "be seen" with another man during that time, in order to deflect attention from himself. To Mosby, during and after the affair, both the cuckolded husband and his wife are merely "clowns"—"funny" creatures to be played with and eventually discarded (MM 182–83). Now, as Mosby recollects the man he has betrayed, he evinces no sign of sympathy or remorse. To the contrary, he reviews Lustgarten's history with detachment, coolly examining him with "the eyes of Comte."

Just as Auguste Comte, the French philosopher and founder of positivism, offered his rational analysis of history, so Mosby analyzes the figure of his former friend, Lustgarten. "Like Napoleon in the eyes of Comte," Lustgarten appears, in Mosby's view, "an anachronism. Inept, he wished to be a colossus, something of a Napoleon himself. . . . Poorly imagined, unoriginal, the rerun of old ideas, and so inefficient." Superfluous to history, "Lustgarten didn't have to happen. And so," Mosby concludes, "he *was* funny." Although Mosby did not, during his affair with Lustgarten's wife, advise her to leave her husband, "his vision of Lustgarten as a funny man was transmitted to Trudy. She could not be the wife of such a funny man" (182–83, Bellow's italics). Serving no viable function or historical necessity, Lustgarten is, in Mosby's eyes, superfluous; devoid of function, he has no value. And though Mosby, as lover, is utterly indifferent to the state of the Lustgartens' marriage, his intellectual disdain for the husband is quickly translated into more immediate terms by the wife—who winds up abandoning her husband.

In marked contrast to the dry-eyed detachment with which Willis Mosby reviews his past, a sea of grief continually threatens to drown Wilhelm Adler. Critics have discussed in detail the ample presence of water imagery in *Seize the Day*.[4] From its opening page, as the elevator "sank and sank" to the lobby of his New York hotel, Wilhelm sinks, like a drowning man, ever deeper into sorrow. "The waters of the earth are going to roll over me," he prophesies with a biblical sense of doom. Wilhelm's misery, moreover, is laced with self-contempt: submerged in despair, he upbraids himself for being a "lousy, wallowing hippopotamus" (SD 55). By contrast, the protagonist of "Mosby's Memoirs" is "elegant and dry," "lean and tight" in "his well-tailored clothes"—the kind of man the French call "*un type sec*" (MM 159).

Comparing these two men, we do not have to wonder how Willis Mosby might react to a man like Wilhelm. In the course of his story, Mosby recalls a telling scene from the past, during which he had the displeasure of confronting just such "a man in tears." When Lustgarten, a man "down on his luck," visits

Mosby and begins to relate his "terrible experience" (including his wife's suspected infidelity!), Mosby's reaction recalls Dr. Adler's repugnance for his suffering son. Like Adler, "[Mosby] did not care to sit through these moments of suffering. Such unmastered emotion was abhorrent" (MM 172–73). No sea of grief, no watery tears for Willis Mosby then or now: only ample quantities of the Mexican mescale he is presently imbibing, throughout the afternoon, at his hillside retreat above the town of Oaxaca. The Mexican liquor cannot, however, replenish the arid desert lying at the heart of this "dry man."

The stark contrast between Wilhelm Adler and Willis Mosby is directly related to the opposition of earthly and spiritual power delineated in *Augie March*. It is in contrast to the earthly powers of a Grandma Lausch, we recall, that the spiritual grace as well as the helplessness of Georgie and Mama clearly emerge. Meek and ineffectual in the world, they possess no power other than love. Like Georgie and Mrs. March, Wilhelm Adler is, to some extent at least, rendered helpless, slated for failure in the harsh world, by his "soft heart" and "sensitive feelings" (SD 25). Wilhelm's "sensitive feelings" place him at an obvious disadvantage, in every worldly sense, with "dry" men like his father or Mosby, whose composure is never unsettled by depth of feeling or concern for others. As an adult in full possession of his mental faculties, Wilhelm is responsible, of course, for the disasters that befall him: the loss of his job, the failure of his marriage and his imminent bankruptcy at the hands of the manipulative Tamkin. Yet Bellow does suggest ways in which Wilhelm's receptivity to life and other people contributes to his vulnerability and downfall. Dr. Tamkin, for one, takes full advantage not only of Wilhelm's emotional neediness but of his humane responsiveness, at the same time maneuvering him into a bad investment.

A telling example of the way Tamkin takes advantage of Wilhelm's sympathy for others occurs near the end of the novel— when Wilhelm demands that Tamkin accompany him to the brokerage office in order to sell the commodities they have purchased together, with Wilhelm's last few dollars. Outside the office door, the two men are waylaid by old Mr. Rappaport, who, nearly blind, is afraid to cross the busy street alone. As Wilhelm and Tamkin approach the door where Rappaport is standing, it is Wilhelm whom Rappaport "somehow recognize[s]"—as if the blind man can perceive, by some internal means of detection, Wilhelm's "sensitive feelings" and humane sympathy. To Wilhelm, therefore, Rappaport blindly reaches out his hand for help (100). Tamkin, apparently eager to get rid of Wilhelm, urges him to do as Rappaport asks. Wilhelm, though reluctant, cannot refuse to help—even though the rich old man, Rappaport, hoards his "information" about the commodities market and refuses to give Wilhelm "the merest sign" or bit of advice (86–87). Wilhelm leads the blind man to the store and there receives from him not a word of thanks—not even one of the cigars that the old man purchases with his help.

Despite his irritation at being delayed by Rappaport, Wilhelm is amused by a story the old man tells him about meeting Teddy Roosevelt. He is especially struck by Rappaport's sudden and uncharacteristic display of feeling. "Man! I love that Teddy Roosevelt," Rappaport declares. "I love him!" Touched by the warmth of Rappaport's affection, Wilhelm thinks to himself, "Ah, what people are! He is almost not with us, and his life is nearly gone, but T. R. once yelled at him, so he loves him. I guess it is love, too. Wilhelm smiled." It is Wilhelm's emotional susceptibility—he is moved by this outpouring of affection from a sickly old man on the verge of death—that distracts him from practical affairs. Helping Rappaport, he momentarily forgets his worries, the shares he has bought and the money Tamkin owes him. By the time he gets back to the brokerage office, the shares have plummeted; Wilhelm has lost his "chance to sell," and Tamkin has disappeared without a trace, failing to reimburse Wilhelm for his portion of the loss (102–03).

The extraordinary capacity for feeling that causes Wilhelm to behave so ineptly is, at the same time, a source of great inner strength.[5] Even the disastrous screen test that he takes, as a college student, for Maurice Venice, highlights this paradoxical reality. Before the test Venice instructs Wilhelm, "Don't be afraid to make faces and be emotional. Shoot the works" (22). As it turns out, the test reveals and points up all of Wilhelm's expressions and "peculiarities, otherwise unnoticeable," with embarrassing results. The screen proves drastically inhospitable to the display of Wilhelm's "emotions," which it picks up and exaggerates grotesquely. If Hollywood represents "the world's business" *par excellence*—that of exploiting illusion for the sake of profit—the screen test emblemizes Wilhelm's incapacity, as a man of feeling, to succeed at it.

Much later in life, after spending ten years as a salesman for the Rojax Corporation, Wilhelm's runaway "emotions" once again prove, as in the screen test, an obstacle to worldly success. As he himself admits, "Feeling got me in dutch at Rojax. I had the *feeling* that I belonged to the firm, and my *feelings* were hurt when they put Gerber in over me" (56, Bellow's italics). What prompts Wilhelm to quit his job is the hurtful discovery that his *feelings* of loyalty to the firm he has served for a decade are irrelevant to those running the business. From a practical viewpoint, Wilhelm's expectations are, of course, unrealistic, his actions foolish and even self-destructive. Yet his "soft heart" has a great deal to do with his blundering. Not only has he "a tendency to be confused under pressure"; he tends to confuse the "world's business" with another kind of "business" altogether—that of achieving a significant fate.

Wilhelm's "sensitive feelings" contribute, then, to his vulnerability in the world. That vulnerability is made glaringly apparent by the screen test. Although, the narrator observes, "the vault of his chest was huge," Wilhelm "really didn't look strong under the lights" (23). Even the huge "vault" of his "chest" calls attention to Wilhelm's prodigious capacity for feeling, which is both his downfall and his source of inner resilience. "It is in the region of the chest," says Eusebio Rodrigues, "the central part of the muscular armor, according to Reich, that Wilhelm experiences severe pains."[6] Whether Wilhelm's severe chest pains are explained by Reich's theories or by the suffering of a "drowning man," his chest provides a focus of attention, as the seat of physical and psychic stress, throughout the novel. One is reminded of C. S. Lewis's observation, in *The Abolition of Man*, that "the chest" is "the seat, as Alanus tells us, of Magnanimity, of emotions organized by trained habit into stable sentiments. The Chest—Magnanimity—Sentiment—these are the indispensable liaison officers between cerebral man and visceral man."

As Bellow makes clear in the novel, Wilhelm's own "chest," the seat or source of feeling, does not receive adequate discipline from "trained habit" or the rule of mind. The huge "vault" of his chest does imply, however, that the prodigious nature of Wilhelm's feelings, the degree of his "Magnanimity," requires exceptional mental discipline, which he has failed to acquire. "Cerebral" men like Mosby, on the other hand, are paragons of "trained habit," subjecting everything to the order of logic and the rule of mind. Yet such men, Lewis cautions, do not always possess the extraordinary intellect that we attribute to them. When the heart or "chest" is inadequately developed, then the "head" or intellect can appear more impressive than it is; what strikes us as exceptional intelligence may only be the result of shallow feeling. In such "Men without Chests," in other words, the "head" looks prodigious because the chest has collapsed. "It is not excess of thought," says Lewis, "but defect of fertile and generous emotion that marks [these Men without Chests] out. Their heads are no bigger than the ordinary: it is the atrophy of the chest beneath that makes them seem so."[7]

Developing Lewis's train of thought, we may say that "atrophy of the chest," or heartlessness, has tended to make Willis Mosby's "head," or intellectual powers, appear all the more impressive to himself and the world. Uncomplicated by sympathy, unhampered by generous emotions, he has pursued a straight course to success; cutting a narrow swath through the world, he has eliminated all obstacles—including other people—with his razor-sharp intellect. Wilhelm's susceptibility to feeling, on the other hand, hampers his progress; where Mosby is brutally decisive, Wilhelm is easily distracted, "confused under pressure." In *Seize the Day*, the "fright and pressure" mount as the specter of Wilhelm's financial failure looms ever larger; at times he has "scarcely enough air in his lungs" to breathe (SD 114). In Mosby's case, on the other hand, the dread experience of suffocation comes as an abrupt surprise, or twist, at the end of the story.

While visiting the ruins of a stone temple at Mitla, Mosby descends to an underground tomb, where suddenly the "erudite, maybe even profound" thinker is caught off guard (157). As if his chest had *literally* atrophied, he finds himself unable to breathe:

> The vault was close. He was oppressed. He was afraid. It was very damp. . . . His heart was paralyzed. His lungs would not draw. Jesus! I cannot catch my breath! To be shut in here! To be dead here! Suppose one were! . . . *Dead*-dead. Stooping, he looked for daylight. Yes, it was there. The light was there. The grace of life still there. Or, if not grace, air. (184, Bellow's italics)

All at once "stone-hearted" Dr. Mosby—"intelligent" and disbelieving" in everything except the "historically necessary"—is brought, by recognition of the "end," to a surprising discovery (158, 167–68). This sudden revelation is instantly undercut, however, by Mosby's habitual cast of mind. His fleeting perception of "grace"—of the gift of life bestowed on all alike, with no human being proving more "necessary" than another—survives only for a moment. Then, as the terror fades, Mosby's mind reasserts control: the "grace of life" is reduced, mentally reconverted, to the positivist's mere "air."

As he hurries to escape from the tomb, Mosby utters the story's final lines: "I must get out. . . . I find it very hard to breathe." Although, we assume, he will manage to find his way out of the tomb, confrontation with death inevitably awaits him. Significantly, "Mosby the thinker" has not grown or developed from this encounter with the unknown, which disrupts his composure for only a moment. Despite his brief glimpse of the "grace of life," a discovery that could lead to a fuller apprehension of reality, Mosby's mind resumes its narrow cast. Clinging to reason, even in the face of the mysteries it cannot probe, he would preserve himself from suffering. By closing himself off from feeling, however, he simply postpones the ultimate terror of confronting his own end.

The terror that strikes Mosby in the underground tomb provides an interesting contrast to Wilhelm Adler's calm recognition that, as he tells his father, "everyone on this side of the grave is the same distance from death." Timid, confused, impulsive, Wilhelm exhibits remarkable steadfastness before the mystery that reduces "erudite" Dr. Mosby to a state of abject terror. Wilhelm does not flinch from the knowledge that life is a preparation for death, that the meaning of the former is inextricably bound to the reality of the latter. It is this knowledge that, for all his training and erudition, Dr. Mosby cannot confront. Similarly, Wilhelm's father, Dr. Adler, "did not like the mention of death" (SD 46). Priding himself, as Mosby does, on strict adherence to logic and the "facts," Wilhelm's father refuses to contemplate any condition that is not empirically defined. "Concentrate on real troubles—fatal sickness, accidents," he instructs Wilhelm (45). That Wilhelm feels fatally wounded by his estranged wife's hatred for him strikes Dr. Adler as so much "voodoo" superstition (48). He characteristically assumes, moreover, that Wilhelm's troubles with Margaret are traceable to a few simple, physiological facts. Thus he queries Wilhelm, "Did you have bed-trouble with her?" (51).

Unable to refute his father's "medical standpoint" with any facts of his own, Wilhelm can only say, "I just couldn't live with Margaret. I wanted to stick it out, but I was getting very sick." The heartsickness that Wilhelm tries to articulate to his father does not have any place, however, in Dr. Adler's diagnostic charts. The son's attempt to "unburden himself" ends in frustration, anger and defeat (51–52). A paragon of Bellow's "head culture," Dr. Adler has, like Mosby, only disdain for modes of knowledge that lie outside the strict purview of rationalistic solutions. From the methods of scientific inquiry and analysis he has built not only a successful medical career but a system of defenses against the "peculiar burden" of human knowledge—Augie March's "oldest knowledge"—and its attendant obligations. Like Dr. Adler, Mosby has managed to shut out this knowledge and deny its burden; yet Mosby appears, unlike Wilhelm's father, to have some inkling of the sacrifice he has made of his humanity.

In those rare moments when his powers of logic and reasoning are unable to maintain control over his consciousness, Mosby is visited by "an odd and complex fantasy." Reliving a car "collision" that took place years earlier in his life, he imagines—in contrast to what actually took place—that he was not "pulled from the car" and saved. In his fantasy, Mosby dies in the wreckage: "He had died. He continued, however, to live. His doom was to live life to the end as Mosby. In the fantasy he considered this his purgatory" (182). Here Mosby's logical mind is invaded by a paradox as old as the human spirit itself—the paradox of death-in-life. He envisions himself as carrying on his material or bodily existence after his essential life, his vital self or soul, has departed. Like the prophetic dreams experienced by so many of Bellow's protagonists, beginning with the Dangling Man, Mosby's "fantasy" hints at the spiritual truth underlying material appearances. The "fantasy" strikes an obvious contrast with Mosby's rational observations on Darwinian nature and historical necessity. It is only in daydream—when, to recall Yeats's phrase, the Emperor's "soldiery are abed"—that Mosby yields to the vision of life as spiritual journey. Then, "in the fantasy," Mosby perceives his life not as a succession of material triumphs but as a "purgatory." In "fantasy" Mosby can admit the knowledge, the burden of human existence, that he spends his waking hours categorically denying: the reality of evil, the meaning of human suffering, the value of remorse.

The knowledge that "Mosby the thinker" consigns to the realm of "fantasy" appears, to Wilhelm Adler, as a form of revelation: "In any moment of quiet, when sheer fatigue prevented him from struggling, he was apt to feel this mysterious weight, this growth or collection of nameless things which it was the business of his life to carry about. That must be what a man was for" (39). Wilhelm's revelation of the real "business" or burden of his life is often singled out by critics to demonstrate his masochistic need to suffer in order to relieve his guilt.[8] Bellow, on the other hand, counters this reductive view by suggesting a religious context for Wilhelm's suffering. The narrator alludes, for example, to Wilhelm's "Buddha's head, too large to suffer such uncertainties" (81–82). Later, talking to Margaret on the telephone, Wilhelm's thoughts echo the words that Christ uttered on the cross: "We could not bear, he thought, to know what we do" (112).[9]

Although Wilhelm occasionally offers up prayers and frequently alludes to the Bible, what finally convinces the reader of the spiritual nature of his struggle are the passages in which ordinary phenomena are suddenly transfigured by Wilhelm's apprehension of mystery. Gazing at the mark left by "a glass of water" on a white tablecloth, Wilhelm suddenly sees it as a "hoop of brightness," an "angel's mouth" announcing the possibility of revelation: that "truth for everybody may be found, and confusion is only—only temporary" (84). Significantly, Bellow draws attention to these "small hoops of brilliance" much earlier in the story, as Wilhelm joins his father in the hotel for breakfast: "Small hoops of brilliance were cast by the water glasses on the white tablecloth, despite a faint murkiness in the sunshine" (31). At this point, however, Wilhelm is sunk in angry resentment, unable to glean any radiance underlying the "confusion" and distress of his situation. Gazing at Mr. Perls, an old man seated next to his father at the table, Wilhelm is repelled by the old man's "skinny forehead," "fish teeth" and "drippy mustache." Characteristically, however, he begins "to relent a little toward Mr. Perls, beginning at the teeth." The old man's ugly face and teeth are soon transformed under Wilhelm's sympathetic gaze. What he now perceives is not accidental, ugly phenomena but matter immanent—virtually "loaded" down—with human meaning: "Each of those crowns," thinks Wilhelm, "represented a tooth ground to the quick, and estimating a man's grief with his teeth . . . , it came to a sizable load" (31–32).

Although Wilhelm's father, Dr. Adler, patently refuses to recognize this human "load" or "burden," his very denial is couched in language that hints at the redemptive nature of suffering. "You want to make yourself into my cross," Dr. Adler angrily tells Wilhelm. "But I am not going to pick up a cross. I'll see you dead, Wilky, by Christ, before I let you do that to me" (110). Instructing Wilhelm to "Carry nobody on your back," he declares, "I want nobody on my back. Get off!" (55). To submit to the "mysterious weight" of this "burden," even in the relatively simple form of aiding a son who needs help, strikes Adler as a senseless act of sacrifice; yet his language recalls, while he explicitly rejects, the model of suffering made meaningful by Christ.

When, moreover, Wilhelm tries to adjust his behavior to his father's demands, warning himself not to aggravate the old man, his efforts are interrupted by "promptings" that issue from "a deeper source": "Therefore he warned himself, Lay off, pal. It'll only be an aggravation. From a deeper source, however, came other promptings. If he didn't keep his troubles before him he risked losing them altogether, and he knew by experience that this was worse" (43). This statement, in John Clayton's view, offers a clear expression of Wilhelm's masochism; only a man who "luxuriates in his suffering" needs to "keep his troubles before him."[10] A different meaning can, however, be found in Wilhelm's statement—one that affirms the potential value of suffering, or of any human ordeal. To confront one's "troubles" is the opposite of trying to escape them, as Wilhelm has tried to do in the past, for example, by changing his name to Tommy Wilhelm. As a young man in flight from his "troubles"—longing "to be freed from the anxious and narrow life of the average"—Wilhelm wasted years pursuing a phantom career, as Tommy Wilhelm, in Hollywood. By striving now to "keep his troubles before him," Wilhelm may well be attempting to stay in contact with his "inescapable self" (23, 25).

Wilhelm's alleged masochism, his perception that suffering is for him "inescapable," takes on a radically different cast when we consider the extent to which other characters in the novel, often inadvertently, validate his vision of universal suffering. In the past, for example, even when Maurice Venice was promising him escape from his "troubles," Wilhelm could feel the "weight" of anguish in the talent scout's sales pitch: "On [Venice's] imagination there was some great weight which he could not discharge. He wanted Wilhelm, too, to feel it. He twisted his large, clean, well-meaning, rather foolish features . . . and said in his choked, fat-obstructed voice, 'Listen, everywhere there are people trying hard, miserable, in trouble, downcast, tired, trying and trying. They need a break, right? A break through, a help, luck or sympathy.' " Having "seized the feeling" behind Venice's words but ignored their meaning, Wilhelm enmeshed himself in the toils of a seductive dream: that he might become, in Venice's words, "a lover to the whole world" (22).

Only much later in life, when he is at a considerable remove, temporally as well as geographically, from Hollywood's dream-factory, does Wilhelm discover another way to handle the shared "burden" of human sorrow. Walking, on "his day of reckoning," through the crowds thronging a subway corridor beneath Times Square, he discovers—in a wholly different sense—the liberation of being "a lover to the whole world": "All of a sudden, unsought, a general love for all these imperfect and lurid-looking people burst out in Wilhelm's breast. He loved them. One and all, he passionately loved them. They were his brothers and sisters. He was imperfect and disfigured himself, but what difference did that make if he was united with them by this blaze of love? And as he walked he began to say, 'Oh my brothers—my brothers and sisters,' blessing them all as well as himself" (84–85).

Later "that very same afternoon," Wilhelm begins to doubt the authenticity of his revelation. "What did it come to?" he asks himself. But just as he tells himself, earlier, not to lose sight of his "troubles," now he "consult[s] his memory": "I must go back to that [experience in the subway]. That's the right clue and may do me the most good. Something very big. Truth, like" (85). Here the subgrammatical phrase, "truth, like," serves to recall Bellow's remarks concerning the difficulty, at this moment in Western culture, of finding an appropriate language for articulating spiritual "truth." The awkwardness of Wilhelm's expression notwithstanding, he has made a remarkable discovery. He has found within the "vault" of his own magnanimous "chest" the radiant source of love and forgiveness—a discovery that sustains him in his own time of "troubles." Unlike Mosby, who begins to choke with fear during his descent underground, Wilhelm finds release from his terror in this underground corridor. Here, in this unlikely setting, he is moved to bless "all including himself"—just as later, at the funeral of a stranger, he achieves the "consummation of his heart's ultimate need."

Viewed from this perspective, "Mosby the thinker" appears, in relationship to Wilhelm Adler, utterly bereft. With his "paralyzed" heart and atrophied chest, Mosby cringes before the mystery that he has sought, throughout his life, to hold at bay. Even while relaxing after an afternoon siesta, Mosby is busy removing himself, mentally, from the intrusive charms of the pastoral setting. Refusing to delight in the florid show of nature or in the musical chirping of birds, Mosby thinks only of the Darwinian struggle for survival. Those apparently innocent birds are, he assures himself, "doing all the things naturalists say they do. Expressing abysmal depths of aggression, which only Man—Stupid Man—heard as innocence." Nature's "liveliness" and "beauty," her ability to stir the heart of "Stupid Man," are for Mosby not a source of delight but a power "very dangerous. Mortal danger." He is disturbed by the "colors, fragrances ready to topple on him," threatening to overwhelm the strict order imposed by his vigilant mind. Behind this seductive beauty lurks something else: something absolute, terrifying, a mystery that disturbs Mosby and from which, as we observe at the end of the story, he strives to escape. "Behind the green and red of Nature, dull black seemed to be thickly laid like mirror backing" (157–58). Only through detachment, the habit of logic, can Mosby preserve himself from the dark mystery that looms behind appearances and threatens to disrupt his view of reality. Like the "dull black" lining of a mirror, the unknown—perhaps death itself—tauntingly suggests that visible reality is a mere reflection, an ephemeral illusion or optical trick. Such ambiguities, lurking behind the the positivist's tangible universe, threaten to "topple" Mosby's mental security.

Later in the story, having regained his mental composure, Mosby once again directs his attention to nature and "the birds of Mexico." In the movements of the hummingbird "so neat in its lust" and of the lizard "drinking heat with its belly," he again detects the Darwinian struggle—Grandma Lausch's "fighting nature of birds and worms." His scientific musings are oddly undercut, however, by another order of insight. "To bless small creatures is supposed to be real good," Mosby suddenly thinks to himself (169). Here the subgrammatical expression, "real good," comments ironically on Mosby's spiritual illiteracy as it recalls Wilhelm's own awkward articulation of "Truth, like." Unlike Wilhelm, however, Mosby cannot open himself to "the grace of life"; nor can he face up to death.

Confronted with the reality of death, "Mosby the thinker" knows nothing except that he "must get out" and away from it. Like other mysteries that he refuses to contemplate, death has "nothing rational to recommend it" (167). Nothing "the naturalists say" offers much help or consolation when the "dull black" of death threatens to obliterate the reassuring "facts" of material existence. It is to such facts that Mosby has rigorously confined his thoughts throughout his long life and busy career. With amused detachment he has enjoyed "making fun of flesh and blood," noting the foibles of his fellow creatures. Culture, art, beauty, religion are to him only "little humanities" inscribed on the Lockean "*tabula rasa*": the "bare skull" of the humble human animal (168).

To the potential meaning of suffering, or to the music that softens even Joseph's "hard-boiled" shell in *Dangling Man*, Mosby has never yielded. He has deliberately sought, instead, to "abstract himself" from the delights of music and nature, using intellection to ward off their influence: "Shut out the piano. Continue thinking about Comte," who bid farewell to "Theology and Metaphysics" in order to welcome in the "Positive Epoch" of the "Enlightened" (168–69). That Mosby is engaged in writing the memoirs of his European experience after the Second World War offers comment enough, one would think, on the inadequacies of Comte's rational faith in the "enlightened" future. It is Augie March's postwar perspective that prompts him, we recall, to regard Paris, the alleged "City of Man," with decided irony. While Mosby does not share Augie's sense of irony, his dread of the unknown—which emerges so dramatically in the underground tomb—betrays the presumed adequacy of his "enlightened" detachment and the "logical tightness" of his views.

If Wilhelm's fastidious father, Dr. Adler, bears a definite resemblance to "dry" Dr. Mosby, the novella's self-styled "doctor" of philosophy, Dr. Tamkin, is a virtual parody of the "erudite" man. So crude is the admixture of reason and superstition, learning and ignorance, fact and falsehood comprising Tamkin's "instruction," that most readers of the novel are as confused as Wilhelm about Tamkin's true identity. Like Wilhelm, every reader can find some buried (and borrowed) truth in what Tamkin says. Shards of Blake's prophetic vision can be gleaned through the bathos of Tamkin's poem, "Mechanism vs Functionalism/Ism vs Hism," just as Reich's theories may be seen to inspire Tamkin's account of "the real soul and the pretender soul" (70).[11] The use that Tamkin makes of ancient, classical or scientific sources hardly suggests, however, that he understands the learning he exploits. Like the advertiser or propagandist, his skill lies in turning received wisdom into immediate advantage. Thus he urges Wilhelm to "seize the day," to grab hold of the "here-and-now" by helping old Mr. Rappaport across the street: "You have to live in this very minute, and you don't want to. A man asks you for help. Don't think of the market. It won't run away"(100).

Despite Tamkin's obvious intention to exploit Wilhelm, he also serves, as does Maurice Venice (another exploiter), to confirm Wilhelm's deepest intuitions about the "load" of grief that is humanity's "peculiar burden." Tamkin inadvertently accomplishes this function—so important to the novel's thematic development—while intending, like the talent scout, to sell Wilhelm on worldly success. Giving every appearance of being a failure as well as a fraud, Tamkin, like Venice, has learned how to pose as a winner. Yet in the same way that Venice, in a sudden access of feeling, inadvertently betrays his firsthand knowledge of human suffering—of being "miserable, in trouble, downcast, tired"—so Tamkin shows continual signs of inner turmoil, confusion and helplessness: "When his hypnotic spell failed, [Tamkin's] big underlip made him look weak-minded. Fear stared from his eyes, sometimes, so humble as to make you feel sorry for him. Once or twice Wilhelm had seen that look" (96). Perhaps it is Tamkin's own failure and suffering that allow him to understand Wilhelm's, just as Wilhelm is here able to detect Tamkin's fear. Tamkin pretends, however, that his understanding of Wilhelm's plight derives not from feeling, or common suffering, but from "science." It is Tamkin's insistence on playing the role of "keen mental scientist," while acting and speaking so erratically, that makes him such a ludicrous but telling character.

Attempting to garner the authority and respect accorded the expert, Dr. Tamkin ingests the homogenized wisdom of popularized "methodologies" (61). At one point he confesses to Wilhelm, "I get so worked up and tormented and restless, so restless!" Then, in the next moment, he professes to have "a calm and rational, a psychological approach" (9–10). He even instructs Wilhelm on how to gamble "scientifically," saying that "the whole secret of this type of speculation . . . is in the alertness. You have to act fast" (8). He drags his feet, on the other hand, when Wilhelm urges him to sell their shares (98). In an effort to impress Wilhelm, Tamkin garbles and misconstrues a host of "scientific" theories. His claim—that his "objective" mind is rigorously engaged in "applying certain principles of observation" to the "study of the ultimates of human and animal behavior"—is a travesty of scientific faith (69, 88, 61). Tamkin assumes, in his ignorance, that the study of "human and animal behavior" will lead to knowledge of the "ultimates"—the "spiritual secrets of life" (69). It is expressly because the "doctor" alludes to these "spiritual secrets" that Wilhelm is drawn to him. As he admits to himself, "I am a sucker for people who talk about the deeper things of life, even the way [Tamkin] does" (69).

Wilhelm comes close to articulating the source of Tamkin's false claims when he reflects to himself: "[Tamkin] spoke of things that mattered, and as very few people did this he could take you by surprise, excite you, move you. Maybe he wished to . . . give himself a lift to a higher level, maybe believe his own prophecies, maybe touch his own heart. . . . Wilhelm could only suspect, he could not say with certainty, that Tamkin hadn't made them his own" (82). If Tamkin has no immediate knowledge of "the spiritual secrets of life," then what he espouses—without having made it "his own"—is by definition worthless. Such truth, as Kierkegaard pointed out, is known through its appropriation by the subject; there can be no knowledge of "ultimates" without subjective participation in what is known. Tamkin, however, is enamored of scientific knowledge, which he mimics and muddles. Thus he says to Wilhelm, "Of course, for simplification purposes, I have spoken of the soul; it isn't a scientific term, but it helps you to understand" (71).

Purporting to give Wilhelm spiritual guidance while apologizing for not having "a scientific term" for "the soul," Tamkin glosses over the question whether or not this entity he calls "the soul" is empirically verifiable or can be scientifically delineated. He appears incapable of making the necessary distinction between mathematical and intuitive modes of knowing and the different "truths" to which they lead. Even Tamkin's most casual statements are a travesty of "scientific" thought. At one point he tells Wilhelm, "The longer [Dr. Adler] lives, the longer your life-expectancy becomes" (62). Tamkin obviously overlooks the fact that statistical probabilities are only valid when describing general trends. They cannot predict an individual's fate.

While it is possible to read everything Tamkin says merely as a smoke-screen for hiding his intention to swindle Wilhelm, the wealth of detail and description Bellow devotes to Tamkin suggests that such a view would be an oversimplification. If Tamkin is, as Bellow says, "a con man who gave his dupes psychological laughing gas," he administers that anesthetic—the hot air of half-truths—on himself as well.[12] Of course Tamkin has his own interests at heart when he encourages Wilhelm to trust in the "ultra-modern electronic bookkeeping machinery" of the brokerage firm, which "won't let you get in debt" (74). But as Tamkin's invocations of scientific magic serve to suggest, he has mesmerized himself into believing that science and technology, as well as psychology, can provide "happy" solutions to profound human problems.

Take, for example, the "proposed inventions" that Tamkin tells Dr. Adler he is working on. One is "an electrical device for truck drivers to wear in their caps," which would "wake them with a shock when they begin to be drowsy at the wheel," its mechanism "triggered by the change in blood-pressure when they start to doze." Another is "an underwater suit" that would allow "a man [to] walk on the bed of the Hudson in case of an atomic attack" (41). Both schemes are travesties of the popular faith in technology, in its power to solve profound human dilemmas as well as everyday practical problems—thus preventing workers from falling asleep on the job or whole populations from blasting themselves off the face of the earth. In the same naive spirit Mrs. Harkavy, in *The Victim*, assures Leventhal that "someday science will conquer death." In *Seize the Day*, Dr. Adler scorns any knowledge that is nonscientific, relegating what cannot be measured to mere "voodoo" superstition; Dr. Tamkin's strange forays, on the other hand, make scientific practice look a good deal like sorcery.

Though a charlatan and impostor, Tamkin proves to be Wilhelm's spiritual guide in one important, though inadvertent, way: he manages to divest Wilhelm not only of his last seven hundred dollars but also of his remaining illusions. With Tamkin's disappearance Wilhelm must surrender any notion of finding escape from the "peculiar burden of his existence." Long ago Maurice Venice had promised Wilhelm an escape or detour from his "troubles," just as Tamkin more recently promises to bail Wilhelm out of his financial difficulties. Even Tamkin's "proposed invention," which would wake up sleeping drivers with an electronic device, falsely implies that human beings are not responsible for their own awakening. Replacing human vigilance with a technological device, Tamkin suggests that scientific "know-how" can somehow relieve humanity of its age-old "burden." In the novella, however, Bellow suggests that only Wilhelm's suffering can provide the means to his awakening.

At the close of *Seize the Day*, Wilhelm Adler must, like Willis Mosby, confront the stark reality of death. Wandering into the funeral of a stranger, Wilhelm quickly becomes that very figure abhorred by Mosby: "a man in tears." As he stands weeping for a dead stranger—weeping "at first softly and from sentiment, but soon from deeper feeling"—Wilhelm is regarded with "wide, glinting, jealous eyes" by a bystander, visibly moved by the intensity of Wilhelm's grief. "Oh my, oh my! To be mourned like that," the bystander exclaims, his "jealous eyes" testifying to the value of Wilhelm's gift, the gift of "deep feeling." To Bellow's readers, the profound nature of this gift is made even clearer; for we, unlike the bystander, know that Wilhelm is weeping not only for the dead stranger, or for himself, but for each and every "human creature" whose final destiny is "the end of all distractions" (117–18). More significant than the "reckoning" of Wilhelm's worldly losses and failures is the value Bellow accords his protagonist's capacity to feel and to suffer—even though, as he makes clear, "there [is] no figure or estimate for the value of this load" (39).[13]

Throughout *Seize the Day*, sorrow and disappointment have threatened to drown Wilhelm in an unrelenting deluge. In the novel's closing passage, the funeral organ's "heavy sea-like music" intensifies the image of Wilhelm as a man drowning in a sea of tears. Yet Bellow's language, echoing the line from Milton's "Lycidas" that recurs throughout the text, allusively links Wilhelm's "death by water" to the immortalized hero of Milton's poem. The poet's drowned friend, we recall, is described as "sunk . . . beneath the watery floor"; at the end of the poem, however, Milton pictures his friend as taken to heaven by Christ. "So Lycidas sunk low, but mounted high" is reborn in the celestial heavens, married to his Maker. That Wilhelm undergoes his own symbolic death, "consummation" and spiritual rebirth is the promise dramatically conveyed in the music of Bellow's highly charged language.

Stripped of every hope of worldly success, Wilhelm Adler nevertheless achieves, in the novella's closing line, "the consummation of his heart's ultimate need." To Bellow's reader the nature of Wilhelm's "need" has been made clear from the outset, when Wilhelm prays for forgiveness and release from the "clutch" of his troubles: " 'Oh God,' Wilhelm prayed. 'Let me out of my trouble. Let me out of my thoughts, and let me do something better with myself. For all the time I have wasted I am very sorry. Let me out of this clutch and into a different life' " (26). At the end of his "day of reckoning," although he has found no practical solution to his dilemma, Wilhelm's prayer is answered. His suffering—and his heartfelt identification with the suffering of others—brings the emotional release for which he has prayed. As a flood of tears unties "the great knot of ill and grief" inside him, loosening the "clutch" of despairing "thoughts" that have paralyzed his will and spirit, Wilhelm, sinking "deeper than sorrow," appears on his way to "a different life."

The promise of renewal is precisely what Willis Mosby denies himself. Spiritually "a dry man," Mosby has made rationalism his faith in order to deny the collective burden of suffering that unites all humankind. Here lies the significance of the "fantasy" emanating from his own subconscious—from a source of knowledge "older" than reason or "the Ganges." Mosby inexplicably "knows" that he has survived, or outlasted *in the body*, his essential death. Such a dreadful condition, that of being a *past* person, is renounced, we recall, by the protagonist of *Mr. Sammler's Planet*. To attempt to detach oneself from others, Sammler recognizes, is not a sign of intellectual strength but of failure: heart-failure. Viewed in these terms—terms that, Bellow suggests, are the most significant in a human being's life—Wilhelm Adler is not simply a "loser." Despite all the distress vexing his "soft heart" and confused head, Wilhelm finds consolation in his loss, resilience in the suffering he shares with others. The nature of Wilhelm's strength is admittedly paradoxical; but paradox has long been the language of spiritual insight. Just as Wilhelm, at the end of the novel, sinks "past reason, [past] coherence" toward a reality "deeper than sorrow"—so the imagination of Bellow's reader is carried "past reason" as well. Only through paradox may we discover the truth that contradicts all worldly notions of success and earthly power: the paradox of the suffering heart, strengthened by the sorrow in which it is steeped.

Chapter 6

Beyond History and Geography: *Henderson the Rain King*

If Wilhelm Adler's suffering tends to obscure his saving grace as a character, the highjinks of *Henderson the Rain King* (1959) prove even more diverting, in both senses of that term. While Wilhelm sinks ever deeper into sorrow, Henderson flies high to escape his misery—so that even his failures seem funny, like a series of pratfalls skirting disaster. Comically bumbling his way through an outlandish terrain, Eugene Henderson may be, as several critics suggest, a "caricature" of the archetypal seeker—his journey a parody of the modern quest. Still, laughter does not disallow the results of Henderson's quest: the sense he gains of having come into contact with the "fundamentals" and "ultimates" of reality (331, 156). "Beneath his bluster and buffoonery," as Sarah Cohen observes, "Henderson is also a serious explorer who has hacked his way through the tangled underbrush and has learned from his mental travels."[1]

Even while he clowns, Henderson hints at the metaphysical nature of his journey. "And I'm still not convinced that I didn't penetrate beyond geography," he tells the reader. "Not that I care too much about geography; it's one of those bossy ideas according to which, if you locate a place, there's nothing more to be said about it" (55). To Henderson, penetrating the African interior has meant "entering the past—the real past, no history or junk like that" (46). To the extent, moreover, that he penetrates "beyond" the epistemological conventions, or "bossy ideas," of history and geography, Henderson moves in a direction beyond finitude. The *terra incognita* he discovers cannot be plotted on the map; this exotic territory eludes spatial coordinates as it defies conventional categories of time. For Henderson, what lies beyond history and geography is not Africa *per se* but a sphere of reality, or a state of mind, liberated from the tyranny of death.

The *terra incognita* to which Henderson's African journey leads is, I shall argue, the world "beyond" death evinced by love. Through love, says Gabriel Marcel, the finality of death is refuted: "to love a being is to say, 'Thou, thou shalt not die.' " To say that the beloved shall not die is not, however, a matter of mere willful assertion; nor is it a simple feat of memory—of preserving, through recollection, what ceases physically to exist. What Marcel means and what Bellow's novel concretely suggests is that love transfigures reality, reveals its "unknown dimensions," by altering the relationship of the lover to all that he loves.[2]

Just as Wilhelm Adler's capacity to love and to forgive others ultimately brings *him* forgiveness and release, the love that transfigures Henderson's perception of reality is all-embracing. Distinct from sentiment or mere sensation, the love Henderson discovers is, in the words of Martin Buber, "a cosmic force." Love "does not," says Buber in *I and Thou*, "cling to an I, as if the You were merely its 'content' or object; it is between I and You [or Thou]."[3] Distinguishing, as Buber does, between the intersubjective relationship of "I and Thou" and the dissociation of "I—It," Gabriel Marcel observes that as "a *Thou* [the individual] is freed from the nature of things," while as "a *that*" he is "a thing" participating "in the nature of things" and "subject to destruction."[4]

To demonstrate just how and in what sense Henderson discovers this "freedom," or salvation, from death is the ultimate goal of my discussion here. What I should like to emphasize at the outset is Henderson's oppressive sense of *un*transfigured "reality"—what he later calls "unreality"—before he embarks on his quest. Blind to the nature and meaning of love, Henderson knows himself—as indeed he knows the world—only as a *thing* "subject to destruction." Unable to believe in any power, or mystery, transcending the "raw fact" of death, he regards love as dubious, inauthentic—the mere product of sentiment or illusion.[5] In contrast to Henderson, Lily, the woman he eventually marries, does not stop "saying 'I love you!' "(10). But to him these spontaneous declarations are a source of pain rather than joy. Lily's "lighted face and joyous eyes" blaze before Henderson with the same undeniable reality as the roses, "piercing and twining and flaming," in the churchyard of Vezelay, where they conclude their tour of French cathedrals. It is Henderson who compares the piercing quality of Lily's love to "the religion and beauty of the churches. Together, Lily's "embraces" and these "great cathedrals" make him a "double captive": they overwhelm him with a reality he would deny. When Lily asks Henderson if he understands what "love [can] do," he tells her to "shut up." Mocking the notion of love's transforming power, he declares, "A single individual can't do the nitrogen cycle all by herself" (16–18).

Even when he marries Lily, therefore, Henderson cannot bring himself to say that he loves her; only after his journey to Africa can he acknowledge and, with increasing conviction, articulate his love (284, 289, 329). As the returned traveler, the person who has voyaged "beyond geography," he gives an account of himself as he was *before* this inner transformation. As early as the novel's first page, Henderson the narrator draws attention to the contrast between his past and present self. "When I think of my condition at the age of fifty-five when I bought the ticket [to Africa], all is grief," he remarks, immediately adding: "However, the world which I thought so mighty an oppressor has removed its wrath from me."

After Henderson's African journey, the world is no longer his "mighty oppressor" because, as he later avows, "I'm not what I thought I was" (328). The man who has scoffed at those who, like Lily, believe in love's transforming power is ultimately transformed by this very power. Whether we attribute the alteration in Henderson's view of reality to himself or to "the world," the radical effects of his voyage into "the interior" are made clear from the outset (331). As a narrator Henderson continues, throughout the novel, to allude to his discovery of an unknown dimension or perspective that, having altered his vision of reality, permeates his account of life before Africa. As he recounts, for example, the events culminating in his breakup with Lily at Vezelay, he interrupts his narration to give thanks for the very love that, as a protagonist, he is anxious to deny. Thus at the end of a paragraph describing, in the narrative *past* tense, the tumultuous development of their affair, Henderson interjects, in the *present*, a prayer of thanks: "Blessed be God for the mercies He continually sends me!" (15).

In this way Henderson prepares his readers not only for his revelations as a protagonist but also for the value he places, as a narrator who has made the journey "beyond" history and geography, upon the meaning and mystery of love. In the novel's concluding pages, he underscores the point by means of repetition—emphasizing the fact that his final affirmation, in the novel's closing chapters, is no sudden or tacked-on affair but the lasting culmination of his experience.[6] Thus Henderson puts it to the reader, as he says, "Once more. Whatever gains I ever made were always due to love and nothing else" (339).

In Africa, Henderson's trials among the Arnewi and Wariri tribes, and especially his ordeal with the lion Atti, bring him into direct confrontation with the "raw fact" of death; yet the paradoxical effect of such experience is to awaken him to a reality "beyond" death, sustained by the absolute power of love. The power that finally "bursts the spirit's sleep" is Henderson's discovered love not only for Lily but also for others—his children, Romilayu, Dahfu—and for the earth itself: this mutable world consigning each mortal to his finite end.[7] From one who reads the sentence of death in all phenomena, who acknowledges the "raw fact" of extinction to be the metaphysical as well as physical law of existence, Henderson is transformed into one who understands the nature of immortality. To understand the alteration that takes place in his consciousness, we must turn, first of all, to Henderson's account of life before Africa. Only from this starting point can the distance spanned by his journey "beyond geography" be accurately perceived.

Before setting out on his quest, Henderson suffers the rage and hostility symptomatic of the enslaved. His antisocial outbursts and impulsive acts of cruelty stem from his fury at mortality itself. He is consumed by a death-ridden vision of reality that denies any possibility for meaning, value or purpose in life. In the manner of all idolaters, he has come to worship that which he most fears: the tyrant death. As King Dahfu, in his particular brand of English, later tells Henderson, "Oh, death from what we do not want is the most common of all the causes" (233). Enslaving himself to what he "does not want" and indeed most fears, Henderson makes his life an advertisement for the "raw fact" of extinction. Having left the Army at the end of World War II, he throws his energies into raising pigs. Hinting at the emblematic nature of his enterprise, Henderson the narrator comments: "When I came back from the war it was with the thought of becoming a pig farmer, which maybe illustrates what I thought of life in general" (20). Much later he acknowledges, "The hogs were my defiance. I was telling the world that it was a pig" (287–88).

Sentenced to slaughter, the pigs startle Henderson with their intelligence. "The discovery that they were so intelligent," he says, "gave me a kind of trauma." Seeing in these "clever doomed animals" a reflection of humanity's own condition, he tries desperately to embrace this vision of mortal doom that inspires him with fear (21). As though hoping to crush the inner voice demanding spiritual enlightenment—seeking knowledge beyond the finite "facts" of existence—Henderson tries, quite literally, to bind himself in pigskin: "And I kept going . . . in my thick padded coat, in pigskin gloves and pigskin shoes, a pigskin wallet in my pocket, seething with lust and seething with trouble" (12). Vehemently extolling the finite gratifications of his "pig kingdom," he announces the tyranny of matter and its laws (33).

Outraged by the doom to which matter subjects even the most ambitious intelligence, Henderson's mind is hostile to the very body that confines it. Even as he drifts off to sleep, he remains peculiarly aware of this Cartesian duality— disclosing to the reader how his "mind and body," which he describes as *separate* entities, "went to rest. It was like a swoon" (204). In their waking state, "mind and body" are even more stridently at odds: "Oh, my body, my body!" Henderson exclaims. "Why have we never really got together as friends?" Echoing Paul in his Epistle to the Romans, he declares, "Oh, who shall deliver me from the body of this death?"—then adds, "Anyway, from these distortions owing to my scale and the work performed by my psyche" (182).[8] The potential answer to Henderson's dilemma is already hinted at in the foregoing sentence. The accursed "body of this death" may not be reality at all, but rather the "distortions" produced by Henderson's overwrought mind— the "work," as he puts it, "performed by my psyche." Before he can be delivered from "*the body of this death*," Henderson must undergo a profound psychic transformation (284, Bellow's italics).

Until this inner transformation occurs, however, Henderson's mind continues to rage against his own body and the world's. With each demonstration of anger, he gains not release but more anger: "Wrath increased with wrath" (24). The material universe in which, as a rich and physically powerful man, he nominally occupies such a comfortable position proves a source of unending torment. Gazing at the sunlit pine trees of his Connecticut farm, delighting in the spicy air that stings his "lungs with pleasure," Henderson nevertheless detects "beneath this grass" an earth "filled with carcasses." And though he knows that "the grass is thriving" because of those carcasses, which "have become humus," he cannot, at this juncture in his life, take solace in "the nitrogen cycle" transforming death into life: "The crimson begonias, and the dark green and the radiant green and the spice that pierces and the sweet gold and the dead transformed, the brushing of the flowers on my undersurface are," he confesses, "just misery to me. They make me crazy with misery. To somebody these things may have been given, but that somebody is not me" (28–29). Yet the narrator's exalted description of this radiant, piercing reality—a world from which he, as protagonist, is painfully alienated—already foreshadows Henderson's ultimate transformation into that "somebody" who is presently, as he says, "not me." To this "given" world or reality, graced by awareness of "the dead transformed," Henderson's journey will ultimately lead. Meanwhile, tyrannized by his vision of "pigdom," he can only ask in misery, "So what am I doing here?" (29).

When Henderson finds his neighbor and occasional cook, old Miss Lenox, dead on the kitchen floor, the longing for rescue becomes an urgent cry for salvation: "The last little room of dirt is waiting. Without windows. So for God's sake make a move, Henderson, put forth effort. You, too, will die of this pestilence. Death will annihilate you . . . and there will be nothing left but junk" (40). As Miss Lenox is carried to the cemetery, Henderson strikes out for Idlewild and takes the first plane to Africa. He embarks on this journey because, as he later tells his guide, Romilayu, "I wouldn't agree to the death of my soul" (277). Yet he has little or no idea how to accomplish this rescue mission.

Like his older brother, Dick, who angrily shot a "balky" fountain pen with his pistol (and absurdly wound up dying as a result), Henderson is more adept at attack than at rescue (34–35). Descending from a long line of soldiers, he instinctively tries to "call on [his] military self" and to exert his "martial blood" in the effort to save his soul (219, 257). When, however, he finds himself among the peaceful Arnewi in Africa, Henderson senses that old Willatale, the tribe's priestess, might teach him an altogether different approach to salvation, grounded in "the wisdom of life." Blind in one eye, both man and woman at the same time, the Queen of Bittahness is, as Duane Edwards says, "a modern Tiresias in African undress."[9] From this monumental presence Henderson hopes to discover "the thing, the source, the germ— the cipher. The mystery, you know" (79, 100). Yet he foils his chances for enlightenment when he impulsively wages war against the frogs plaguing the tribe's water supply.[10]

Henderson's attack upon the frogs is, on one level at least, inspired by his gratitude to Willatale for her understanding and wisdom. "You[r] heart is barking," she notes with sympathy, encouraging him to continue his quest for reality "beyond" death (82). In a well-known passage she instructs him, "Say, you want to live. Grun-tu-molani. Man want to live." Henderson's response reflects only partial understanding of her advice. Rejoicing in Willatale's insight, he at first declares, "Me molani. She sees that? God will reward her . . . for saying that to me." Yet in his next breath, he takes matters into his own hands—resolving to play "God," or at least the god of war, himself: "I'll reward her myself. I'll annihilate and blast those frogs clear out of that cistern, sky-high" (85).

Before this devastation occurs, the ambiguous motives underlying Henderson's "act of gratitude" have already been suggested. Fashioning a bomb by which to blow up the frogs, he experiences a heady sense of power: "I lay grinning at the surprise those frogs had coming and also somewhat at myself, because . . . I went so far as to imagine that the queen would elevate me to a position equal to her own" (94). Summoning, as he tells the reader, "all the know-how I had," Henderson mistakes technique for enlightenment (102). His attempt to rid the "problem water" of its frogs betrays more than a misguided faith in mechanical solutions; Henderson is fundamentally confused about the nature of salvation (61). In unwitting worship of death, he seeks deliverance through the power of his self-proclaimed "murder technique" (66).[11] Aware, in retrospect, of the contradictory impulses spurring him on at this point, he confides to the reader: " 'Poor little bastards' was what I said [about the frogs], but in actual fact I was gloating. . . . My heart was already fattening in anticipation of their death. We hate death, we fear death, but when you get right down to cases, there's nothing like it. . . . I hungered to let fall the ultimate violence on these creatures in the cistern" (89).

Henderson's impetuous behavior, Bellow makes clear, is both an act of *hubris* and a travesty of the true quest. Not until he has brought catastrophe upon the Arnewi does Henderson pause to consider whether his "dangerous know-how" and Western technique—the Austrian lighter, the fancy H & H Magnum rifle, even the pith helmet on his head—afford him the ability, let alone the right, to tamper with the complex relationships governing the Arnewis' mode of life (65). But this period of reflection is itself short-lived. After a bout of shame and guilt, Henderson soon begins to rationalize his failure as one that all practitioners of modern "know-how" are bound to experience: "Is there a surgeon anywhere who doesn't lose a patient once in a while?" he rhetorically asks (115). Later, when he arrives among the tougher, warlike tribe of the Wariri, he tries to impress them, too, with various modern appurtenances. The aggressive Wariri, who possess plenty of "dangerous know-how" (including guns) of their own, simply ignore the sundry "cigarette lighters," the "magnifying glass" and other trinkets that Henderson produces from his pack. Yet he persists in overestimating the security afforded by "advanced" Western "know-how." When, for example, he is told that the Wariri do "not permit outsiders to carry arms in their territory," Henderson, now dispossessed of his firearms, reacts with a confidence that seems naive, if not obtuse. He merely wonders "whether these characters know much about [the] high-grade equipment" they have carefully removed from his possession (130, 132).

Henderson's impulsive acts are fueled, as I have suggested, by an admixture of ambition, pride and longing for spiritual salvation. When, with characteristic impetuosity, he resolves to lift the Wariri's statue of the goddess Mummah, the connection between his ambition and his fateful conduct among the Arnewi is overtly drawn: "I burned to go out there and do it. Craving to show what was in me, burning like that bush I had set afire with my Austrian lighter for the Arnewi children" (185). His expressed confusion of technique with spiritual salvation comically underscores his need for enlightenment. After he succeeds in lifting the Mummah, Henderson becomes the Sungo, or Rain King, of the Wariri. But as he later discovers, it is the duty of the Rain King to lift the statue each year until, having failed to do so, the Sungo is killed. It is no coincidence that with each succeeding attempt to demonstrate his prowess and superior technique Henderson finds himself confronting, once again, the "raw fact" of extinction. As Marcel points out in his discussion of the nature of salvation, "it is inconceivable that technique . . . can ever overcome death."[12] It is inconceivable, in other words, that any humanly devised technique or method can refute or transcend the "raw fact" of extinction governing mortality. For Henderson to achieve salvation—deliverance from a death-ridden existence—a profound alteration in his view of reality must take place.

Essential to this process of inner transformation is Henderson's gradual recognition of "how much mind, just mind . . . lies at the root of my complaints" (164). Because his "complaints" are largely about the nature and condition of reality, it is possible, he begins to recognize, that the operations of his mind—the "work performed by [his] psyche"— may lie "at the root" of this reality, or "unreality." While, as he says, "the world of facts is real all right," there is also "the noumenal department, and there," he adds, "we create and create and create. As we tread our overanxious ways, we think we know what is real" (167). Indeed, as Henderson narrates his own story, he exposes the process of "mental deceit" by which he, like the "reality instructors" in *Augie March*, has schooled himself in a "reality" that proves to be "nothing but pedantry" (HRK 322, 167). He shows us, moreover, that through his ordeals among the Wariri, his friendship with King Dahfu and his confrontation with the lion Atti, he comes to shed his most oppressive assumptions about reality.

Among the Wariri, Henderson first becomes aware of the world as "an organism, a mental thing, amid whose cells I had been wandering." At the time, he attributes such awareness to the "peculiarity of my mental condition." He is mistaken, however, to assume that because the world he perceives is a mental construct, it is under his control and direction. "From mind the impetus came and through mind my course was set, and therefore nothing on earth could really surprise me," Henderson glibly announces (156). Almost immediately, however, the stark reality of the *terra incognita* into which he has ventured shatters his assumptions—especially the assumption that his "course was set" and nothing "could really surprise" him. Seated next to King Dahfu at the Wariri tribal ceremonies, Henderson watches a man's chest being lightly carved by a priest's "old green knife"; and a visceral "shock" registers in the "depths" of his body—"like the ones big buildings get from trains which pass beneath" (172). This is only the first, and the slightest, of innumerable shocks to the system—both his nervous system and the system of mental habits and ideas ruling his perception—that will gradually transform Henderson's relationship to reality. Still, as the novel demonstrates, his habits of mind are deeply ingrained, and "pedantry" offers plenty of resistance to illumination.

One way in which Bellow suggests the intellectual resistance, or "mental deceit," that Henderson habitually exercises is to call attention to his insistent wearing of a pith helmet—the headpiece still in his possession after the Wariri divest him of his firearms and other equipment. This helmet, which the white man wears to shield himself from the blazing African sun, becomes the focus of a recurrent motif emblemizing Henderson's militant resistance to reality. Practically speaking, of course, Henderson requires the protection of a helmet against the sun's fierce rays. Yet as he tells King Dahfu, "I always have some headpiece or other. In Italy during the war I slept in my helmet, too. And it was a metal helmet." Even when stripped of his Western attire and swathed in the Rain King's billowing "green drawers," Henderson refuses to part with his helmet. Noting the weird effect of Henderson's costume, Dahfu gently protests, "But surely a headcover indoors is not necessary." As Henderson the narrator observes, however, he "refused to take [Dahfu's] hint. I sat before him in my white pith hat" (206–07).

Later, when Henderson undergoes his ordeal with the lion Atti, his terror—so intense that it makes him "half deaf, half blind, with my throat closing and all the sphincters shut"—is measured by his failure to "reset my helmet when it sank over my brows." And as the lion stares intently at Henderson, breaking down his "blind" resistance to her presence, he feels his "hair, though cramped by the helmet, stir all over [his] head" (224). Henderson's frozen posture and closed "sphincters" markedly contrast, moreover, with the "relaxed" and "easy positions" assumed by Dahfu in Atti's presence. Similarly, his "cramped" hair pointedly contrasts with the sheer vitality of Dahfu's springy locks: "and on his head," Henderson observes of the king, "the hair lived (to say that it grew wouldn't be sufficient)" (207). Henderson's "carapace-like helmet," with its cramping of head and hair, emblemizes the "cramped conditions" under which he is living—constrictions for which his mind, doing battle with the world, is largely responsible (287, 224). Just as the helmet fails to serve as "a weapon for protection" against the beast that slaughters his friend Dahfu, so Henderson discovers the "unreality" of the mental carapace enshrouding his perceptions (295).

This process of discovery begins among the Arnewi, where Henderson's attack upon the frogs brings destruction as well as defeat. His experience among the Wariri undercuts more drastically still his assumption of knowledge and expertise. As the Wariri prepare, for example, for their rain dance ceremonies, Henderson makes a bet with Dahfu that it will not rain; he confidently points out to the king that the "sun is still shining," that "there aren't any clouds" in the sky. Obviously cognizant of these facts, the king suggests to Henderson that reality may be more mysterious, less predictable than he supposes. Perhaps, he gently points out, Henderson is too easily taken in by appearances. Thus Dahfu says, "Your observation is true, to all appearance, I do not contest you. . . . Nevertheless, I have seen all expectation defied."[13] Henderson gives the king a skeptical look, mounting the following challenge: "Do you think it's so easy to get what you want from Nature? Ha! ha! I never have got what I asked for." Then, adopting the scientific vocabulary he has previously used to disparage Lily's faith in love, Henderson begins a disquisition on "the rain problem." Citing the failure, reported in the *Scientific American*, of one modern "technique" devised to create rain, he rehearses some other "recent ideas" and voices his preference for a "theory" based on the assumption "that the salt spray of the ocean . . . is one of the main ingredients of rain" (177–78).

As it turns out, Henderson is dead wrong: at the conclusion of the tribal ceremonies, the sky fills with clouds and it begins to rain. Even before this happens, however, Henderson's scientific posture is ironically undercut by his own impetuous behavior—fueled, once again, by his admixture of pride, ambition and longing for salvation. As the ceremonies begin, he can hardly wait to try his luck at lifting the statue of the goddess Mummah, the difficult feat that must be performed if, according to the Wariri, rain is to arrive. Henderson's eagerness to demonstrate his physical prowess thus leads to his direct participation in the rituals at which he initially scoffs. As he confronts the statue of the Mummah, he experiences a sudden change in perception. Having ceased to debate "the rain problem," he employs a different vocabulary altogether.

Echoing Bellow's own, earlier cited account of the "two different speeches" operating in contemporary culture, Henderson now heeds the "silent speech of the world" that registers beneath the busy "growling of [his] mind" and is apprehended only by the "soul": "I heard it," he declares. "The silent speech of the world to which my most secret soul listened continually now came to me with spectacular clarity. Within—within I heard. Oh, what I heard!" (162, 187). *"You are blind,"* Henderson is told. *"Should you be overcome, you slob, should you lie in your own fat blood senseless, unconscious of nature whose gift you have betrayed, the world will soon take back what the world unsuccessfully sent forth. . . . The purpose will appear at last though maybe not to you"* (187–88, Bellow's italics). In this moment of "inward communication" Henderson understands that he is in danger of dying. Having "betrayed" the "gift" of life, he is in the process of forfeiting it. Not the world but his own spiritual sloth threatens to destroy him as he sleeps, "senseless" and "unconscious," in his "own fat blood."

As Henderson strains to lift the statue of Mummah, his former preconceptions about reality are even more radically disrupted. Caught up in the overwhelming desire to "raise her up," Henderson, in a flash of feeling, suddenly perceives the statue not as a dead object but as "a living old woman. Indeed . . . a living personality not an idol. We met as challenged and challenger, but also as intimates." In an access of tenderness, he lays his "cheek against her wooden bosom," and the "benevolent Mummah with her fixed smile yielded to [him]" (192). Thus, Henderson succeeds in lifting the Mummah. Through his participation in this rite, he symbolically enters an "unknown dimension" of reality. His triumph is not the result of "technique," the skillful manipulation of an object or thing; it springs, instead, from the perceived interrelationship between two subjects—the creative relationship of Buber's "I-Thou," not the mechanical "I-It." Suffused with happiness at his success, Henderson also basks in the warmth of this discovered bond with creation. His "whole body," he says, "was filled with soft heat, with soft and sacred light. . . . My spirit was awake and it welcomed life anew." Directly "after this feat," he adds, "when the sky began to fill with clouds, I was not so surprised as I might have been" (193–94). In this world "beyond geography" no rational explanation for the sudden appearance of clouds, and subsequently of rain, is provided; their significance lies elsewhere. As Henderson's psyche awakens to its bond with matter, the world no longer appears to him as a hostile enemy, or "body of death," but as a living entity.

That the world is not his enemy but rather an "intimate" is Henderson's ultimate discovery, the "reality" into which King Dahfu initiates him. According to some of Bellow's critics, Dahfu, as his name suggests, contains more than a hint of the "daffy."[14] Yet Dahfu's insights into Henderson's plight are telling, if not profound. From the outset of their friendship, Dahfu instructs his American friend on the "connection between insides and outsides, especially as applied to human beings" (236). "You are," he tells Henderson, "in the flesh as your soul is" (268). By "speaking somatically," Dahfu strives to illustrate the "utterly dynamic," non-Cartesian union of body and mind—"the flesh influencing the mind, the mind influencing the flesh, back again to the mind, back once more to the flesh" (236).[15]

Though fascinated by Dahfu's instruction, Henderson cannot help, as he says, "thinking of mind and flesh as I knew them"—as forever at odds. He tends, therefore, to conceive of spiritual "awakening" as disembodiment, adamantly resisting Dahfu's instruction. "If this body, if this flesh of mine were only a dream," he insists, "there might be some hope of awakening" (265). While Dahfu may speak to him "somatically," emphasizing the relationship between mind and flesh, spirit and body, only Henderson's immediate experience can convey the truth of what Dahfu, in a lyrical passage that recombines elements of Psalm 19, tells him: "You are related to all. The very gnats are your cousins. The sky is your thoughts. The leaves are your insurance, and you need no other. There is no interruption all night to the speech of the stars" (266).[16]

By urging Henderson to come face-to-face with the lion Atti in her den, Dahfu compels his friend to confront "somatically" rather than abstractly the fact and terror of death. Whether the word catharsis or Reichian terminology is used to describe what happens to Henderson in the lion's den, the process he undergoes is clearly a liberating one.[17] By, as Dahfu says, "absorb[ing] lion into himself," Henderson is no longer enthralled by fear (265). "When the fear yields," Dahfu says, "beauty is disclosed in its place. This is also said of perfect love" (262). It is Henderson's love and admiration for Dahfu that compels him, in the first place, to confront his fear. Only this love, the heartfelt desire not to lose Dahfu's friendship, is powerful enough to make Henderson, a congenital "avoider," face the lion in her den (259–60). Confronting the "unavoidable," Henderson gradually enters into relationship with the lion, until dread—his abject terror of this savage beast—no longer paralyzes him. To perceive the lion as subject—to gauge her reactions, understand her gestures, participate in her otherness—is a process, moreover, that partakes of love. In both cases, as Dahfu says, "ego-emphasis is removed" (262). Relinquishing the "military self" perpetually in combat with adversary and object, Henderson finds release in participation: "And so I was the beast. I gave myself to it, and all my sorrow came out in the roaring. My lungs supplied the air but the note came from my soul" (267).

The spiritual release Henderson gains through his physical ordeal with the lion verifies the "connection between insides and outsides" proposed by Dahfu. This sense of connection is, moreover, granted a Judeo-Christian context by the narrator himself. In the poignant yet comical account of his ordeal, Henderson illustrates Bellow's earlier cited statement: "In *Herzog* and *Henderson the Rain King* I was kidding my way to Jesus." As contact with Atti stimulates Henderson to empathize with her and to "act" like a lion himself, he begins to roar. But the "roaring," he remarks, is really "a cry which summarized my entire course on this earth, from birth to Africa; and certain words crept into my roars, like 'God,' 'Help,' 'Lord have mercy' . . . plus snatches from the 'Messiah' " (274).

Although terrifying, Henderson's confrontation with the "unavoidable" brings revelation of something more fundamental than fear or dread. When he first learns that he cannot avoid entering the lion's den, a trembling Henderson drops to his knees and, from his "deepest feelings," addresses a plea to "you . . . you Something because of whom there is not Nothing. Help me to do thy will. Take off my stupid sins. Untrammel me. Heavenly Father, open up my dumb heart and for Christ's sake preserve me from unreal things. Oh, Thou who tookest me from pigs, let me not be killed over lions" (253). An unholy mixture of slang and reverence, Henderson's prayer, uttered in sheer desperation, has an obviously comic impact. Yet we cannot ignore his explicit recognition here of the connection between his "stupid sins" and the "unreal" scheme of things to which he has been mentally enslaved. Henderson's repeated encounters with the lion establish his intimacy with a universe from which his fear—fear of death and thus of life—has served to alienate him. By confronting his fear, he turns "unreality" into "reality." During the rain-dance ceremony, we recall, it was the power of Henderson's love that transfigured his perception of the Mummah and enabled him to lift not a dead object but a "living woman." As this ritual enactment symbolically suggests, love is the key to Henderson's spiritual awakening. Entering into a subjective "I-Thou" relationship with creation, he achieves release, as he has lifted the Mummah, from his "burden of wrath" (214).

Engaged in this process of awakening, or rebirth, Henderson recalls a time, "very early in life," when he had been not estranged from the world, but bound to it by love: "*It is very early in life,*" he says, recalling his childhood, "*and I am out in the grass. The sun flames and swells; the heat it emits is its love, too. I have this self-same vividness in my heart. . . . I put my love-swollen cheek to the yellow of the dandelions. I try to enter into the green*" (283, Bellow's italics). In Africa, in middle age, Henderson rediscovers this intimate bond with the universe. Gnats, people, stars—all, of course, live and die; they are "figures and not abiding realities." Each of us must contemplate a time when, as Henderson puts it, "I will never be seen again." Yet at the same time, he says, "everyone is given the components to see: the water, the sun, the air, the earth" (333). All share in this "given," each comprises a part of the whole; and what abides is a living entity, not a "body of death." No longer alienated from these "given" phenomena, Henderson is now that "somebody" he formerly was "not"—transformed by his very awareness of "the dead transformed."

That the world is not his adversary but rather an "intimate" is the discovery Henderson makes on his quest. This is the insight that liberates him from bondage to a universe of death. Reality now takes on a radically different meaning. The world is not set against the ego but contains it, nurtures it. Immortality, as Henderson discovers, is neither a reduction of the self nor an abstraction of the mind. As he says to Romilayu at the end of the novel, "the universe itself being put into us, it calls out for scope. The eternal is bonded onto us" (318). Extinction no longer threatens him because he experiences himself, his self, as part of an enduring whole—a whole that embraces difference just as it creates difference. To this enduring universe, Henderson now recognizes, he is bound by love. What *binds* him to this world, in other words, also *frees* him: releases him from bondage to fear and the tyranny of death.

In an Africa "beyond" history or geography, Henderson abandons "unreality" for its "opposite." And this discovered reality, Bellow makes clear, is no Cartesian machine, no world explained by "schemes" and abstractions, no object of disinterested inquiry. To the contrary, Henderson discovers that "it's love that makes reality reality. The opposite makes the opposite" (286). Under the agency of love "the body" of this world, no longer estranged from the self, is transformed from soulless machine to incarnate creation. Evincing the "gains" he has made "due to love," Henderson begins to contemplate a world in which "corporeal things are an image of the spiritual and visible objects are renderings of invisible ones" (338–39).

In a passage that casually reintroduces the helmet-motif discussed earlier, Henderson affirms the union of mind and flesh, soul and body, that he is beginning to achieve: "The hair on my head, especially at the back," he notes, was "thriving. I was growing black curls, thicker than usual, like a merino sheep, very black, and they were *unseating my helmet*. Maybe my mind, beginning to change sponsors, so to speak, was stimulating the growth of a different man" (272, italics added). This "change" in "sponsors" refers, of course, to the transformation of Henderson's perception and psyche. Exorcising his doom-laden identification with the pig, he "absorbs," under Dahfu's tutelage, the lion's pride and strength. By acknowledging, moreover, the intrinsic connection between his "mind" and his body—in the growth of new hair and "the growth of a different man"—Henderson signals a more radical alteration in his consciousness. As the impression of his "thriving" locks suggests, his regenerated psyche appears to be "unseating" the "carapace-helmet" along with the dread that has enslaved him.

Unseating the dead weight of his old hostility, "the burden of wrath," Henderson does not discard his helmet but adopts a new relationship to it. In a scene occurring near the end of the novel, after King Dahfu has been killed, Henderson and Romilayu stage their escape from the Wariri. Refusing to abandon the lion cub believed by Dahfu and his people to embody the dead king's soul, Henderson risks his own safety to bring the cub out of Africa with him. Insisting that his beloved friend has "got to survive in some form," he tells Romilayu: "I can't leave the animal behind and I won't. . . . I can carry it in my helmet" (326). This willing divestment of his headgear is best understood in the light of Henderson's former dependence on the helmet. Earlier in the novel, after being stripped naked during the tribal rain dance, he literally panics when he finds himself without it. "Pick up my clothes—my helmet," he shouts to Romilayu, "I've got to have my helmet" (202). But now, as he and

Romilayu embark on their escape from the Wariri, Henderson does not hesitate to forfeit his helmet for the sake of the cub.

The timing of Henderson's action, moreover, intensifies its impact. Only a few hours earlier, we realize, he has witnessed firsthand the death of his beloved friend. Horrified but helpless, he has watched a savage lion, far more brutal than Dahfu's Atti, tear the king's proud body to pieces. The bloody death of this noble being does not, however, obliterate Henderson's faith in life or in Dahfu's immortality. Quite the opposite, he embraces the lion cub, the very "child of [his] murderous enemy," as Dahfu's "enigmatic form" (328, 333). By this action, "enigmatic" in its own right, Henderson evinces both his love for Dahfu and love's power to transfigure reality. No longer at war with the world, Henderson is confident that Dahfu endures: he is part of the whole that embraces, just as it creates, both difference and death.

Like the helmet, Henderson's old "military self" is gradually put to rest by his awakened spirit. Although his grief at Dahfu's death is fierce and unremitting, it moves Henderson to forgiveness rather than the old "wrath." Of course he would like, as he tells Romilayu, to crush "like old beer cans" the Bunam and his men, whom he blames for the king's death. But now Henderson tempers his impetuous nature, entreating Romilayu, who is "quite a Christian fellow," for his help: "Revenge is a luxury. I've got to be canny. Hold me back, Romilayu" (316–17). Then, as Henderson turns his attention to planning their escape, even these traces of his old warring self give way to contemplation of his love for Dahfu and what he has learned from him. With newly opened eyes, Henderson is able to recognize his dead father's love for him, whereas before he felt only blind resentment. Thus, he says to Romilayu, "I suppose my dad wished, I *know* he wished, that I had gotten drowned instead of my brother Dick, up there in Plattsburg. Did this mean that he didn't love me? Not at all. I, too, being a son, it tormented the old guy to wish it. Yes, if it had been me instead, he would have wept almost as much. . . . Oh, I don't blame the old guy" (317–18, Bellow's italics).

Even while digging "on all fours" to escape the stockade where he and Romilayu have been locked up by the Bunam and his assistant, Henderson— this new Henderson—can speak of love and forgiveness. By returning love for hate, he stops the cycle of "wrath increased by wrath" that he has, for so long, blindly perpetuated. As Dahfu once told him, a brave man "will not want to live by passing on the wrath. A hit B? B hit C?—we have not enough alphabet to cover the condition. A brave man will try to make the evil stop with him" (214). It is this bravery, rather than the old resentment and hostility, that Henderson now undertakes to enact. Instead of rushing to slay the offspring of the lion that has destroyed Dahfu—"the child of [his] murderous enemy"— Henderson nurtures the tiny cub in an effort to "continue [Dahfu's] existence" (314). Instead of cursing "the body of this death" Henderson kneels "to kiss the earth" in gratitude (318).

The earth, in turn, offers up its humblest creatures for Henderson's own survival. As he and Romilayu make their escape through the wilderness, a grateful Henderson cries out, "So at last I'm living on locusts, like Saint John." Demonstrating the truth of Dahfu's declaration—that "the gnats are your cousins," the "leaves are your insurance"—Henderson is nourished by the "cocoons and the larvae and ants" that also succor the cub: "I had to mince grubs and worms with the knife in my palm and make a paste, and I fed the little creature by hand" (326–27). Providing the means to sustain Dahfu's "enigmatic form," the physical world is no longer "the body of this death" but rather the fount of life.

During their ten-day trek through the wilderness, Henderson, growing delirious from fatigue and lack of water, has no idea whether he will survive to see his family or home. What he does know for certain, however, is "that the sleep is burst, and I've come to myself." He understands, furthermore, that "much" has been "promised" between "the beginning and the end" of mortal life, even though he cannot formulate the exact nature of this promise (328). Perhaps the promise is of salvation itself: the salvation from despair and a world of death that Henderson himself has undergone. At the end of the novel he emerges not only from the wilderness but also, like Lazarus, from the "grave of solitude" where he has lain "buried"—to embrace the world of the living (265, 277).

In the novel's final pages, Henderson bids farewell to Romilayu—the black man who, he declares, has "saved [his] life"—and embarks with the lion cub on his journey home. *En route* to America he dons his helmet once again, as he takes the now sturdy lion cub "on a leash" to visit the Acropolis in Athens. On the plane flying over the Atlantic, however, Henderson removes the helmet one final time and places it "inside the wicker basket with the cub." The cub, he tells us, "needed a familiar object to calm him" during the flight (331–33). Although the helmet is still in his possession, Henderson regards it, at the end of his ordeal, in an altogether different light—as a "familiar object" rather than a shield. Yet for the reader, the pith helmet still bears the weight of its symbolic role. Unseated from its crowning position of authority, it betokens the triumph of love over the tyranny of death in Henderson's consciousness.

Roused from his "spirit's sleep," Henderson gazes, at the novel's close, into the clear, wide eyes of a little Persian boy seated next to him on the plane. In those eyes so "new to life" he perceives, paradoxically, an "ancient" power: "They had that new luster. With it they had ancient power, too. You could never convince me that *this was for the first time*" (Bellow's italics). Not even the extreme youth of this child, whose "smoothly gray eyes" are still un- clouded by worldly experience, belies this "ancient power"—what Augie March calls the "oldest knowledge, older than the Euphrates," which comes with the territory of being human. Beneath the shining "new luster" of a fledgling existence Henderson discovers no Lockean "*tabula rasa*" but an immortal soul "trailing [its] cloud of glory" into the earthly sphere—knowing what it knows, as Mr. Sammler might say, and never "for the first time" (339).

Tenderly administering to both the orphan child and the lion cub, the Henderson who flies home from Africa has clearly been "called from nonexistence into existence" (284). In his own existence he has realized the "promise" that sounds, throughout the novel, in recurring lines from Handel's *Messiah*. On the airplane bearing him home to Lily and his family, Henderson sings aloud the words to Handel's music: "And who shall abide the day of His coming (the day of His coming)? And who shall stand when He appeareth (when he appeareth)?" (334). For bravery of spirit—that ideal courage which, as Dahfu tells Henderson, puts an end to the cycle of "wrath increased by wrath" and returns love for hate, good for evil—there is, in the Western tradition at least, no greater model than Christ. If Bellow has, in his own words, been "kidding his way to Jesus" throughout *Henderson the Rain King*, his protagonist's ebullient singing marks the point at which he arrives at the novel's destination. Signalled by music that springs from Henderson's "secret soul," this point—located "beyond" history and geography—is marked by no other coordinates.

Chapter 7
The Antic and the Ontic:
Herzog

In *Herzog* (1964) Bellow elaborates the odd marriage of highjinks and spiritual contemplation, the antic and the ontic, created in *Henderson the Rain King*. The "kidding" of both comedies apparently prepared their author "to bare himself nakedly" in his subsequent novel, *Mr. Sammler's Planet*. While Eugene Henderson embarks on a series of strenuous physical ordeals, however, Moses Herzog's struggles occur mainly in his head. That he is physically inert during much of the novel—collapsed on the sofa of his New York apartment and supine on mattress, couch or hammock in his Ludeyville retreat—only underscores the turmoil of Herzog's hyperactive mind. The novel is, among other things, a resounding though comic culmination of the multifarious arguments, explanations and methodological approaches that the modern mind has brought to bear on human experience.

This "critical, recursive, ratiocinative" activity constitutes what Giles Gunn, in another context, calls "the characteristic [intellectual] experience of our time." As Gunn points out in *The Culture of Criticism and the Criticism of Culture*, the process "centers on the human mind itself as it moves in brilliant but sometimes fitful and ever more disbelieving steps toward the end of its own tether."[1] Nearing the end of his own tether, Herzog ultimately breaks the mental chain that binds him. After sifting through mounds of verbal persiflage, his mind comes to rest not in conclusions but in silence—a suspension of those critical operations that have tended to drown out his "primordial" self.

"In almost everything I write there appears a primordial person," Bellow told Matthew Roudané in 1984. The novelist's remarks, briefly cited in the chapter on *Augie March*, are especially pertinent to the themes of *Herzog* and thus bear further consideration. The "primordial person," Bellow goes on to say, "is not made by his education, nor by cultural or historical circumstances. He precedes culture and history. . . . This means that there is something invariable, ultimately unteachable, native to the soul. A variety of powers arrive whose aim is to alter, to educate, to condition us. If a man gives himself over to total alteration I consider him to have lost his soul."[2] In a world deluged with information, media events and global crises, the individual is particularly susceptible to the forces of "alteration" that distract and assail the "primordial person" or self. If an abyss can be said to underlie human existence, it is not, in Bellow's view, the much-touted modernist void undermining every human attempt to create meaning and value. To Bellow, "the Void" is not the inescapable condition of existence; rather, it is a state of spiritual emptiness, the terror of nonbeing, which overtakes the individual who has surrendered the "primordial person" and, in the novelist's words, "lost his soul."

Insisting upon the "primordial person," Bellow implicitly honors, in Paul Tillich's words, "the ontological priority of being over nonbeing." Even before thought itself, Tillich observes in *The Courage To Be*, there exists "the astonishing prerational fact that there is something and not nothing." Just as Bellow finds that "there is something invariable, ultimately unteachable, native to the soul," Tillich asserts that the primordial *is* something: we cannot speak of "the primordial night of nothing," he points out, because "such an aboriginal nothing would be neither nothing nor something": "it becomes nothing only in contrast to something."[3] Similarly, Bellow's "primordial person" originates not in chaos, Nothingness or "the Void," but in "Something"—in the ground of being which Eugene Henderson, echoing Tillich, identifies as the "Something because of whom there is not Nothing" (HRK 253).

The priority of being over nonbeing—and of the soul or "primordial person" over the conditioned self—does not imply, however, either to Tillich or to Bellow, a secure or complacent existence. The "primordial" self is a "given" of creation; and like any gift that is undervalued or taken for granted, it may be lost through carelessness, inattention or distraction. Bellow suggests as much when he says that a person who "gives himself over to total alteration" by the conditioning forces has "lost his soul." From Wilhelm Adler to Moses Herzog, Bellow's protagonists are aware, at least intermittently, of the dangers of spiritual sloth—and of the "ontic self-affirmation" crucial to personal salvation. "Ontic," says Tillich, comes "from the Greek *on*, 'being,'" and describes "the basic self-affirmation of a being in its simple existence." "The subject of self-affirmation," he adds, is "an individualized self"—"this unique, unrepeatable, and irreplaceable individual." Bellow's implicit identification of the "primordial" self with the "soul" is also clarified by Tillich: "The theological assertion that every human soul has an infinite value is a consequence of the ontological self-affirmation as an indivisible, unexchangeable self."[4]

Bellow explicitly delineates this connection between "ontic self-affirmation" and spiritual salvation in both *Henderson* and *Herzog*. Henderson, for example, understands that the quest for being, as opposed to becoming, is crucial to the salvation of his soul. In the ceaseless process of becoming—what Herzog calls the "Faustian spirit of discontent"—Henderson locates the threat to his being, or "ontic self-affirmation" (H 68). "I've just got to stop Becoming," Henderson declares. "Jesus Christ, when am I going to Be?" (HRK 191). Similarly, Herzog must, as Bellow comments to Roudané, "look for repose in what he was before he had accumulated this mass of 'learning.' He returns to Square One. There he asks himself the essential question. . . . What was my created soul? And, where is it now?"[5]

The "primordial" self or "created soul" that precedes culture and history is the polar opposite of Sartre's existential man who, lacking essence, creates his own existence. Sartre, as Daniel Fuchs observes, denies "essence in the sense of God-given soul, a belief to which Bellow finally subscribes."[6] It follows that Bellow's understanding of human freedom is markedly different from that of the French existentialists. "Pure freedom," as even the Dangling Man acknowledges, is attained in the quest "to know our purpose, to seek grace" (DM 154). Freedom is located, therefore, in the condition of *religio*—the individual's recognition of being *bound* to the transcendental principle or divine source from which his being springs. As Tillich points out in *Theology of Culture*, the "unconditional" power or ground of Being—that mystery the religious address as God, the *Deus est esse*—is the source of a human being's ontic "self-affirmation."[7] In order to affirm their own being, then, both Henderson and Herzog must move "beyond" contemporary culture and history—beyond the hegemony of rational argument and theoretical constructs—in order to clear a space, or a silence, in which the soul's own promptings may be heard.

An intellectual and academic, Herzog is even more deeply identified with the language and "know-how" of Western culture than Henderson. Yet a parallel exists, as I have suggested, between Henderson's strenuous physical antics among the Arnewi and Wariri and Herzog's equally strenuous mental voyage through the landscape of contemporary thought and values. As Henderson stumbles through the tricky undergrowth of a symbolic Africa—to emerge, at the end, like St. John from the wilderness—so Herzog, with equal desperation, hacks his way through a verbal forest of philosophical, scientific and legal formulations. Through the deterministic thickets of psychoanalysis, historicism and countless fashionable ideologies, he presses forward in search of his soul.[8]

The torrent of words, formulations, hypotheses that swell Herzog's private monologues and unsent letters recall, yet again, William James's observations concerning the "loquacity" of rationalistic thought. Continually voicing its demands, says James, rationalism "can challenge you for proofs, and chop logic, and put you down with words." It is this voice that Herzog hears insistently ringing, day and night, in his own head. Like an incubus, this "*someone inside*" Herzog, a "little demon," has "impregnated" him "with modern ideas" that challenge and "chop" his every attempt at ontic self-affirmation (11, 93, Bellow's italics here and throughout the chapter, unless otherwise indicated). Of this analytic voice, with its rage for order and explanation, Herzog declares: "*I am in his grip. When I speak of him I feel him in my head, pounding for order. He will ruin me*" (11). Through the endless maze of his own words, therefore, Herzog must cut a swath—rehearsing, challenging and finally discarding their "logic" and argument—before he can arrive at spiritual "repose." Only at the end of the novel is Herzog left, significantly, with nothing to say. Only after this arduous process of divestment—after his restless "Spirit," in Trilling's words, has descended in a "downward movement through all the cultural superstructures to some place where all movement ends, and begins"—does Herzog achieve the experience of authentic being. Then, in the sweet calm of a late summer afternoon in the Berkshires, the mental clamor finally subsides, supplanted, for awhile at least, by the singing of birds. "Not a single word" is, with an appropriate note of paradox, Herzog's parting word to the reader. Having arrived at a "place where all movement ends, and begins," he attunes himself to the harmonious silence that moves him, in a special sense now, "out of his mind."

It is the re-reader of *Herzog* who notes the special meaning of the novel's first sentence, in which Herzog declares, "If I am out of my mind, it's all right with me." Introducing the novel when his protagonist is already in the Berkshires, and nearing the end of his mental journey, Bellow creates an opening "frame" from which Herzog will review, in an extended series of flashbacks, the misadventures that have brought him to his country retreat. From the beginning of the novel, therefore, the reader is given a partial, penultimate glimpse of the "repose" at which Herzog, in the end, will arrive. When the novel opens, it is "the peak of summer" in Ludeyville, and Herzog has already written "endlessly, fanatically, to the newspapers, to people in public life, to friends and relatives and at last to the dead." The "need to explain, to have it out, to justify, to put in perspective," which began "late in spring," has by now almost played itself out. True, Herzog still trundles to "the kitchen, his headquarters," to write down "some new thought" when, with demonic tenacity, it "gripped his heart"; yet he is aware, "all the while, [that] one corner of his mind remained open to the external world" (1–2).

From this symbolic "corner," Herzog appears to be clearing a psychic space for his soul, attuning himself to a world permeated with the mystery of being: "When he opened his eyes in the night, the stars were near like spiritual bodies." The metaphor expresses Herzog's revelation of a universe mysteriously rescued from the mechanistic laws of matter. These remote bodies, and the universe itself, are no longer a distant abstraction but something "near" to him, a world to which he is intimately connected. Herzog's perception of these "spiritual bodies" is decidedly more than a figure of speech; his vision reflects a profound change that has taken place within him. As Tillich points out, such symbols open up "levels of reality which otherwise are hidden and cannot be grasped in any other way. . . . But in order to do this, something else must be opened up—namely, levels of the soul, levels of our interior reality. . . . So every symbol is two-edged. It opens up reality and it opens up the soul."[9]

After this premonitory opening in Ludeyville, the novel moves back in time, recounting successive stages of Herzog's emotional and intellectual crisis. An academic who has made "a brilliant start" in his career but lately lost his way, Herzog is in a special position to register what Bellow calls, in his remarks on the novel, the "enfeeblement of the educated man" by the conditioning forces of culture and history (4).[10] Midway through Herzog's research on a book intended to investigate "the social meaning of Nothingness" and its influence upon "the modern condition," he finds his faith in explanations and theoretical programs critically shaken (39). The crisis emerges during the bleakest months of his marriage to his second wife, Madeleine, but it is not just the result of domestic misery. Rather, the misery of his marriage brings to Herzog's attention certain unresolved questions—questions that his "elaborate abstract intellectual work" cannot help him answer. Far from helping him, his intellectual projects have only made him, "with his own soul, evasive" (265, 5). As he later discerns, "he, Herzog, had committed a sin of some kind against his own heart, while in pursuit of a grand synthesis" (207).[11] Engaged in research for his second book, Herzog soon realizes that "he couldn't deceive himself about this work. He was beginning seriously to distrust it. His ambitions received a sharp check. Hegel was giving him a great deal of trouble" (6).

It was Hegel's systematic account of reality, we recall, that Kierkegaard ostentatiously lauded—while regretting, with his customary irony, that such a marvelous abstraction has nothing to do with actual human existence.[12] The disjunction Kierkegaard delighted in pointing out—between the enchanting symmetry of philosophical models dreamed up by the human mind and the unfinished muddle of human existence—serves as an implicit source of comedy in Bellow's novel. We laugh, for example, at the naive assumption of Herzog's friend, the zoologist Asphalter, who assumes that Herzog must have known or suspected Madeleine's infidelity because, as he tells Herzog, "your intelligence is so high—way off the continuum" (43). On a larger scale, this disjunction between spheres of knowing, or reality, fuels the painful domestic farce of Herzog's second marriage. Living with Madeleine in the country, Herzog is busy on his research, confidently working out "problems [he] had become involved with in *The Phenomenology of Mind*" and preparing "to wrap the subject up, to pull the carpet from under all other scholars, show them what was what" (119). Purporting to have mastered the principles by which "reality oppos[es] the 'law of the heart,' alien necessity gruesomely crushing individuality," Herzog cannot abide or control the forces grinding his own domestic life to a halt. On the intellectual who "appeared to know how everything ought to go," actuality takes its revenge (123).

The muddle of Herzog's immediate existence is mirrored in the frightful physical mess of the house in which he and Madeleine are living: "The kitchen was foul enough to breed rats. Egg yolks dried on the plates, coffee turned green in the cups—toast, cereal, maggots breeding in marrow bones, fruit flies, house flies, dollar bills, postage stamps and trading stamps soaking on the formica counter" (121). While Herzog studies Hegel with that "proud air of abstraction in which," as he later comments, "M. E. Herzog, Ph.D., had once been clothed"—Madeleine vents her frustration by purchasing expensive clothes, antiques and food (246). As the bills and bounced checks mount, she accuses Herzog of being "sick with abstractions" and punishes him with "*lessons of the Real*" (123, 125).

Beyond the immediate failure of Herzog's second marriage, the novel illustrates more profound dangers incurred by the individual who gets carried away by "harmful Prussian delusion[s]." By taking on "the problem of the world's coherence, and all responsibility for it," the thinker assumes an insuperable burden that can lead to internal as well as external disaster (155). When Herzog's faith in his own systematic explanations collapses, the disappointment is crushing, his self-condemnation unrelenting. "Lacking clear ideas," he is also "losing self-respect" (104). Slowly Herzog must free himself of the "dream of intellect, the delusion of total explanations." He must recognize how "thought" itself can create a "realm of confusion" rather than clarity, especially when insuperable demands, for "total explanations," are placed upon it (166). Such intellectual overreaching leads not only to delusion but, as his own experience demonstrates, to a crippling sense of impotence, failure and "*self-contempt*" (161). By "*asserting too much*," he discovers, a person winds up "*suffering from self-hatred as a consequence*" (164). The process is verified by Bellow throughout the novel; time and again, Herzog's rage at Madeleine and Gersbach, his bitter lust for revenge, also manifests his "self-contempt." Noting the "ugly" confusion of his life, Herzog "despised himself for creating it" (104).

Although few of the other characters in the novel share Herzog's "dream of intellect," they are caught up in delusive ideologies of their own. Each believes, in his own way, in a systematic "explanation" of life—preaching, like Ramona Donsell, the doctrine of sexual pleasure or, like Sandor Himmelstein, the brutal facts of predatory existence. Most of the secondary characters are shown, in other words, to live in their own "realm of confusion"; and even those who betray Herzog are linked to him by the same "lunatic" anger and despair that they exacerbate in him (104).[13] Madeleine Herzog, for example, is both the object of Herzog's fury and the victim of her own "hatred" of him, hatred complicated by a "fringe of insanity" (299). Although Madeleine's psychological traits—which include "Pride, Anger, Excessive 'Rationality,' " and "Competitiveness"—may, as Herzog points out, be attributed to a classic case of paranoia, they also suggest that she suffers some of the same disorders manifested by her estranged husband.

While still married to Madeleine, Herzog explains to Dr. Edvig, a psychiatrist, that his wife thinks—as "to some extent many of us do"—that she has "to recover from some poison, need[s] saving, ransoming. Madeleine wants a savior, and for her I'm no savior," he adds. While Herzog openly criticizes this "Christian" vision of the world in crisis, "some fall from classical greatness, some corruption or evil to be saved from," he fails to see that he and Madeleine are both infected by a common "poison," the poison of mutual hatred and blame from which they sorely need saving (54). Herzog's recollection of one of their ugly marital squabbles underscores the point. In this scene, Madeleine actually denounces Herzog for being a false, or failed, savior: "So now we're going to hear how you SAVED me. Let's hear it again. . . . You SAVED me. You SACRIFICED your freedom. . . . Your important time and money and attention" (124). The "poison" of Madeleine's fury would seem to declare her need for salvation, just as it manifests the "corruption or evil" that prevents her from finding it. Thus, even before she and Herzog are married, he notes her "desperate," contradictory attempts at "purifying herself with angry vigor" (110).

Madeleine's short-lived conversion to Catholicism is an obvious attempt to save herself from the vision of Nothingness, or "the Void," whose influence on modern culture Herzog had intended to examine in his second, unfinished book. Although the rituals of devotion she practices seem closer to the spirit of theatrical role-playing than to true religious worship, it is clear that Madeleine's conversion expresses—in distorted and abortive fashion—Herzog's own "longing for reality, for God" (208). Her conversion cannot last, however, because it derives from fear rather than faith. As she tells Herzog, "I believe in my Savior, Jesus Christ. I'm not afraid of d-death now, Moses" (117). That Madeleine stutters when she pronounces the word "death" belies her declaration. She has no more rid herself of the fear of death than of the anger poisoning her existence. Soon afterward, as Herzog observes, "culture" and "ideas" take "the place of the Church in Mady's heart" (71). In yet another parody of Herzog's own quest, she courts, with characteristic desperation, the intellectual's faith in ideas that Herzog has begun to discard as inadequate.

Bound together by mutual confusion, fear and wrath, Madeleine and Herzog are joined in their little circle of hell by Valentine Gersbach, formerly Herzog's "dearest friend" and the man with whom Madeleine betrays him (36). "I sometimes see all three of us as a comedy team," Herzog remarks from hindsight, "with me playing straight man. People say that Gersbach imitates me—my walk, my expressions. He's a second Herzog" (190). As Herzog comes to recognize, Gersbach's adultery with Madeleine is also an odd attempt at intimacy with her husband, an expression of his admiration for, as well as rivalry with, the man he has cuckolded. The lectures that Gersbach writes on Martin Buber and other religious thinkers strike Herzog, moreover, as "a parody of the intellectual's [i.e., Herzog's] desire for higher meaning, depth, quality" (60). As Gersbach's estranged wife, Phoebe, tells Herzog, "He fell for you. Adored you. Tried to become an intellectual because he wanted to help you. . . . You wore him out. It nearly killed him trying to back you up." In reply Herzog admits that "some of what you say is right enough, Phoebe" (261). Trying to save Herzog, as Herzog initially tried to save Madeleine, Gersbach is another travesty of the "savior." Even his sexual betrayal may be seen as a grotesque expression of his bond with Herzog; for, as Herzog later writes, Gersbach *"tried to reach me through her,"* to seek *"me in [Madeleine's] flesh"* (318).

Further underscoring the bonds of love-hate, and offering yet another parody of salvation, Dr. Edvig, Herzog's psychiatrist, also falls in love with Madeleine—his fascination sparked by Herzog's account, during office visits, of his wife's beauty and intelligence. Adding to the "comedy team," Edwig winds up as Madeleine's therapist, courting his patient during sessions, *"at twenty-five bucks a throw,"* which he devotes to *"lectures on Eastern Christianity. After this,"* Herzog wryly comments, *"she began to develop strange symptoms"* (55). The relationship of Edvig and Gersbach to Herzog—as rivals who parody his role as Madeleine's lover and would-be savior—is antically, and ontically, mirrored in yet another love triangle. George Hoberly, the ex-boyfriend of Herzog's current mistress, Ramona, actually stalks Herzog on his way to her New York apartment, waiting below in the street while Herzog is wined and dined by Ramona. "Crushed by failure," Hoberly strikes Herzog, still suffering from his own sense of failure, as an appropriate double. As Herzog observes to Ramona, "while in New York I am the man inside, in Chicago [where Madeleine and Gersbach live] the man in the street is me" (199).

Even Sandor Himmelstein, the hard-headed Chicago lawyer who takes Herzog into his home after Madeleine throws her husband out, echoes the theme of failure and uncontrolled wrath that permeates so many of the characters' lives. And though Himmelstein scorns the very notion of salvation, taking great pride in "knowing the score," his desperate behavior belies his outward confidence. In long harangues, ostensibly delivered for Herzog's benefit, Himmelstein preaches the brutal facts of existence. As Herzog observes, "the very Himmelsteins, who had never even read a book of metaphysics, were touting the Void as if it were so much salable real estate" (93). Only a matter of minutes after extolling his life of practical success and material reward, Himmelstein breaks down, weeping with anger at his family, to whom he has given "everything," and "also at himself, that he should have such emotions." He screeches to Herzog, "Moses—they're killing me! Killing their father!" (89). Himmelstein, then, is afflicted by a sense of despair and meaninglessness derived from "the Void" he purports to celebrate.

The tirade of murderous accusations and counter-accusations that breaks upon Herzog from every side, and from within his own angry heart, testifies to the validity of his insight: "People are dying—it is no metaphor—for lack of something real to carry home when day is done" (28). Herzog's insight is not a judgment on his fellow human beings but a recognition, like Wilhelm Adler's, of mutual suffering and confusion. The persistence of this theme in Bellow's fiction should by now be obvious, and it is further evinced by the title of his latest novel, *More Die of Heartbreak* (1987). "People are dying," Bellow suggests, not physically but spiritually; they are heartsick, heartbroken. In despair, frustration and self-contempt, they turn, like Himmelstein or Madeleine, against those closest to them, if not against themselves. In the red face of a truck driver, therefore, Herzog reads the same fury that is written on Madeleine's forehead (286). Similarly, Herzog's wealthy brother, Shura, is a man who "despised everyone" (78). Shapiro, the historian, coolly discourses on intellectual matters, but his speech is punctuated by a "snarling wild laugh"— "the white froth forming on his lips as he attacked everyone" (70). The discord registered in so many lives lends urgency to Herzog's rejection of "the Void" and underscores the universal implications of his "desperate longing for reality, for God" (208). The "realm of confusion" evinced by these characters girds Herzog, like Augie March, to resist their various forms of "reality-instruction." He perceives that the lessons "administered by Madeleine, Sandor, et cetera" are meant to "destroy his pretensions to a personal life so that he might disintegrate and suffer and hate, like so many others" (94).

So excruciating, on the other hand, is the effort of "ontic self-affirmation" that, as Herzog says, "it was enough to make a man pray to God to remove this great, bone-breaking burden of selfhood and self-development." Burdened as he is, Herzog refuses to sink down "in the mire of post-Renaissance, post-humanistic, post-Cartesian dissolution, next door to the Void." He refuses to surrender his soul to the loquacious "demon" of "modern ideas," whose "terrible little heart" is "excited" by "one [idea] in particular": that "you must sacrifice your poor, squawking, niggardly individuality—which may be nothing anyway (from an analytic viewpoint) but a persistent infantile megalomania, or (from a Marxian viewpoint) a stinking little bourgeois property— to historical necessity. And to truth. And truth is true only as it brings down more disgrace and dreariness upon human beings, so that if it shows anything except evil it is illusion, and not truth" (93–94).

Salvation from "disgrace and dreariness" comes, then, not from more "ideas," systematic explanations and formulations but from within the "primordial" self anterior to them all. Not in the outward "alterations" imposed by culture and history, in other words, but only through inner transformation can Herzog be delivered from the poisonous wrath that keeps him in thrall to Madeleine and his disastrous past. In contrast to Madeleine, who "with angry vigor" seeks to "purify herself" through outward gesture and ritual—first by joining the Church and imitating piety, then through her zealous pursuit of academic knowledge and an advanced degree—Herzog perceives that true salvation comes only through "a great change of heart." "Let the enemies of life step down," he declares in a flash of insight. "Let each man now examine his heart" (51). Thus begins the arduous process of introspection, recollection and confrontation that culminates in Herzog's liberation from Madeleine and, still more important, the "delusion of total explanations."

The road to salvation, the recovery of Herzog's endangered soul, is riddled with comic setbacks and temporary delusions. Midway through his "vague pilgrimage," joyfully aware that he is "changing," he suddenly proclaims "the miracle of his altered heart" (17, 165–66). Yet this euphoric sense of confidence is shown to derive largely from Herzog's imminent visit to his mistress's apartment. There he anticipates being regaled with "food, music, wine, conversation, and sexual intercourse" (166). When he arrives at Ramona's, Herzog's immediate expectations are not foiled. Comically confusing his lust with his longing for salvation, Herzog hopes that by possessing Ramona he will be delivered from wrath. The next morning, however, "as soon as he was alone in the rattling cab," he realizes the deception, asking himself: "No freedom? Only impulses? And what about all the good I have in my heart—doesn't it mean anything?" (206–07).

Something more than pleasurable "impulses" will be required of Herzog before he can answer this question. His heart must be cleansed of the poisonous hatred he bears Madeleine and Gersbach before the "spell" under which he has been living appears, on the novel's last page, "to be passing, really going." Buried under the weight of the conditioning forces of culture and history, modern man also suffers attack from within. Collapse is fostered by that internal vacuum or spiritual "Void" that is, in Bellow's view, the prime legacy of "modern ideas." The power of these ideas, coupled with the disorder and chaos of contemporary urban life, tends to overwhelm Herzog's essential "faith" in life's "sacred quality" (93). At one point, the turning point, in the novel, he too becomes convinced that "anything except evil" is "an illusion."

Evidence in support of this dire judgment is delivered to Herzog at the Magistrate's Court in New York City. Here the deprived and dispossessed declare their confusion and hatred in a vicious cycle of dehumanizing violence. And here Herzog, having witnessed the trial of a woman who has abused and finally killed her own child, resolves to enact his own murderous revenge. Fending off his impulse to pray for the dead child, he asks himself in despair: "And what was there in modern, post . . . post-Christian America to pray for?" (240, ellipsis Bellow's). With a sinking sense of "the monstrousness of life," he resolves to seek his own justice, to kill Valentine Gersbach and thereby rescue his little daughter, June, from the clutches of Madeleine and her lover. The viciousness of Herzog's mental state eradicates both the antic tone and the "ontic self-affirmation" that have saved him from despair. Now he intensifies his bondage to Madeleine by surrendering to the very "hatred" that is "the most powerful element in her life." Yielding—as Sammler does when he kills the German soldier in the Zamosht Forest—to the "orgiastic rapture" of evil, he thrills to "the sweet exertion" of "inflicting death" (255).

In order to carry out the murder, Herzog visits his dead father's home in Chicago and steals from the desk Father Herzog's old pistol, still loaded with two bullets. Then, with the "flat but deadly flavor" of hatred, "a metabolic poison," in his mouth, he proceeds to the home of Madeleine and Gersbach—appropriately "gunn[ing] his motor with threatening impatience" (253–55). Here, feeding "his rage, to keep it steady, up to full strength," Herzog sneaks up to the bathroom window and finds his intended victim administering a bath to his (Herzog's) little girl. As he narrowly observes this man, Gersbach, whom he loathes—the man who has usurped his role as lover, husband and father—Herzog is nevertheless confronted by some "facts" that are neither brutal nor nasty: "The man washed her tenderly. . . . The hated traits were all there. But see how he was with June, scooping the water on her playfully, kindly" (256).

Despite his recognition of Gersbach's "fraudulence" and gross sentimentality, Herzog acknowledges the kindliness with which the burly, red-haired man is bathing his daughter. Confronted by this concrete *actuality*, he realizes that "firing this pistol was nothing but a thought": "To shoot him!—an absurd thought. As soon as Herzog saw the actual person giving an actual bath, the reality of it, the tenderness of such a buffoon to a little child, his intended violence turned into *theater*, into something ludicrous" (257–58). At this moment, in which concrete actuality exerts its priority over sheer abstraction, Herzog is cleansed of the poison that has infected him. Killing Gersbach now belongs to the same order of hollow ritual, of meaningless gesture, as Madeleine's *theatrical* show at becoming a Catholic. At this moment Herzog perceives, moreover, the destruction that hatred, like a poison, inflicts upon the hateful: "Only self-hatred," he observes, "could lead him to ruin himself because his heart was 'broken.' " Although Herzog now "congratulated himself on his luck," it is not luck but liberating insight—"a true change of heart"—that effects his recovery. From severe "atrophy of the chest," to recall Lewis's phrase, Herzog is redeemed by his own generous feelings: "His breath came back to him; and how good it felt to breathe!" (258).

Herzog credits luck rather than insight with this "change of heart" because, I would suggest, he is used to thinking of himself as a passive rather than active agent. Yet his confrontation with actuality constitutes much more than a passive reaction. By facing up to his own murderous impulses, Herzog, like Sammler in Bellow's subsequent novel, confronts in himself the reality of evil. Recognizing that he participates in the mystery of human evil—even in the horrors graphically exposed at the Magistrate's Court—Herzog ceases to be, as he says, "with his own soul, evasive." Previously, Herzog has suspected himself of "potato love," of sustaining false "innocence" by "willingly accepting the necessary quota of consequent lies" (266). He has also discerned a connection between such ontological evasion—escape from his "soul," or primordial self—and his emotional passivity: "He wondered at times whether he didn't belong to a class of people secretly convinced they had an arrangement with fate; in return for docility or ingenuous good will they were to be shielded from the worst brutalities of life" (154). By confronting actuality Herzog's own capacity for the "worst brutalities" is tested; through this ordeal he discovers that for him, murder is "nothing but a thought." Yet he could not have made this discovery—of his potential for evil and his capacity to overcome it—by means of abstract thought.

Herzog's emotional and ontological crises are, then, intrinsically linked. Confrontation with actuality—"the actual person giving an actual bath"— brings dramatic revelation of his primordial self as it brings him face-to-face with a reality that cannot be reduced to ideas. As opposed to the mental schemes comprising "nothing but a thought," actuality consists of "*everything horrible, everything sublime, and things not imagined yet*" (258). In actuality, Herzog discovers, paradox is everywhere: good and evil exist in the same being, within the same heart; Gersbach is both a cad and a kindly man; Madeleine's lover steals from Herzog, he loves Herzog; hatred is a poison directed at others but fatal to the self; forgiveness is freedom.

Before Herzog makes this discovery, while he is still pursuing his mission of vengeance, he passes by "a Polish church with a Christ in brocades exhibited in a lighted window" (254). This casual reference to the image of Christ neatly situates within the text a symbol of that deeper "level of reality," in Tillich's phrase, to which Herzog's soul is ultimately opened as it opens to itself. Later, having consigned his murderous intent to "nothing but a thought," Herzog rejoices not only in his failure to murder but also in his knowledge that "Father Herzog had never—not once in his life—pulled the trigger of this gun" (259). In the deepest recesses of his primordial self, Herzog celebrates the mystery symbolized by Christ's statue—that love can overcome hatred, transform evil into good. Thus, as he gazes at his young daughter, he reflects, "I had this child by my enemy. I love her. . . . Isn't it mysterious how I love the child of my enemy?" Grounded in this mystery, Herzog finds that love renders superfluous his previous search for theoretical explanations of life's meaning. The individual "does not need meaning as long as such intensity [of love] has scope. Because then it is self-evident; it *is* meaning" (289).

"What starts out as a novel of revenge," Daniel Fuchs remarks of *Herzog*, "becomes more and more a novel of redemption."[14] Herzog moves from death to life, despair to rebirth as he works out his salvation from nonbeing. He finds the courage to confront his own fear, hatred and guilt by confronting actuality; loosening the stranglehold of "modern ideas" upon him, he discovers that he can both accept himself and bless others—even those, like Madeleine and Gersbach, who are his "enemies." What he says about Madeleine to Phoebe Gersbach is not saintly, but neither is it hateful: "Bless the bitch! Good luck and good-by. I bless her. I wish her a busy, useful, pleasant, dramatic life. Including *love*" (263). Shortly after delivering this comic blessing on his enemies, Herzog's "change of heart" is both tested and confirmed. As a result of a traffic accident involving a Volkswagen truck, he is taken to Police Headquarters for questioning. The police have found him carrying Father Herzog's pistol, still loaded with the two unfired bullets; and Herzog possesses no permit. To him the gun is only a remnant of his former, foolish condition—belonging to what he now regards as "an earlier period" (300). To the police, however, it is an incriminating piece of evidence.

When Madeleine arrives at the police station to pick up June, she tries to incriminate Herzog further, declaring to the sergeant, "He's jealous and a troublemaker. He has a terrible temper" (301). Forcibly struck, once again, by Madeleine's fury, "as reminiscent of poison as chemical sweet acids," Herzog resists infection (299). Neither the humiliating situation nor Madeleine's efforts to implicate him in a criminal action can erode his persistent sense of well being. Now, no longer "heavy-hearted," Herzog feels "rather free" (302). Freed of hatred, he has no impulse to judge, condemn or explain. "I make no last judgment," he says. "That's for them, not me. . . . I'm out of this now. Count me out. Except what concerns June" (299). Gazing at Madeleine's face, he thinks to himself, "Ultimately unknowable, the processes behind it. See, Moses? We don't know one another. Even that Gersbach, call him any name you like. . . . He was unknowable. And I myself, the same" (299).

Abandoning the search for "total explanations," Herzog finds himself *"much better now at ambiguities."* The real human *"disorder,"* he observes, is the desire for *"super-clarity"* (304). Clinging to the delusion that absolute clarity, hence judgment, is possible, Madeleine does not hesitate to condemn Herzog. In her eyes he reads "a total will that he should die. This was infinitely more than ordinary hatred. It was a vote for his nonexistence" (301). But for Herzog final judgments, his own or Madeleine's, no longer matter. Like his brother Will—who tells him, "I'm not making any judgments on you"—Herzog finds that charity, mercy, love are essential; they enable us to forgive others and ourselves as well (306). No longer driven to justify his past mistakes, he does not try to explain to Will why he married Madeleine in the first place. Instead Herzog tells his brother, "God ties all kinds of loose ends together. Who knows why!" (305).

When, at the end of the novel, Herzog announces that he *"has no arguments to make"* and does not want *"a solitary thing,"* he is rejoicing in a state of awareness that transcends his former passivity. He has found that condition of *being* which Henderson sought in his journey to "the interior" and regarded as the salvation of his soul. By means of his own inward journey, Herzog has recovered his "primordial person" and reversed the process by which, according to Bellow, a man "gives himself over to total alteration" and "loses his soul." Thus Herzog finds himself, near the end of his quest, *"pretty well satisfied to be, to be just as it is willed, and for as long as I may remain in occupancy"* (340). Far from the empty or hollow affirmation that many critics detect here, Herzog's new-found capacity to accept rather than explain the mystery of existence is concretely demonstrated at the close of the novel.[15]

The protagonist's inner transformation is not, admittedly, characterized by any dramatic conclusion or resounding event; it is signalled, however, by subtle changes in Herzog's responses and behavior. This focus on the ordinary is, moreover, entirely in keeping with the novel's central meaning and emphasis. After all, it is Herzog who notes, early on in his letter-writing, that *the question of ordinary experience is the principal question of these modern centuries. . . . The strength of a man's virtue or spiritual capacity measured by his ordinary life"* (106). If "the question of ordinary experience" is the principal question, Bellow suggests, then it must be resolved not by explanations or theories but by the specific behavior of each human being in his "ordinary life." Whereas Herzog formerly had a theoretical understanding of this principle, he is now able to realize its meaning concretely in his own life.

It is, then, Herzog's immediate response to "ordinary life"—the decisions he makes and the conduct he adopts—that validates for the reader his acknowledged "change of heart." In contrast to his former urge to escape, for example, Herzog now rejects the role of passive observer or victim. At the novel's opening, he had been "hoping for some definite sickness which would send him to a hospital for a while," so that "he would not have to look after himself" (13). At the novel's close, however, Herzog refuses his brother Will's offer to place him under hospital care. Admitting that "only a while back, in New York, I had fantasies about being put in the hospital," he explains that now, in Ludeyville, "I'm excited, not sick. I don't want to be treated as though I were sick in the head" (332).

Other superficially mundane signs of Herzog's inner transformation emerge in his relationship to Ramona at the end of the novel. Offering to make dinner for her at his country retreat, he is at first apprehensive. If he picks some flowers for the table, he wonders with customary anxiety, will his guest think they are a pledge of commitment? Yet Herzog's doubts are quickly dispelled by the recognition that he is no longer tempted to "escape," as Tillich puts it, from being "into neurosis." With telling relevance to Herzog's own situation, Tillich defines neurosis as *"the way of avoiding nonbeing by avoiding being."*[16]

Herzog's neurotic "self-absorption," says Victoria Sullivan, "leaves him capable of infatuation or obsession, but hardly of love. Thus, for Herzog, women necessarily fall into the category of either victim or victimizer; he can have no other relationship with a woman."[17] Yet while playing the part of ardent prince, or "king of hearts"—perpetually "embracing his Wandas, Zinkas, and Ramonas"—"amorous Herzog" has longed for a more meaningful existence (94). He has yearned for that "wider range of human feelings" he experienced as a child—when, despite material poverty, existence was richly permeated by love in many forms: love for family, for one's fellow human beings, for a physical and social environment to which one belonged, and (in contrast to his recent self-contempt) for oneself (140). Like other aspects of his psychic life, I would argue, Herzog's "paranoid anxiety" about women—which Sullivan deems a permanent feature of his character—is dramatically transformed by the "change of heart" taking place within him. The fact is, once Herzog has freed himself of the urge to *escape* into Ramona's arms—in the "evasive" attempt to avoid "nonbeing by avoiding being"—he can adopt a healthier, more generous attitude toward her.

It is a freer, more confident Herzog—a man beginning to "know his own mind"—who at the end of the novel seeks candles for the dinner table "because Ramona was fond of them." Confident that "the flowers couldn't be used; no, they couldn't be turned against him," he brings them into the house for his guest to enjoy (340–41). Alhough still wary, as Sullivan points out, "of being exploited . . . in sexual combat," Herzog is for once the assertive host rather than Ramona's passive guest.[18] Earlier, in New York City, she had been "emphatic about the wine," refusing to let him bring a bottle along for dinner. At that time Herzog attributed her insistence that he not bring wine to the "feeling of protectiveness" he "produced" in people (154). Now it is Herzog's turn to insist on supplying all the provisions for dinner—and the "emphatic" tone is his. "You'll do nothing of the sort," he tells Ramona when she offers to bring the wine (337). These are small matters, admittedly; yet as Herzog has acknowledged, it is in the specific details of "ordinary experience"—in the realm not of "ideas" but of concrete actuality—that a person's "change of heart" proves real or illusory.

The last letters that Herzog composes, in Ludeyville at the close of the novel, further testify to his inner transformation. Released from the demonic grip of "modern ideas," total "explanations" and final judgments, he once more—and this time in a most heartfelt manner—extends his blessing to his former "enemy": "*Dear Madeleine, you are a terrific one, you are! Bless you! What a creature!*" (318). In another letter composed during his "final week of letters," Herzog contemplates the nature of suffering, shedding light on the ordeal he has undergone. While rejecting the notion that suffering has independent value, Herzog acknowledges that "*with the religious, the love of suffering is a form of gratitude to experience or an opportunity to experience evil and change it into good. They believe the spiritual cycle can and will be completed in a man's existence and he will somehow make use of his suffering, . . . and he will die transfigured*" (317). Herzog's recognition of suffering made meaningful by the transformation of evil into good, hatred into love, explicitly recalls Wilhelm Adler's experience as it does Henderson's. Like them Herzog has made "use of his suffering" and, in his own way, been "transfigured"; he has "experienced evil," faced it within himself and "changed it into good."

In achieving a profound "change of heart" Herzog has exercised the freedom that Bellow's earliest protagonist, Joseph in *Dangling Man*, identifies as "the freedom to seek grace." Grace, Paul Tillich points out, is the theological term for that ultimate or divine morality which transcends strict moralism and judgment. It is "forgiveness of those who are unacceptable"—as we all know ourselves to be—"and not of those who are good people." Tillich adds, "Grace unites two elements: the overcoming of guilt and the overcoming of estrangement. The first element appears in theology as the 'forgiveness of sins,' or in more recent terminology, as 'accepting acceptance though being unacceptable.' The second element appears in theology as 'regeneration,' or in more recent terminology, as the 'entering into the new being' which is above the split between what we are and what we ought to be. Every religion, even if seemingly moralistic, has a doctrine of salvation in which these two elements are present."[19]

If salvation means healing this deep psychic "split" through the operation of grace—then Herzog has, by the end of the novel, entered a state of grace. He discovers that he can accept his own flawed nature and the world's; he can ask God for forgiveness of his trespasses as he is able to forgive those who have trespassed against him. It is in prayer, therefore, that Herzog concludes the letter he composes at Police Headquarters, right after Madeleine has treated him with lashing contempt. "*Dear God! Mercy! My God!*," he supplicates, pronouncing the Hebrew words, "Rachaim olenu . . . melekh maimis. . . . *Thou King of Death and Life. . .*!" (304, ellipses Bellow's). Later, in "several lines" that he addresses to God from Ludeyville, Herzog notes "*how [his] mind has struggled to make coherent sense*" and admits that he has "*not been too good at it.*" Yet he accepts his failure, as he accepts his "*desire to do your unknowable will*" (325–26). Finally, in his closing prayer Herzog affirms, "*Thou movest me*" (340). That Herzog is moved by "*a holy feeling*" is the actuality that now takes precedence over any system of "total explanations." No logical method can test or prove the validity of "a holy feeling"; but as Herzog has already observed, "*we have no positive knowledge of [the] void*" either (314).

Repeating at the close of the novel what was announced at the beginning, Herzog once more declares, "But if I am out of my mind, it's all right with me" (315). Having arrived at the end of all the theories, systems and abstractions through which he has mentally sifted, Herzog may be "out of his mind," but he is by no means crazy. If he resembles anyone, it is not a certified lunatic but "daffy" King Dahfu, of whom Henderson observes: "And when I say that he lost his head, what I mean is not that his judgment abandoned him but that his enthusiasms and visions swept him far out" (HRK 235). If Herzog too is swept "far out," beyond the conventional boundaries of argument and assertion— to be "contained by everything about him *Within the hollowness of God*"— he still knows that he abides in truth (325). Riven for so long by the conflict between the "demon" of "modern ideas" and the "primordial person," Herzog understands—like the protagonist of Bellow's subsequent novel, *Mr. Sammler's Planet*—that he had "willfully misread [his] contract": "Evidently I continue[d] to believe in God. Though never admitting it" (231). Now, however, he can "*admit what I never stopped asserting anyway, or feeling. The light of truth is never far away, and no human being is too negligible or corrupt to come into it*" (314). Such is the awareness of grace. Able "to accept ineffectuality, banishment to personal life, confusion," Herzog can also accept the truth that no argument in the world either proves or disproves: that in his essence, his primordial self—his soul—he is, for as long as he remains "in occupancy," bound to God.

Chapter 8
The Legacy of *Humboldt's Gift*

Like Moses Herzog, the protagonist of *Humboldt's Gift* (1975)—the novel published after *Mr. Sammler's Planet*—spends a good deal of time lying on a couch, thinking.[1] Citrine's inner explorations result in more unlikely attitudes, however, among which the headstand figures prominently. The practice of standing on one's head—though it might strike Henderson, Herzog and certainly Mr. Sammler as bizarre—can be related to these characters' efforts to realign their position in the world and their relationship to reality. Advised by his friend, George Schweibel, a physical-fitness freak, to stand on his head to relieve an "arthritic neck," Citrine finds that this "upside-down position" not only cures his physical "neck pains" but relieves some profound psychological "strictures" as well (48–49).

Citrine makes this discovery one December day when, having found his silver Mercedes brutally "beaten and clubbed" by thugs hired to terrorize him, he attempts to quell his anxiety by turning to "the one Yoga exercise" he knows: "I removed my shoes, took a position on the floor, advancing my toes, and, with a flip, I stood on my head" (35, 47). As he waits for the police to arrive, Citrine—balancing his "trembling aching legs in the air"—takes solace in the deep red of his Persian carpet: "one of those surprises that seem to spring straight from the heart" (48). At this critical moment he is both surprised and heartened by the unusual perspective afforded by his "upside-down" posture. As he observes, "standing on my head did relieve me. I breathed again. But I saw, when I was upside-down, two large circles in front of me, very bright. . . . The weight of the body set upon the skull buckles the cornea and produces an illusion of big diaphanous rings. Like seeing eternity. Which, believe me, I was ready for on this day" (50). Citrine's anxiety, like his longing for "eternity," is only exacerbated—not caused—by the wreck of his Mercedes. Like Henderson and Herzog, he has arrived at a crisis point in his life. Entangled in a seemingly endless divorce suit with an angry and vengeful ex-wife, regarding himself as having "bungled" previous relationships as well as "the whole money thing," Citrine is most troubled by having lost touch with his "inmost being"—Bellow's "primordial person" (48). "I knew everything I was supposed to know," he says, "and nothing I really needed to know" (50). In his mid-fifties, Citrine has developed an "arthritic neck" because, he explains, as "I grew older my head seemed to become heavier, my neck weaker. The strain was largely at the top. In the crow's-nest from which the modern autonomous person keeps watch" (171).

The "strain" derives, in other words, from psychic rather than physical stress: the burden of sustaining that "crow's-nest" vantage, the detached observation-post of the "autonomous" member of contemporary "head culture." The latter term, as Bellow points out in his 1977 interview with Jo Brans, is explicitly used by the protagonist of *Humboldt's Gift*, who understands that "head-culture opposes" his belief in the soul and his longing for "individual connection with the creation" (350, 441). Citrine is acutely aware, then, of the hazards wrought by divided consciousness. The "strain" felt "largely at the top" of his spine registers the heavy "weight of the sense world" pressing on his confused soul. Contributing to that "weight" is the mass of material objects, information and data erected, like Sammler's "superstructures of explanation," upon a spiritual void (293).

Almost a year before the demolishment of Citrine's Mercedes, during a spring vacation with his mistress, he had already grown weary of the splendid "veil" of "appearances" distracting his vision. By refusing to look at the charming view of the French countryside outside his train window, he explains, "I rejected the plastered idols of the Appearances. These idols I had been trained, along with everybody else, to see, and I was tired of their tyranny. I even thought, The painted veil isn't what it used to be. The damn thing is wearing out. . . . I was thinking of the power of collective abstractions, and so forth. We crave more than ever the radiant vividness of boundless love, and more and more the barren idols thwart this. A world of categories devoid of spirit waits for life to return" (16–17).

It is not the phenomena from which Citrine recoils but their existence, according to "rational orthodoxy," as "categories devoid of spirit" (363). Credited as the sole reality accessible to man, physical phenomena have become the "barren idols" of present culture. In *Saving the Appearances: A Study in Idolatry*, Owen Barfield, a British philosopher known to have influenced Bellow, offers a penetrating discussion of this development.[2] In the recent "history of the West," Barfield points out, analytic thought (which he designates as "alpha-thinking") gave rise to a new form of idolatry:

> It had temporarily set up the appearances of the familiar world . . . as things wholly independent of man. . . . But a representation, which is collectively mistaken for an ultimate—ought not to be called a representation. It is an idol. Thus the phenomena *themselves* are idols, when they are

imagined as enjoying that independence of human perception which can in fact only pertain to the unrepresented.[3]

By the "unrepresented" Barfield means that "supersensible" reality—alternately designated as God or as the posited waves, quanta and particles of modern physics—existing "behind the appearances" of the humanly perceived world.[4]

Sick of idolatry and impelled "to look behind the appearances," Citrine seeks to discover a "*personal* connection with the external world" (167, 202, Bellow's italics). The detached, analytic world-view of the "modern autonomous person" has spelled not freedom from matter but its "tyranny." Like Henderson's "carapace-helmet," the burden of "collective abstractions" places a strain on Citrine's body and soul. "Keeping up its indefatigable pedantry," his "lexical busybody mind" creates an uncomfortable sense of top-heaviness (102). Citrine's "neck pains" are symptomatic of psychic strain, which wears him out and from which he escapes into sleep. "The truth about sleep," he avows, can "only be seen from the perspective of an immortal spirit. I had never doubted that I had such a thing. But I had set this fact aside quite early. I kept it under my hat. These beliefs under your hat also press on your brain and sink you down into the vegetable realm" (109).

Because "communications" concerning the spirit are "prohibited under the going mental rules of a civilization that proved its right to impose such rules by the many practical miracles it performed," Citrine has "no one but [him]-self to turn to" (50). Over the objections of nearly everyone, from his mistress to his closest relatives and friends, he seeks relief in another "upside-down" maneuver for which his headstands provide a suitable emblem and introduction. He seeks guidance in the writings of "the famous but misunderstood Dr. Rudolf Steiner" (109). By performing Steiner's spiritual exercises Citrine executes a kind of mental headstand. Overturning "the ruling premises" of "head culture," he eases his "neck pains" by lifting the lid of the "mental coffin" entombing his spirit (433).

When Citrine's mistress, Renata, asks him if he seriously believes "all this stuff" Steiner writes about "higher worlds" and "knowledge that doesn't need a brain," he answers in terms that attest to the "strictures" of contemporary thought: "I take it seriously enough to examine it," Citrine tells her. "Only my head-culture opposes it" (349–50). And when his ex-wife Denise needles him by asking, "Renata doesn't want you to be a mystic, does she?", Citrine objects: "I'm not a mystic. Anyway . . . it doesn't mean much more than the word religion, which some people still speak of with respect. What does religion say? It says that there's something in human beings beyond the body and the brain and that we have ways of knowing that go beyond the organism and its senses. . . . Test me on the scientific world-view and I'd score high. But it's just head stuff" (227–28).

Significantly, Citrine's growing awareness of the "head stuff" weighing down his spirit extends to others as well. As he contemplates his ex-wife and her "estimable beauty," he observes that although "the strength of the social order was on her side," Denise is "a burdened woman. . . . The beautiful head was a burden to the beautiful neck." Even her hairdo emphasizes the strain that she, another "modern autonomous person," unwittingly shares with her ex-husband: "Her hair was piled on top of her head and gave it too much weight. . . . The very fact that she wasn't aware of the top-heavy effect of her coiffure seemed at times a proof that she was a bit nutty" (224). The same may be said of numerous other characters in the novel, from Renata Koffritz to Citrine's brother Ulick, who, unaware of the peculiar "burden" of materialist culture, still manifests the strain.

Grappling self-consciously with his "burden," Citrine asks himself why he "enjoy[s] no relations with anyone of my own mental level"—preferring "bumptious types" like Rinaldo Cantabile, the Chicago wheeler-dealer who has connections to the underworld. The answer is rather clear, he admits: "These matters of the spirit are widely and instinctively grasped. Except of course by people who are in heavily fortified positions, mental opponents trained to resist what everyone is born knowing" (173, 91). By entangling Citrine in bizarre relationships with members of the *demi-monde* and in confrontations with lawyers and the police, Cantabile actually serves as a catalyst for certain fundamental revelations on Citrine's part. "Pale and crazy," pushy and persistent, Cantabile crashes into the intellectual's quiet domain like a "demon, an agent of distraction." In exasperation, Citrine wonders whether it is Cantabile's "job," or mission, "to make noise and to deflect and misdirect and send me foundering into bogs" (287, 180).

At the time that Citrine asks himself this question, Cantabile is playing a significant role in the other man's life. Pestering Citrine to tell him about the movie scenario that the dead poet, Von Humboldt Fleisher, wrote with Citrine years ago, as a lark, Cantabile maintains that it might have "commercial" possibilities (179–80). Citrine dismisses the suggestion as outrageous. As he later discovers, however, the movie scenario is part of the "gift" that Humboldt bequeathes to him "from the grave, so to speak" (6). Left in a sealed envelope, the unearthed manuscript eventually provides evidence that Humboldt and Citrine wrote the pirated scenario for the recent movie, *Caldofreddo*. It is Cantabile who brings the movie's popular success and huge box-office revenues to Citrine's attention. Subsequently, the money that the movie producers are compelled to pay Citrine rescues him from imminent financial collapse and frees him to pursue his spiritual quest.

The "gift" of the novel's title, as Jeanne Braham observes, "is also a human legacy of forgiveness for old disputes and past indifference." In the end, the mutual friendship of these two men, Humboldt and Citrine, outlasts their petty quarrels and shameful betrayals. In this novel, as in *Henderson*, the power of love to survive the grave is a dominant theme. *Humboldt's Gift*, as Braham says, "suggests not only a tangible bequest but an intangible legacy—Humboldt's voice from beyond the grave, which transcends the 'fact' of death."[5] Cantabile performs an important role in the novel by bringing both the tangible "gift" and the intangible legacy to Citrine's attention. Near the end of the novel, Cantabile arrives in Spain to jolt Citrine out of his isolation—bringing him news that everyone *but* Citrine, who has become increasingly hermetic, has heard. Long before he is made aware of these developments, however, Citrine begins to suspect that Cantabile's role in his life might be altogether different from his initial view of it. As the novel progresses, Cantabile "seemed [to Citrine] to have a spiritual office to perform. He had appeared in order to move me from dead center" (287–88). Reminiscent, in certain ways, of the pickpocket whose outrageous actions move Artur Sammler off "dead center"—summoning him from distant moon-thoughts back to his "planet"—Cantabile plunges Citrine into "a world from which," he admits, "I had the illusion that I was withdrawing" (287).

Recognizing that "no normal and sensible person" can help him out of his stasis, or crisis, Citrine contrasts Cantabile's possible "spiritual office" to the lack of communication he experiences with "a man like Richard Durnwald. Much as I admired him, I couldn't be mentally comfortable with Durnwald," Citrine avows (288). Yet Durnwald, a "great scholar, one of the most learned people on earth," seems inadvertently to have performed a "spiritual office" as well, having introduced Citrine to the works of Rudolf Steiner. A strict "rationalist," whose "analytical power" Citrine greatly admires, Durnwald "had simply been joking about Steiner during one of their conversations." Citrine, on the other hand, "was not joking"; but he cannot admit this to Durnwald for fear of being "thought a crank" (109, 186).

Scorned by most members of the intellectual establishment, Steiner, with his reputation for "crank theories" and "kinky" ideas, creates a particular dilemma for Bellow's readers, who tend to share Durnwald's attitude (350, 363).[6] How seriously, they ask, does Bellow himself take Steiner's views? In contrast to some of the novel's "incredulous reviewers," as Ben Siegel puts it, Bellow has expressed his outright admiration for Steiner, whom he describes as having "a great vision." Steiner was, Bellow insists, "a powerful poet as well as philosopher and scientist."[7] Attempting to shed some light on the matter, Daniel Fuchs—while acknowledging that *Humboldt's Gift* contains the author's "confession of faith"—notes Bellow's wariness, as a novelist, of proclaimed "absolutes." Fuchs cites some relevant notes that Bellow made at the time he was composing the novel:

> In notes for a lecture [says Fuchs], Bellow speaks of Valery's hostility to novelists. Valery "often says there is no principle of necessity in the facts they offer. Other facts can easily be substituted. In a novel things are

entirely too relative to interest him." Bellow notes this insight with disapprobation and comes to the novel's defense. "The novel," he says, "is the highest form of human expression so far attained. Why? Because it is so incapable of the absolute."[8]

Far from aiming to restore the "lost content" of an "honorific culture"— to recall Charles Newman's charge against Bellow—the novelist here celebrates the genre's inherent ambivalence and freedom. In the novel's anti-authoritarian structure, so "incapable of the absolute," Bellow appears to locate its moral and linguistic superiority—"the highest form of human expression so far attained." This viewpoint calls to mind the writings of the Russian critic, Mikhail Bakhtin, who lauded the uniquely liberating tendencies of the novel's language and structure. In *The Dialogic Imagination*, Bakhtin outlines, at great length and in terms by now familiar to most practicing critics, the essential difference between the genres of poetry and the novel. To the "unitary and indisputable discourse," or "language system," of poetry he contrasts the social and linguistic "heteroglossia" of the novel's "hybrid" form. According to Bakhtin's formulation—which is, despite its abstruseness, in striking agreement with Bellow's—the novel "denies the absolutism of a single unitary language" and liberates discourse from assuming the "absolute form of thought."[9]

The novel's "hybrid" linguistic structure so strongly undermines any single perspective or language that, Bakhtin contends, even "when the novelist comes forward with his own unitary and fully affirming language, . . . he knows that such language is not . . . in itself incontestable."[10] Suggestively verifying Bakhtin's contention are the patterns of "structural irony" in *Humboldt's Gift*, which, as Fuchs notes, persistently undermine the author's "confession of faith." In *Humboldt* as in *Henderson* and *Herzog*, the "structural irony" embedded in the novel's plot and narrative voice undercuts any tendency on the reader's part to regard the character's (or author's) language of affirmation as "absolute." Thus, for example, in the midst of Citrine's "lofty reflections" on Steiner and the soul, "Renata has," as Fuchs puts it, "her gourmand footsy orgasm."[11] Throughout the novel, I would add, Citrine's escapades with various Chicago thugs and his relationship to his sexually "turned-on" mistress repeatedly suggest just how how tenuous his grasp of "eternity" is—how easily he slips from contemplation of "higher worlds" to confrontation with banal actuality.

Within the text, moreover, occasional stylistic evasions recreate, at the syntactical level, the "structural irony" detected in the larger pattern of events. Take, for example, the casual phrase, "and so forth," which Citrine interjects in several passages of "lofty reflection," including the passage cited earlier: "I was thinking of the power of collective abstractions, and so forth."[12] The urgent but unfocused state of Citrine's mind tends to bear out his later contention—that he is "only in a state of preparation, not an initiate" in Steiner's spiritual philosophy (440). Nor does Citrine declare, by the novel's end, any "absolute" faith or certainty. Quite late in the novel, in fact, he admits that "there were passages in Steiner that set my teeth on edge. I said to myself, this is lunacy. Then I said, this is poetry, a great vision" (439). By this time he has resolved, however, to pursue his studies at the "Swiss Steiner Center, the Goetheanum," near Basel (481–82).

Most important for Citrine, his interest in Steiner's philosophy takes him beyond the "respectable empiricism in which [he] had been educated," to contemplation of the "strangeness of life." Dismissing "ordinary spiritualism," Citrine nevertheless senses "a core of the eternal in every human being. Had this been a mental or logical problem I would have dealt logically with it. However, it was no such thing." He is convinced that "the more the mind opposed the sense of strangeness [of life] the more distortions it produced." Steiner's vision serves, then, to free Citrine from the dominant "mental respectability of good members of educated society," who assume that scientific rationalism can account for this "strangeness" or mystery. Thus, "whenever the esoteric texts make [him] uneasy," Citrine reminds himself of, and is "sustained by," his "contempt" for the reductive account of life offered by "respectable empiricism" (438–39).

It is hunger for news of the soul that impels Citrine to study Steiner; and it is as an aspect of Citrine's internal dilemma or conflict—between the mind's knowledge and the soul's understanding—that the discussions of Steiner in *Humboldt's Gift* should primarily be regarded. Aware, like Sammler, of the distinction between mystery and knowledge, Citrine observes: "The old philosophy distinguished between knowledge achieved by effort (*ratio*) and knowledge received (*intellectus*) by the listening soul that can hear the essence of things and comes to understand the marvelous." But rationalist culture is so overbearing, manufactures so much "distraction," that the "listening soul" has difficulty heeding "the essence of things" (306). By immersing himself in Steiner's philosophy, Citrine seeks to loosen the "strictures" on his "lexical busybody mind" and open himself to other modes of knowledge (102). The materialist view of existence has reduced the "inner self" to a biological function, metaphysics to an intellectual game. Failing to credit as real anything but that which is seen by the eye, grasped with the hand or digested in the belly, "the modern autonomous person," says Citrine, embraces "five different epistemologies in an evening. Take your choice. They're all agreeable, and not one is binding or necessary or has true strength or speaks straight to the soul" (390).

Stressing the *dramatic* importance of Citrine's study of Steiner does not, however, exonerate the critic from paying some serious, though necessarily brief, attention to the actual premises on which Steiner bases his epistemology. In however tentative a manner and to however qualified a degree, it is Steiner's epistemology that inspires the fresh perspective Citrine is able, by the novel's end, to adopt toward reality and, most significantly, toward his dead friend, Von Humboldt Fleisher.[13] In Citrine's view, Humboldt was silenced as a poet, and finally destroyed as a man, by the noisy distractions and massive pressures inflicted by a culture enslaved to the "plastered idols of the Appearances": "A wonderful man like my late friend Humboldt was overawed by rational orthodoxy," laments Citrine, "and because he was a poet this probably cost him his life. . . . Must the imagination be asked to give up its own full and free connection with the universe—the universe as Goethe spoke of it? As the living garment of God?" (363). To Steiner, whose philosophy grew out of his own scholarly interest in Goethe, Citrine turns for an answer. To Steiner, therefore, Bellow's readers ought to direct at least cursory attention.[14]

When asked, near the end of his life, which of his writings would last the longest, Rudolf Steiner immediately replied, *"The Philosophy of Spiritual Activity* will outlive all my other works."[15] The significance of this statement becomes even more pronounced when one considers the range of Steiner's output, which totals, in the complete German edition, fify volumes of written works and nearly two hundred volumes of lectures. In *The Philosophy of Spiritual Activity*, Steiner lays out with philosophical rigor the tenets of his epistemology, which serves as the foundation for his later anthroposophical texts. Offering critiques on the philosophies of Kant, Hegel, Berkeley and others, he attempts to demonstrate the primary reality of the soul and the essential unity of subject and object, inner and outer reality.

According to Owen Barfield, Steiner wrote *The Philosophy of Spiritual Activity* "at the same time that he was editing Goethe's scientific works in Weimar."[16] Like Goethe, his mentor, Steiner opposes the traditional distinctions between experience and idea, matter and mind, reality and spirit. In his Introduction to *The Philosophy of Spiritual Activity*, Hugo Berman, a professor of philosophy at the Hebrew University of Jerusalem, identifies the aspects of Goethe's thought that influenced Steiner:

> Goethe had conceived . . . the world [as] a manifestation of ideal forces in the world of the senses. All plants, for example, are nothing but materializations of the one, ideal archetypal plant. The archetypal plant is the fundamental design of all plants: the [node] and the leaf. We have to think of this fundamental design as a living, working idea which cannot be seen by means of our sense organs but which manifests itself in the world of the senses.

In opposition to the premises of scientific materialism, Berman continues, Goethe argued that "there was no fundamental difference between the spiritual and physical view," that "the idea and the sense perception *complete* each other."[17] In *Humboldt's Gift*, Citrine even comments on this aspect of Goethe's thought as he reflects on Steiner's philosophy: "according to Goethe the blue of the sky *was* the theory. There was a thought in the blue. The blue became blue when human vision received it" (363, Bellow's italics). Human sense perception, in other words, completes the idea or the "thought in the blue."

Building upon Goethe's theory of knowledge, Steiner demonstrated that, as Barfield says in *Romanticism Comes of Age*, "we owe it to our concepts that we perceive a world of shapes, forms, 'things' at all. 'The picture of the world with which we begin philosophical reflection,' wrote Steiner in *Truth and Science*, 'is already qualified by predicates which are the results solely of the act of knowing.' " By analyzing the act of cognition Steiner demonstrates that, contrary to the tenets of positivism, the sense-experience constitutes neither an objective nor the ultimate element in our knowledge of reality.[18] Furthermore, it is by thinking—a dynamic process that, according to Steiner, engages the imagination as well as the reason—that the individual knows he exists and participates in a spiritual world of which the sense-world is only a partial manifestation. By carefully examining the implications and consequences of this activity of thinking, Steiner sought to redefine, indeed to overturn, the "ruling premises" of scientific materialism and, in Citrine's phrase, its "categories devoid of spirit."[19]

Discussing Steiner's teachings with the anthroposophist, Dr. Scheldt, Citrine alludes to the tenets of *The Philosophy of Spiritual Activity*, saying: "Let me see if I understand these things at all—thought in my head is also thought in the external world. Consciousness in the self creates a false distinction between object and subject. Am I getting it right?" Dr. Scheldt answers, "Yes, I think so, sir" (261–62). Dr. Scheldt's "I think so" is a highly appropriate response; for Steiner labors to demonstrate that the human activity of "thinking" is itself anterior to this elementary "distinction between subject and object":

> Insofar as the human being observes an object, it appears to him as given; insofar as he thinks, he appears to himself as active. He regards what comes to meet him as *object*, and himself as thinking *subject*. . . . It must, however, not be overlooked that it is only with the help of thinking that we can define ourselves as subject and contrast ourselves with objects. For this reason, thinking must never be understood as a merely subjective activity. Thinking is *beyond* subject and object. It forms these two concepts, just as it forms all others.[20]

Challenging the perceived duality of subject and object, which the activity of thinking both creates and can transcend, Steiner's self-declared "monism" stresses the immanence of spirit and thought in the material world and the active participation, by means of thinking, of the individual in so-called objective or "external" reality.

According to Steiner, if thought or spirit participates and manifests itself in the "appearances," then what we see—the phenomena—is only the visible portion or dimension of the unseen world of spirit. Death is only the visible, limited end of a life whose reality originates in spirit and therefore transcends the physical world of the senses. Thus, Citrine says, "under the recent influence of Steiner I seldom thought of death in the horrendous old way. I wasn't experiencing the suffocating grave. . . . Instead I often felt unusually light and swift-paced, as if I were on a weightless bicycle and sprinting through the star world" (221). The primacy of spirit having been revealed to him, matter and the pull of gravity no longer weigh down, or "suffocate," Citrine's consciousness.[21]

This sudden sense of weightlessness, of "light-in-the-being," while it may suggest a desire to escape from the burden of mortality, affords Citrine a new perspective and allows him to bear up under daily pressures (177). Outside the judge's courtroom, where he must appear in connection with Denise's ongoing alimony suit, Citrine observes his situation, as he stands flanked by two lawyers, with unusual calm: "three creatures belonging to the lower grade of modern rationality and calculation" (221). What has seemed a life-and-death matter is suddenly placed in a wider perspective. The legal settlement is a pressing but ultimately ephemeral issue, a problem handled and solved by the very institutions of "modern rationality and calculation" that have created it. And even when these blissful moments of "detachment" end—as this one does, abruptly, when the judge charges Citrine to come up with "half a million dollars more"—he is consoled by an enlarged perspective. Suppressing his "longing for passionate speech" and "taking a chance on heartbreak through tongue-holding," he concedes that his punishment, while hefty, is confined to this "lower grade" of human affairs: "Besides, as suffering went, I was only in the middle rank or even lower. So out of respect for the real thing I clammed up" (231–32).

While Fuchs correctly notes Bellow's wariness, as a novelist, of offering his readers spiritual certainties or "absolutes," Bellow's novels testify, as I have shown, to his comparable wariness of the "ruling premises" of contemporary culture. These premises have assumed such "respectability" in a technological society that they are rarely subjected to scrutiny or question. Implicit in nearly every form of social as well as scientific discourse, they operate as virtual or tacit "absolutes" (as Bellow's term, "rational orthodoxy," implies). The rendering of life, in all its contradictory and mystifying "strangeness," is one way that Bellow, employing the concrete medium of the novel to greatest effect, challenges the hegemony of "collective abstractions." In *Humboldt's Gift*, he reveals the strange forms that contemporary idolatry, the worship of matter raised to the level of the "absolute," has taken. The most striking example occurs in the depiction of Citrine's older brother, Ulick, a "wizard with money" who has devoted, indeed subjugated, his life to "the idols" of materialism. In the service of that faith he has erected numerous "shopping centers, condominiums, motels" that have transformed the face of the earth in "his part of Texas" (245).

The seat of Ulick's real-estate operations is the town of Corpus Christi, Texas—whose name ironically underscores the radically different "metaphysical assumptions" by which he and his younger brother exist (244). Implicitly contrasting the teachings of Christ with the profit-motive, "Corpus Christi" recalls that spiritual vision Citrine is struggling to discover. Ulick's whole life, on the other hand, is devoted to the power and pride of material objects—and to the active denial of whatever cannot be seen, touched or digested. "In principle [Ulick] was not in favor of strong family bonds," Citrine says; in his businessman's view, "brotherly love [was] an opening for exploitation" (244). "Hardheaded" Ulick thus makes a point of denying all memory of the past "except for business transactions" (391, 386). ("Plato," Citrine elsewhere reminds us, "links recollection with love" [348].) The only form of exchange Ulick credits is "business," the exchange of objects or property. Thus, although Citrine knows in his heart that his brother loves him, Ulick will not acknowledge any family feeling—except by offering his younger brother a business "deal" (381). His faith in the profit-motive does not allow him, moreover, to bring off such a "deal" without making a little respectable profit for himself. He could not "do such an unbusinesslike thing"; failure to turn a profit goes against his highest principles. "Of course," he avows to Citrine, "I have to take a little advantage"—but of his brother, "it would be the minimum basic" (392).

When Citrine visits his brother at home, shortly before Ulick is to undergo heart surgery, this man of property appears to be unafraid of death. Citrine senses, however, that beneath the silence Ulick is "terrified by the approaching blank" (391). His only acknowledgment of imminent events is to tell his younger brother that, should he die on the operating table, Charlie must marry his widow. "She's a better woman than you'll ever find by yourself," he tells Charlie. "You'll never have another financial problem, I can tell you that." Admitting that he has not discussed the matter with Hortense, he adds: "She probably guesses that I want her to marry a Citrine, if I die on the table" (398). By bequeathing Hortense, his most cherished possession, to his brother, Ulick is perhaps expressing that "brotherly love" he cannot articulate in any other way. In any case, he seems to regard himself, genetically bound to his brother, as somehow materially *interchangeable* with him—so that the next best thing to being married to the woman he loves is to have his brother Charlie, also "a Citrine," marry her. His bizarre offering, as Bellow arranges for us to see, bears testimony not only to "the strangeness of life" but to the primitive consciousness of the idolater: the blinkered view of reality that, in a culture which celebrates "material conveniences" and "creature comforts" as the highest good, passes for practical wisdom (383).

While Ulick presumes to bequeath his unsuspecting widow to his brother, she—out of concern for his health—has tried to keep him from indulging his gluttony, which threatens to ruin his chances for a successful operation. When Citrine visits his brother before the operation, Ulick takes the opportunity, while showing Charlie the site of his latest and biggest property deal, to stuff himself with the food he has not ceased to crave, with "extraordinary greed," since childhood (393):

> The fish had been eaten. We sat with him under a tree sucking at the breast-sized, flame-colored fruit. The juice spurted over his sport shirt, and seeing that it now had to go to the cleaner anyway he wiped his fingers on it as well. His eyes had shrunk, and moved back and forth rapidly in his head. He was not, just then, with us. (397)

As Bellow's extraordinary rendering of the "strangeness of life" again illustrates, Ulick's adoration of the material clearly exceeds the strictly logical premises that foster and purport to explain such "orthodox" devotion. Citrine's perception of his brother contradicts the image of a "hardheaded" man of property and practicality. It is not just that Ulick's greed is "excessive"—the silent expression, perhaps, of his desire to grasp hold of life as he sucks, like a babe, at the "breast" of a juicy persimmon. No, by blotting out all consciousness of the past or apprehension of the future, Ulick seems to be suffocating the soul altogether. In escape from the human plane ("he was not, just then, with us") he descends to some lower scale of the evolutionary ladder—consciousness devolving into sheer instinct and the rapacity of blind appetite. By arranging "the phenomena" in this way Bellow suggests, rather literally, the "tyranny" of matter over the "modern autonomous person" who would deny the reality of spirit.

After Ulick's successful surgery, Citrine visits his brother in the hospital, unable to "get over" the miracle of medical technology: "they had pried open the man's rib cage and taken out his heart; they had shut if off like a small motor and laid it aside and started it up again when they were ready" (399). Ulick's comment on his experience is itself eerily detached, a clear reverberation of the technician's objective viewpoint. "A heart can be fixed like a shoe," he assures Charlie. "Resoled" (400). The last word, with its buried pun, suggests the reductive view Ulick takes of his own heart or soul.[22]

Before Citrine, who is about to leave for Europe, says goodbye to his brother, Ulick makes an odd request: "Listen, Chuck," Ulick says, "there's something I've always wanted that you can buy for me in Europe. A beautiful seascape. I've always loved paintings of the sea. Nothing but the sea. I don't want to see a rock, or a boat, or any human beings. Only mid-ocean on a terrific day. Water water everywhere" (400). Later, as Citrine wanders through Spanish art galleries, fruitlessly seeking a painting devoid of all phenomena but the sea's "pure element, the inhuman water," he wonders at his brother's peculiar taste. Perhaps, he thinks, it is a sign that even this man of property, this idolater of the material, longs in his heart of hearts to be released from earthly bonds. "What did a seascape devoid of landmarks signify? Didn't it signify elemental liberty, release from the daily way and the horror of tension? O God, liberty!" (421–22). Citrine's speculations may more accurately reflect his own longings for spiritual release. In Ulick's case, the reader is left with an impression of surrender, of a consciousness so weighed down by "the sense world" that it sinks into oblivion, or sleep (293).

As Citrine has earlier observed, the weight of phenomena can "press on your brain and sink you down into the vegetable realm." To the mineral realm, the sea's "inhuman water," Ulick himself may be attracted by the lure of oblivion. In rendering the "strangeness" lurking beneath Ulick's seemingly ordinary behavior, Bellow employs the novel's concrete medium to overturn the materialist vision and premises that, in Ian Watt's well known phrase, fostered "the rise of the novel" during the eighteenth century—the Age of Reason. Bellow's own novelistic rendering of reality, while building on the genre's formal traditions and techniques, increasingly challenges that vision and those premises: what Citrine calls "the alleged rationality and finality of the oblivion view" (357).

Like his brother Ulick, Citrine's mistress, Renata Koffritz, declares her worship of matter, though she prefers the word "nature"—of which her first name is a near-perfect anagram.[23] "I believe I live in nature," she writes to Citrine in her farewell letter. "I think that when you're dead you're dead, and that's that. And this is what Flonzaley [the mortician she has just married] stands for. Dead is dead, and the man's trade is with stiffs, and I'm his wife now" (431). Previously married to a man named Koffritz, a salesman of crypts and tombs, Renata emblemizes—in her last name (koff-ritz, ritzy coffin or, perhaps, the Ritz as "mental coffin") and her two marriages—not so much "nature" as the authority of death in the physical world. To "accept the finality of death" is as much a "part of [her] package," Citrine observes, as it is of Ulick's (392). In the materialist faith, the "raw fact" of "death," to recall Marcel's phrase, becomes the supreme metaphysical as well as physical law. Nothing—not love or honor, thought or belief—can challenge its "finality"; the ultimate end, it consumes all other human ends. The death-principle underlying Renata's materialist faith is highlighted when Citrine says to her, "Renata, let me quote you a text: 'Though you are said to be alive you are dead. Wake up and put some strength into what is left, which must otherwise die.' That's from the Revelation of Saint John, more or less" (320).

It was from such a death-ridden existence that Eugene Henderson fled, abandoning his "pigdom" in order to save his soul. Renata, on the other hand, remains true to "her beliefs," abandoning Citrine for the mortician. Although she remains true to the "rationality of pleasure," a certain "strangeness"—a "solid mass of improbabilities" and contradictions—undermines the logic of her theory and practice (164, 374). Her voluptuous beauty and flagrant dedication to Eros notwithstanding, Renata is far less "natural" or sexually spontaneous than she wishes to appear. Despite her splendid biological attributes, which she expertly deploys, she is "by no means fully at ease in sex. There were times," Citrine notes, "when she was sad and quiet and spoke of her 'hangups' " (191). He repeats the observation later in the novel: "How easy and natural she made everything seem—goodness, badness, lustfulness. . . . At the same time I didn't really believe that it was all so very natural or easy. I suspected—no, I actually *knew* better" (360, Bellow's italics).

The occasion prompting Citrine's latter observation bears particular discussion. At this moment he is seated with Renata and his cohort, Thaxter, at a table in the Palm Court of the Plaza Hotel. Bored by the high-minded conversation the two men are having, Renata covertly makes love, under the table, to Citrine's foot—or to herself by means of his foot, from which she has tacitly removed the shoe. "This had happened before," Citrine acknowledges, noting at the same time the "enjoyment of secrecy" lighting up Renata's face as she achieves, in Daniel Fuchs's phrase, her "footsy orgasm" (360). Amusement at her own cleverness, the thrill of covert action, her power to undermine Citrine's lofty speculations—these elements obviously complicate Renata's motives and quicken her "natural" appetites. The keen pleasure she derives from her manipulations reveals how very mental, how idea-ridden, is her devotion to the "facts" of nature. To idolize nature—to worship the "plastered idols of the Appearances"—is, Citrine recognizes, not "natural" at all. Posing as an earth-goddess, Renata is actually an ideologue; she has succumbed, in her own way, to "collective abstractions." As Citrine says, "I knew her *theory* well. Whatever was said, whatever was done, either increased or diminished erotic satisfaction, and this was her practical test for any idea" (365, italics added).

When, at an earlier point in the novel, Renata drives Citrine downtown, dropping him off at "a handsome russet and glass skyscraper," he leaves her car to make the following observation:

> And there was the insignificant Picasso sculpture with its struts and its sheet metal, no wings, no victory, only a token, a reminder, only the *idea* of a work of art. Very similar, I thought, to the other ideas or reminders by which we lived—no more apples but the idea, the pomologist's reconstruction of what an apple once was, no more ice cream but the idea, the recollection of something delicious made of substitutes, of starch, glucose, and other chemicals, no more sex but the idea or reminiscence of that, and so with love, belief, thought, and so on. (218)

Among these "ideas" or imitations of the real thing—Renata herself may be counted.

Adorned in "wonderful, soft, versatile" costumes, her "belly and thighs under an intermediate sheath of silk," Renata advertises herself as an agent of Eros; yet Citrine's firsthand knowledge of her once again contradicts appearances. Recollecting his initial attraction to her, he recalls thinking that "Eros was using my desires to lead me . . . toward wisdom." He quickly refutes this reassuring "interpretation," however: "That was nice, it had class, but I don't think it was a bit true. . . . The big name if I must have one, . . . was not Eros, it was probably Ahriman, the principal potentate of darkness" (211–12). "In Steiner's *An Outline of Occult Science*," Fuchs points out, "Ahriman originally is the spirit of awareness of the material world. An excessive awareness has made him a destructive force."[24] That Renata's sexuality is hypertrophied—manifesting an "excessive awareness" that distorts and destroys "nature" or the life-force—is already suggested by her respective marriages to Koffritz and Flonzaley, both of whom trade in death. Unlike Citrine, whose financial prospects are dubious, Flonzaley can offer Renata all the creature comforts. An unending supply of corpses ensures that he will "never run out of money" (417).

Renata's association with death goes beyond her choice of husbands, however. The first time that Citrine tries to make love to her, the apparent earth-goddess takes on the semblance of a beautiful corpse. In the rented hotel room to which she and Citrine repair after imbibing cocktails in the bar below, Renata passes out from too many martinis. "She was damp and felt cold," Citrine observes as he proceeds "to unbutton her coat to help the breathing." Finding that she is naked "under the coat," he gazes at her impassive but exquisite body; then, feeling "more like an art lover than a seducer," he "buttoned her up from sheer respect." Renata's carefully preserved body— "every tissue was perfect, every fiber of hair was shining"—sustains the impression of a carefully wrought work of art (217). Like a "graven image," she embodies the *idea* of erotic pleasure but remains "damp" and "cold," like marble (or a corpse), to the touch.

Through this unlikely association of live beauty with the deathly pallor of a statue or corpse, Bellow implicitly draws upon the biblical wisdom concerning idols, idolaters and their suggestive affinity. When Citrine says, for example, "Ye have eyes and see not," he directly invokes the relationship of idol to idolater expressed in numerous passages of the Old Testament, including the book of *Isaiah* (Chapters 6 and 44) and several of the Psalms (HG 46). Psalm 135, for example, states, "The idols of the heathen are silver and gold,/The work of men's hands./They have mouths, but they speak not;/Eyes have they, but they see not." The psalmist adds, "They that make them are like unto them:/So is every one that trusteth in them." It is clear, Owen Barfield observes, "that the Hebrew writers associated with images [idols] the almost opposite notion of *emptiness* or *nothingness*—the absence of any spirituality whatsoever." They conceived this condition of spiritual emptiness, Barfield adds, "as likely to be transferred to the subjective state of the idolater."[25]

Although Citrine appears the passive party in his breakup with Renata, it is his active decision to pursue "a different kind of life" that brings it on. And just as his breakup with Renata marks a step in his gradual disengagement from the driving forces of materialism—"the American dollar-drive"—so the collapse of their love affair throws into relief his enduring attachment to Humboldt (430). Indeed, the most dramatic indication of Renata's status as both idolater and "idol" may well occur when she says, in her farewell letter to Citrine, "Your passion for Von Humboldt Fleisher speeded the deterioration of our relationship" (432). If, as I have tried to show, Renata suggests only the idea— not the reality—of love, then her resentment of the dead poet is especially noteworthy. Whereas she abandons Citrine for Flonzaley, who trades in death, Humboldt's love for his friend is so powerful that he can "act from the grave"—effecting, as Citrine says, "a basic change in my life. . . . I came into a legacy" (6).

The second movie scenario that Humboldt leaves Citrine as a "legacy" (the first is the one pirated by the producers of *Caldofreddo*) is, as Citrine later observes, also Humboldt's "affectionate opinion of me. . . . It was an act of love" (351). "Be sure," Humboldt writes in his posthumous letter to Citrine, "that if there is a hereafter I will be pulling for you" (347). In terms of the novel's time-scheme, the "hereafter" to which Humboldt refers contains the "present" in which Citrine exists. Upon this immediate present, already Humboldt's "hereafter," the poet continues to exert tremendous influence. Indeed, the love by which Humboldt "acts from the grave" is a mutual bond, one that Citrine shares with his dead friend. "One infallible sign of love," Citrine tells us, "was that I dreamed of Humboldt so often. Every time I saw him I was terribly moved, and cried in my sleep" (10).

At first Citrine is unwilling to acknowledge the bond that ties him to Humboldt. After fifteen years of estrangement, and only two months before the poet's death, Citrine, in New York City on business, had spied Humboldt walking down the street. "I knew that Humboldt would soon die," he admits years later, "because . . . he had death all over him" (7). Sick, "gray" and "dusty," the poet already appeared a ghost. Later, "after Humboldt's death," Citrine threw his energies into keeping fit, attempting to define himself *against* the dead poet. Recollecting the savage pleasure he took in contrasting the corpse's rotting bones to the warmth of his cohabitation with Renata, Citrine sums up his attitude: "So my pal Humboldt was gone. Probably his very bones had crumbled in potter's field. Perhaps there was nothing in his grave but a few lumps of soot. But Charlie Citrine was still . . . in terrific shape and lay beside a voluptuous friend" (8).

The macabre note in this description sounds with added irony when the novel's re-reader ponders this "voluptuous" friend's subsequent marriage to the undertaker, Flonzaley, satirized by Citrine as Pluto, the "Prince" of the underworld (431). Long before Renata's marriage, however, Citrine begins to recognize the "illusion and idiocy" inherent in such posturing. No matter how much prowess he may demonstrate to his mistress on the "Posturepedic mattress," his own aging and death are inevitable (9). Ceasing to deny his bond with Humboldt, Citrine both mourns his dead friend and acknowledges his legacy. "As time went on," says Citrine, "I found certain of [Humboldt's] characteristics beginning to stick to me. . . . I found myself becoming absurd in the manner of Von Humboldt Fleisher. By and by it became apparent that he had acted as my agent" (107). As Citrine's "agent," or alter ego, the poet provides a focus for Citrine's own struggle against the burden of worldly distractions and materialist formulations.

Reviewing Humboldt's tragic life, Citrine conjures a picture of the romantic artist weighed down and finally crushed by a culture that no longer values the poet's vision or "passionate speech" (232). Humboldt's tragedy, Citrine speculates, was the poet's loss of faith in his own soul. "Pure, musical, witty, radiant, humane," the poems in Humboldt's first published book were, says Citrine, "Platonic. By Platonic I refer to an original perfection to which all human beings long to return" (11). But after this perfect "love-offering" from the poet to the world, Humboldt became increasingly transfixed by the world's own siren song, the clamorous ring of material power. So distracted was he by the "babbling and grunting and TV commercials"—the cacophony of "matter creaking and hissing"—that he could no longer hear the "voice that sounds in [the poet's] soul" (264–65, 312). The poet's voice, Citrine maintains, "has a power equal to the power of societies, states and regimes": the "power to cancel the world's distraction, activity, noise, and become fit to hear the essence of things" (312). Yet Humboldt, seduced by the material world, apparently ceased to believe in his Orphic power. A poet, after all, "can't perform a hysterectomy or send a vehicle out of the solar system" (118). Surrendering his faith in the poet's sacred office, Humboldt sought to establish himself as an intellectual authority; placing his trust "in victorious analysis, he preferred 'ideas' to poetry" (269).

In *Humboldt's Gift*, Alvin Kernan has deftly argued, "Citrine is a poet too." Yet despite Citrine's "Wordsworthian intimations that he was singled out for some great work in the world," most of his *oeuvre*, says Kernan, is "historical and political writing in which the facts, not the imagination, control the work. . . . This is not the oeuvre of a poet or any great imaginative writer, but the marketplace-determined writing of a man who gives the world what it wants and will buy."[26] In the movie scenario that Humboldt writes and bequeathes to Citrine, he parodies his friend's factual art by inventing a writer named Corcoran, loosely modelled on Citrine himself. After Corcoran's ecstatic sojourn to an exotic island with his mistress, Laverne, he returns home to write a novel describing his enchanting adventure. But he realizes he cannot publish it, because his wife, Hepzibah, would know from reading the novel that he had been unfaithful to her. In a further parody of the factual artist, Corcoran decides not to transform imaginatively the "facts" of his adventure but to make the same trip again, this time with Hepzibah. Then, he thinks, he can safely publish his novel. Hoping to get all the "facts" right, he has his literary agent prepare the island's natives to repeat every circumstance and event that characterized his sojourn with Laverne. When the trip is repeated and the novel published, both Laverne and Hepzibah are outraged: Hepzibah knows she cannot be the heroine of such tender, erotically charged scenes, and Laverne knows he has betrayed their intimate and unique experience by repeating it with another woman. The parable embedded in Humboldt's scenario, Kernan points out, suggests that "the modern writer, like Citrine, in his anxiety for the public fame which comes from publication and his desire for social acceptance and respectability, the marriage to Hepzibah, covers up the original experience, and in so doing makes a clown out of himself."[27]

At the end of *Humboldt's Gift*, the story of Corcoran is bought by the producers of *Caldofreddo*. The fact that both scenarios have been bought by Hollywood producers testifies, in Kernan's view, "to the power of the material world itself" upon the modern artist. Kernan observes,

> The old romantic figure of the poet disappears into the grave with Humboldt, and Charles Citrine, the poet of the next generation, at last accepts that disappearance forever when he reburies Humboldt in a decent place, appropriately enough using the money the movie plot has earned. The machinery of the modern world, bulldozer and crane, bury the poet deep beneath "brown clay and lumps and pebbles," first placing a concrete slab on top of the concrete case for the casket. Gazing at that concrete slab being lowered over Humboldt's coffin, Citrine asks himself, "But then, how did one get out?" Immediately the answer follows, "One didn't, didn't, didn't! You stayed, you stayed!" (487).

Here, says Kernan, Citrine accepts the material world "in its most potent and inescapable form of death," articulating "the ultimate admission of defeat for . . . poets who lived to tell us in their lives and poetry of realms of gold not subject to decay and death."[28]

Granted, the coffin in which Humboldt's bones lie has been sealed; but that casket should not be equated with the "mental coffin" from which Citrine has struggled to release his entombed spirit. Nor can several other important developments in the novel be overlooked. To begin with, both the movie scenario about Corcoran—in which Humboldt spoofs the modern writer who depends on mere "facts" rather than on imaginative vision—and the letter with which Humboldt prefaces that gift offer evidence that Humboldt did not succumb as completely as Citrine has thought to the distractions of American culture. Rejecting its "rational orthodoxy," the poet writes in his last letter to his friend: "we are not natural beings but supernatural beings" (347). While many readers have dismissed Humboldt's provocative statement as arbitrary and unconvincing, it underscores Citrine's own developing awareness of Humboldt's "supernatural" existence: the poet's felt presence, the bond he shares with Citrine and the influence he exerts "from the grave."[29] As I suggested earlier, Citrine's study of Steiner not only grants him an independent, or "upside-down," perspective on the materialist's view of reality; it also frees him to meditate on Humboldt's life and career from that altered perspective.

The change in Citrine's views begins to manifest itself quite early in the novel, as he comments on his recently revised reading of a poem by Humboldt, the very last one the poet had sent him. "Eight or nine years ago," says Citrine, "reading this poem, I thought, Poor Humboldt, those shock-treatment doctors have . . . ruined the guy. But now I saw this as a communication, not as a poem. The imagination must not pine away—that was Humboldt's message" (111–12). Humboldt, in other words, is already "acting" upon his friend "from the grave"; the "basic change" he helps to effect in Citrine's life is fueled by the transformation taking place in the latter's consciousness. As Citrine inwardly disengages himself from the "higher realism" of those "sensible people" who cannot take poetry seriously, who deem its power illusory because it is not material, he is able to discern, as he does in the last poem Humboldt sent him, the poet's enduring resistance to these claims as well (442). It is this new perception of Humboldt, as witness rather than victim of materialist culture, that is confirmed, at the end of the novel, by Citrine's receipt of Humboldt's concrete "gift."

By the time, therefore, that Citrine travels to Coney Island in order to seek out Humboldt's Uncle Waldemar, who has in his possession Humboldt's posthumous letter, he feels like a changed man. Buoyant and in "glorious condition," Citrine cannot ascribe his sense of joy to mere "physical well-being" or the delights of "sleeping with Renata." "I was inclined to think," he says, "that I owed it to a change in my attitude toward death. I had begun to entertain other alternatives." And then, just as he is entertaining such an "alternative," the supposedly dead past suddenly springs to life before him (328). At the nursing home where Humboldt's Uncle Waldemar resides, Citrine encounters Menasha Klinger, an old man who, in Chicago half a century ago, had boarded with the Citrine family, when Charlie was a little boy. This is the same Menasha Klinger, "an amateur physicist," who used to explain to the boy how "human beings could affect the rotation of the earth" if the entire race agreed "to scuff its feet" at the same moment. Recollecting Menasha's lesson early in the novel, Citrine comments: "Of course Menasha's real topic was not physics but [human] concord, or unity" (77–78).

Now, as he relives with Menasha details from their shared but distant past, Citrine thinks to himself, "Love made these things unforgettable" (330). Guided to this unlikely place by love for his dead friend, he reflects upon the way that love's "bounteous" gift highlights, and puts in perspective, the poverty of the materialist view. "I was thinking," he says, "that life was a hell of a lot more bounteous than I had ever realized. It rushed over us with more than our senses and our judgment could take in. . . . It rushes up also from within" (331). Even before Citrine opens the letter containing Humboldt's "gift," his declared belief in a reality transcending the physical laws of existence is confirmed by an access of love "rushing up from within." Having guided Citrine to this spot, and to this revelation, the memory of Humboldt, "acting from the grave," already attests to his status as a "supernatural" rather than a "natural" being.

In the cemetery where, at the close of the novel, Humboldt is reburied next to his mother, Menasha Klinger is once again united with Citrine. It is here, at the gravesite, that Citrine is struck by the terrifying finality of death. Not even Houdini, he thinks, could escape from that coffin, sealed beneath a concrete slab. But as Citrine's earlier musings on Houdini, who once hung "upside-down" from "the flagpole of the Flatiron Building in New York," have already indicated, he no longer identifies with "the great Jewish escape-artist" (435). "Dazzling rationality" and "the most ingenious skill" cannot, he observes, "overcome the final fact of the material world" (435–36). Nor is Citrine any longer the zealous "physical culturist," attempting to stave off aging and death with rigorous exercise and sophisticated techniques of self-preservation. Like Henderson before him, Citrine has faced the fact that, as Marcel points out in his previously cited statement, "it is inconceivable that technique can overcome death." That Humboldt's *body* cannot escape the dirt grave where his coffin lies buried is, of course, a physical fact (already that material body has ceased to exist). It does not follow, however, that the "raw fact" of "death" holds ultimate sway over Citrine's consciousness. The "up-side-down" perspective afforded by Steiner's philosophy reveals a different reality than the one to which Houdini's "upside-down" physical maneuvers are confined.

In the novel's closing paragraphs, in lines that succeed the passage cited earlier by Kernan, Citrine and Menasha Klinger walk away together from Humboldt's fresh grave. Menasha, still radiating that sense of "bounteous" love, unity and "concord" among human beings, espies a spring flower beneath the pile of "last autumn's leaves." Wondering what kind of flower it is, the old man says to Citrine:

> They used to tell one about a kid asking his grumpy old man when they were walking in the park, "What's the name of this flower, Papa?" and the old guy is peevish and he yells, "How should I know? Am I in the millinery business?" (487)

Significantly, Menasha's joke is not on the artist who, as Kernan says of the invented writer, Corcoran, "makes a clown out of himself." Rather, the joke is on the "hardheaded" (or "hard-boiled") businessman—on the idolatrous worship of "business" whose authority, and "higher realism," Citrine has begun to challenge: "Business, sure of its own transcendent powers, got us all to interpret life through its practices" (475). In Menasha's story, the stereotypical Jewish merchant, his consciousness burdened by practical matters, betrays the "commonsense absurdity" by which he lives (477). His worship of the "plastered idols of the Appearances" is underscored by his absurd inattention both to nature and to the reality of flowers. To him, a flower that does not serve the profit-motive has no authority—it is not real. Only the imitation, the false representation, is perceived as real: the flower on a hat has become an idol.

Satirizing the "ruling premises" of materialism, Menasha's story recalls an earlier scene in the novel, when Citrine is negotiating with the Harvard lawyers who represent the producers of *Caldofreddo*. Although his financial future and a considerable sum of money are at stake, Citrine is struck by the shallowness of such transactions: "And was this the famous Romance of Business? Why it was nothing but pushiness, rapidity, effrontery. The sense it gave of getting your way was shallow. Compared with the satisfaction of *contemplating flowers* or of something really serious—trying to get in touch with the dead, for instance—it was nothing, nothing at all" (469, italics added). Nor are such observations mere idle speculation on Citrine's part; later, when Barbash, the lawyer, offers to pay him two thousand dollars a week to work on the Corcoran scenario, Citrine—in contrast to Corcoran, his fictional parody—turns down the lucrative offer. Indirectly referring to his plans to study at the Steiner Center in Switzerland, he tells Barbash he has other business to attend to: "No, I'm engaged in a very different kind of activity," Citrine says, adding that he plans "to take up a different kind of life" (482–83). Furious with Citrine for turning down such a splendid offer, Cantabile curses Citrine and is then summarily dismissed by him. Citrine is no longer willing to waste time with those who, like the grumpy businessman in Menasha's joke, do not credit the "serious" business of "contemplating flowers."

Menasha himself takes the business of contemplating flowers seriously, concluding his story by asking Citrine to name the flowers they have stumbled upon. "Here's another [flower]," Menasha says, "what do you suppose they're called, Charlie?" "Search me," Citrine answers in the novel's closing lines, "I'm a city boy myself. They must be crocuses." This verbal shrug, "I'm a city boy myself," hardly serves as a convincing disclaimer. As though recognizing his attempted evasion, Citrine, unlike the Jewish businessman in the story, does proceed to name the flower. By this apparently simple act— naming the crocus—he pays homage not simply to the reality of flowers but to a nexus of linguistic, historical and philosophical relationships that exist between, and unite, the flower and the human being who perceives it.

Let the reader consider, as Bellow's novel closes on this scene of two men united in the act of "contemplating flowers," all of the physical and perceptual processes that contribute not only to the evolution of the flower as an organism, but also to the evolution of its name and of the system of botanical classification by which it is identified in both laboratory and park. (These "phenomena," the laboratory and the park, themselves emerged at different stages in the history of Western consciousness.) During the course of this evolution— of nature, human consciousness and the culture that formalizes the relationship between the two—human beings have come to associate, through observation and memory, the dawn of spring with one of its flowers, the crocus, which appears early in the season. By means of still other, intricately related perceptual processes, many human beings regard the material "phenomenon" of the crocus, which flowers around Easter, as an embodiment not only of nature's cyclical regeneration but also of spiritual rebirth. By naming the crocuses, Citrine has, consciously or unconsciously, placed himself in relation to all of these processes of creation. (Even the etymology of the word rehearses the development of Judeo-Christian culture; according to the *OED*, the English "crocus" derives from the Latin *crocus*, the Greek *krokos* and a Semitic original, akin to the Hebrew *karkom*.)

While Citrine has sought, throughout the novel, to discover a "personal connection" to "the creation," the novel's linguistic and structural patterns remind us that such connection is already latent or immanent in existence—for each individual to discover, or rediscover, on his own. As Citrine has already observed in discussing Goethe's approach to natural science, "the blue [of the sky] became blue when human vision received it" (363). Failure to acknowledge the processes by which mind, Steiner's activity of "thinking," embraces matter to create a distinctively known world has the gravest consequences for human beings. One has only to think of Ulick, Renata and other characters whose "premises" for defining reality derive from a set of "collective abstractions" as narrow, in Bellow's view, as the grumpy father's in Menasha's joke. The novel's last laugh is on those who dwell among lifeless replicas, worshipping "the plastered idols of the Appearances."

The "crocuses," literally and figuratively, have the last word in *Humboldt's Gift*. As he utters their name to Menasha, Citrine situates himself in a reality that implicitly comments upon, and qualifies, the weight of the cement slab lowered upon Humboldt's coffin.[30] Strategically located in the text, these linguistic signs—like the delicate harbingers of spring they are meant to signify—recall the "unseen" processes of rejuvenation ceaselessly at work in the world. To say that death is "the final fact of the material world" implies little about ultimate reality. The crocus, after all, is reborn each spring from its burial ground. And though each particular flower bears the sentence of death, the flowers themselves persist. Which, then, is ultimately more real: the transitory moment of the bulb's annual flowering or the enduring reality of these "flowers" we know to be "crocuses"?

The ending of Bellow's novel may appear ambiguous; still, its final word—"crocuses"—hardly suggests, as Kernan maintains, Citrine's "thralldom to material fact" or to "the material world in its most potent and inescapable form of death." Admittedly, the reader does not know how Citrine will fare with his spiritual studies; yet his decision "to take up a different kind of life" is clear. Rejecting the determinist vision of a world reified by scientific materialism, Citrine acts upon the truth of his earlier stated conviction: "It is not the world, it is my own head that is disenchanted. The world *cannot* be disenchanted" (203, Bellow's italics). By unsettling the "collective abstractions" of contemporary "head culture," literally standing them on their head, Citrine resolves to find a "personal connection" to creation. To the possibility of discovering such connection the novel itself bears witness.

Chapter 9

A Contemporary Fall:
More Die of Heartbreak

"Contemplating flowers"—a more serious occupation to Charlie Citrine than the customary business of America—receives even more prominent attention in Bellow's latest novel. In *More Die of Heartbreak* (1987), the protagonist, Benn Crader, is an internationally renowned botanist who, in the words of his nephew, the novel's narrator, is both a research scientist and a "plant clairvoyant" (234, 305). Working "like a contemplative, concentrating without effort," Uncle Benn, a university professor, not only studies plant anatomy but appears to see "behind the appearances" (253). "Studying leaves, bark, roots, heartwood, sapwood, flowers, for their own sake," Uncle Benn, says his nephew, "contemplated them"—that is, "he saw into or looked through plants. He took them as his arcana. An arcanum is more than a mere secret; it's what you have to know in order to be fertile in a creative pursuit, to make discoveries, to prepare for the communication of a spiritual mystery" (27).

This visionary enterprise, "contemplating flowers," delineates only one of the numerous thematic and structural affinities between *Humboldt's Gift* and Bellow's most recent novel. Because *More Die of Heartbreak* takes up, in so many ways, where the earlier novel left off, I have chosen to alter slightly the chronological pattern traced thus far (with the initial exception, of course, of *Mr. Sammler's Planet*) and devote immediate attention to *More Die of Heartbreak*. Thus *The Dean's December* (1982), the novel that appeared directly after *Humboldt's Gift* (1975), will be discussed in the succeeding chapter of this study.

Charlie Citrine, the narrator of *Humboldt's Gift*, reviews the tragic history of his old friend, the poet Von Humboldt Fleisher, as he tells his own story. In *More Die of Heartbreak*, Benn Crader's nephew, Kenneth Trachtenberg, is compelled by a similar bond of love to recount the story of a man he reveres. By reviewing the life of his uncle, whom he regards as his spiritual father, Ken attempts to put that life as well as his own in perspective. Citrine, furthermore, attributes the demise of Humboldt's personal life and artistic vocation to the poet's loss of faith in his visionary imagination. Similarly, Ken Trachtenberg pays tribute to his uncle's gift of seeing, as a "plant clairvoyant," and attributes Benn's recent "fall" to loss of confidence in that visionary power.

The author of many "books and articles," Uncle Benn enjoys a "big reputation" in the field of botany (32). Yet despite Crader's eminence as a scientist, says his nephew, "not even the 'laws' of physics or biology were permitted to inhibit him" (15). "Uncle was sure," Ken later explains, "that nature had an *inside*" (128, Bellow's italics). In his research on plants, Benn Crader has worked "like a contemplative, concentrating without effort, as naturally as he breathes, no oscillations of desire or memory" (253). To his own, characteristically modern "oscillations of consciousness," Ken contrasts his uncle's mode of contemplation—one that, in Ken's description, bears a definite resemblance to Rudolf Steiner's account of "inward" vision: Benn "really *knew* the vegetable kingdom. He practiced the scrutiny of secret things—total absorption in their hidden design." "There were times," Ken also notes, "when you felt [Benn's] power of *looking* turned on you. . . . This is the faculty of seeing; of seeing *itself*; what eyes are actually for" (317, 14, Bellow's italics).[1] In the end, however, Uncle Benn fails to "make the psychic transfer to human relations"; the complexity and deviousness of personal relationships disturb and ultimately foil his powers of insight (106).

Born and raised in Paris, Ken accepts a teaching post at his uncle's midwestern university in order to be near his mentor. It is from Benn that his nephew, a man in his middle thirties, hopes to learn something of the "higher spheres" of existence, knowledge to which Ken's natural father, Rudi Trachtenberg, is wholly indifferent. An American expatriate who remained in Paris after the Second World War, Ken's father is a cosmopolitan whose many accomplishments belong strictly to the sexual and social spheres of life. In "tennis, [his] war record, . . . in sex, in conversation, in looks," Rudi Trachtenberg is, according to Kenneth, an unqualified success. In an era that celebrates physical fitness and erotic invention, Rudi is a paragon—a "Hegelian . . . Master Spirit" (65). "The historical thing which millions of sex-intoxicated men were trying to do and botching, he did with the ease of a natural winner" (37).

The very type or product of those "conditioning forces" against which Augie March seeks to defend the "primordial person," Rudi Trachtenberg is indifferent to the "fundamentals" his son urgently seeks to discover (10–12). Like Herzog, Ken Trachtenberg admits that he "used to be sold on" theories and ideas but "discovered that they were nothing but trouble if you entertained them indiscriminately." There are some "matters"—including the "matter" of Uncle Benn's "fall"—"for which theorizing brings no remedy" (19).[2] Ken's "partial deafness," moreover, directly links him to Artur Sammler, whose partial blindness emblemizes the Bellovian hero's divided consciousness, oscillating between the "superstructures of explanation" and the soul's "natural knowledge" (47). "Modern life, if you take it to heart, wears you out," Ken reflects. "Even my hearing aid was off, and when I fiddled my finger under my long hair and tapped on it, something like a sonic boom went off in my skull" (118). Turning on his hearing aid, Ken tunes into "modern life"; like a "sonic boom" in the "skull," the impact of his re-entry is shattering.

With his uncle, a widower, Ken shares a propensity for ineffectual and "confused relations with women"; he cannot even persuade Treckie, the "childlike" but willful young woman he adores, to marry him. Instead, Treckie has removed herself, along with their little girl, Nancy, thousands of miles away from Ken—to live in Seattle with another man. Aware that he lacks his father's sexual talent, Ken tries "to right the balance" by giving himself "more mental weight." Yet this attempt to compensate mentally for lack of physical or sexual authority only goes to show, in Ken's view, "how far we've fallen below the classical Greek standard. We've split things in two, dividing the physique from the mind" (39–40). Searching for a way to mend this "split," Ken wants to realize his "soul in the making" (37).

Looking to his uncle for guidance, Ken finds, instead, that Benn Crader is also prey to divided consciousness. As Ken says, "I had come to America to complete my education, to absorb certain essential powers from Uncle, and I learned presently that he was looking to *me* for assistance" (92, Bellow's italics). What happens to Benn in the human sphere, Ken discovers, is partly due to his special nature as "a man of feeling"; for Benn, a middle-aged widower, proves acutely susceptible to "*love* longings" and their peculiarly modern distortions (278, Bellow's italics). When, in his mid-fifties, Benn suffers an onslaught of erotic longing—impulses that Rudi Trachtenberg is much more adept at handling—he impulsively sets out to achieve conjugal bliss. Believing himself to have fallen in love with a "perfect" beauty, a woman much younger than he, Benn peremptorily marries Matilda Layamon. Unfortunately, the marriage brings him neither peace nor love. It is a disaster— one that could have been averted if he had paid heed to the warning signals emitted by his "prophetic soul" (326). Distracted by desire, failing to trust in his intuitive powers because they strike him as "irrational," Benn becomes prey to those "oscillations of consciousness" Ken has sought, under his uncle's influence, to quell.

When Ken initially sets out to absorb his uncle's influence, he is not sure whether Benn's gift for "contemplating flowers" may be carried over into the human sphere. Eventually he discovers that Benn's insight into plants does "overlap," to a considerable degree, with the sphere of "human relations" (106). Alarmed, however, by what he sees, Benn decides, like Von Humboldt Fleisher, not to credit his visionary powers. As a poet Humboldt "wanted to drape the world in radiance" but lacked "enough material" (HG 107). The "short supply" of "material," which Citrine attributes to the poet's failure to trust in his visionary imagination, similarly plagues Uncle Benn. As his nephew observes, "the whole vegetable kingdom was [Benn's] garment—his robe, his coat. . . . Still, Uncle's garment was incomplete. It didn't quite button" (119). This tragic incompleteness is partly due, of course, to the fact that human beings make far more complex demands on one's powers of insight than members of the "vegetable kingdom." But as Benn and his nephew both come to realize, Benn's failure also derives from his refusal to heed the promptings of his inmost self.

Characterized as a mysterious "daemon" or "inner spirit," Benn's inmost self—which he also calls "that second person of mine"—has guided him at crucial moments in his life. (This "daemon" is the polar opposite of Herzog's "demon" of "modern ideas," whose insistent demand for theories and explanations must be silenced before Herzog can commune with *his* inner spirit.) It was "that second person inside" him that prompted Benn to "become a botanist" in the first place (58, 84). By the same clairvoyant power that allows him to see into plants, he detects something repellent in the "hidden design" beneath Matilda's lovely outward appearance. Not liking what he sees, he attempts to dismiss these "visions" as mere "irrational reactions" (263). Exposed to his uncanny insight, which he cannot explain, certain features of his fiancée, despite her "classic face" and form, appear malign (124). Whether Matilda's "sharp teeth" or wide, mannish shoulders *objectively* reveal her true nature is a moot question (143). For Benn they have disturbing significance, provoking a troubling response that he ought not to ignore. By this time, however, the wedding has been planned, the invitations engraved; thus he chooses to "go against [his] deeper instinct" and marry Matilda (326). Weakly attempting to justify that decision to his nephew, from hindsight, Benn tells Kenneth, "I was warned . . . not to marry. It was a sin to disobey the warning. But a man like me, trained in science, can't go by revelation. You can't be rational and also hold with sin" (298).

By marrying the wrong woman Benn also entangles himself in her family—becoming the pawn of her father's elaborate financial schemes. A rich and prominent physician, Dr. Layamon is far more dedicated to empire-building than to the art of healing. Embroiling his son-in-law in a financial maneuver designed to yield millions of dollars, Dr. Layamon tells Benn, "If you're going to share the bed of this delicious girl of high breeding and wallow in it, you'll have to find the money it takes." By urging Benn to regain several million dollars he has been "screwed out of," Dr. Layamon proposes to help his son-in-law earn the right to "wallow" in Matilda's bed. (Dr. Layamon is obviously heir to the "pigdom" that Henderson summarily abandons.) Years earlier, Benn's Uncle Vilitzer had purchased from Benn and his sister, for a modest sum, a piece of family property that Vilitzer secretly knew would soon be worth millions. Shortly after the purchase, Uncle Vilitzer was able to resell the

Craders' family property, for no less than fifteen million dollars, to a multinational corporation as the prospective site of the Electronic Tower, a monstrous skyscraper that presently dominates the skyline of the midwestern metropolis where Benn and the Layamons reside. By threatening to reopen a lawsuit against Uncle Vilitzer at this time, Benn will, according to Dr. Layamon, force his uncle to pay him several million dollars (167–68). In this way, Layamon tells his son-in-law, "you can be made whole" (171).

The ironic effect of Dr. Layamon's pledge is not lost on the reader, who later observes how the purported goal, to make Benn financially sound or "whole," shatters his psychic well being. Instead of making the "psychic transfer" from the plant kingdom to the human sphere, as his nephew had hoped, Benn's vision is severely impaired by his entry into the Layamon family and his descent into the maelstrom of American greed, ambition, desire. His remarkable "marine blue, ultramarine" eyes—eyes that, before his ordeal with the Layamons, seemed to embody "the power of seeing itself, created by the light itself"—are soon beclouded by "sorrow" and guilt, "sin and punishment" (14, 234, 240). The Layamons thus serve "to bring Benn in, that is, to bring him back" into the world of property and power, "down from the sublime regions" of lofty contemplation. They are not, however, entirely to blame. "Benn," says his nephew, "had *wanted* to come down, he had a special wish to enter into prevailing states of mind and even, perhaps, into the peculiar sexuality associated with such states" (165–66, Bellow's italics). By insisting that his fascination with Matilda's alluring beauty *is* love, Benn undergoes his version of the West's current "ordeal of desire"—implicating him in the "fallen state" in which, says Ken, "our species finds itself" (100, 19). Dwelling in "the absence of love" and attempting to compensate for "inner poverty" with "sexual enchantments," contemporary humanity is in dire straits (241, 118, 155). Whether conscious or not of their "human impoverishment," plenty of people are, as Citrine already notes in *Humboldt's Gift*, "oppressed to the point of heartbreak" (HG 350).

Even before Benn Crader's disastrous marriage to Matilda Layamon and his subsequent "fall," he has gone on record affirming the universal need for love and the "heartbreak" brought on by its absence. To a journalist who interviews him about the "dangers of radioactivity from Three Mile Island and Chernobyl," Benn makes the unexpected reply that serves as the novel's title and suggests its central theme: "It's terribly serious, of course, but I think more people die of heartbreak than of radiation" (197, 87). Implicit in Benn's unorthodox statement is his perception of two invisible yet deadly forces. While science has made the first one clear to us—warning of the terrible dangers produced by extreme levels of radiation—the lethal condition of "heartbreak" cannot be detected by instruments. As invisible to the naked eye as radiation, the misery of "human impoverishment" is registered, Bellow makes clear, not by scientific instruments but within the human heart.

Nothing less than a new vision of human life—one that breaks through the current "claustrophobia of consciousness" and places love squarely at the center—must be found, Benn's nephew is convinced, if more people are not to "die of heartbreak" (33). Just as Ken traces his uncle's unique visionary powers to an extraordinary "heart" and the love it generates, so he is able, under Benn's influence, to perceive how "an overflow of feeling" transforms the very nature of a person moved by love. When, for example, Ken tells Uncle Vilitzer's son Fishl of the schemes being laid by the Layamons against his father, Fishl's filial piety is profoundly aroused. Right before Ken's eyes, Fishl metamorphoses from a vulgar "entrepreneur and seed-money man" to a dignified and devoted son:

> He didn't even look like the double-chinned suave man who had received me. . . . The eyes, the nose, not a single particular of his appearance remained the same. I thought, You don't even begin to know a person until you've seen the features transformed in an overflow of feeling. A totally different Fishl came before me as soon as he saw that he might be in a position to defend his father, save him from his enemies. (182)

The impact of this transformation becomes even more pronounced when one considers that Fishl has been cut off, financially as well as emotionally, by his father. Heartless and, by all reasonable standards, utterly *un*deserving of affection, Harold Vilitzer continues, up to the moment of his death, to be loved unrequitedly by both his son Fishl and his nephew Benn. Thus Uncle Vilitzer occupies the unusual, and paradoxical, position of denying the reality of love while being its recipient.

Although Ken's revelation of the power of love centers upon Fishl rather than his father, a brief digression on the character of Harold Vilitzer helps to clarify the reality old Vilitzer would deny. Annoyed by Fishl's many bizarre, and failed, business ventures, Harold Vilitzer has refused, for fifteen years, even to see his son. Nor does he appear, in extreme old age, to have any regrets about his behavior—anymore than he regrets having cheated Benn by turning a fifteen-million-dollar profit on the Craders' family property. "Where money is concerned," Uncle Vilitzer declares, "the operational word is *merciless*" (282, Bellow's italics). From Vilitzer's "message" of mercilessness, Ken traces the logic of unalloyed materialism:

> Death is merciless, and therefore the ground rules of conduct have to include an equal and opposite hardness. From this it follows that kinship is bullshit. You can see how this would reflect on my attachment to Uncle [Benn], on Uncle's attachment to me. Against us there stood Vilitzer's exclusion of his son Fishl. . . . Fishl's emotions towards his father were further evidence [in his father's eyes] of his unfitness, his ignorance of the conditions of existence. (282)

When Benn and his nephew visit Uncle Vilitzer, in order to talk about his swindling of the Craders, the old man gets angry and even tries to "take a sock" at one of them. Catching the octogenarian in his arms, Ken notes that Vilitzer "felt as light as an empty plastic egg carton. . . . He was scarcely even a tenement of clay; he was wickerwork, porous plastic. Only the pacemaker unit under his shirt had any weight" (286–88). Ken's impression is of a man whose heart has been virtually replaced by the tiny machine fitted to his breast. Nearly a corpse, Vilitzer is not so much a skeleton as a hollow shell. A mere semblance of humanity, he honors no human bond that would hamper his grip on his hundred-million-dollar financial kingdom. Nor can this desiccated creature acknowledge the final irony of his existence: that death, to which Vilitzer has opposed his "equal and opposite" code of "mercilessness," will soon arrive to sever his (death)grip on his money. Uncle Vilitzer has built his kingdom not in opposition to death, but under its yoke.

Through Ken's bond with his uncle—the warmth of an "attachment" deemed worthless by Vilitzer—he has become more "receptive" to phenomena and "the power behind" them (299). Gazing at Fishl, who now looks "totally different," Ken recalls Benn's "second person inside"; there may be, he suspects, "such a person also in Fishl" (182–83). Almost immediately, he has the extraordinary "impression" of *seeing* this "second Fishl": "As I watched closely, the singularity of this seemingly comical fatty seemed to detach itself from him and, with a tremor, move away. I give my impression of this just as it came to me. Another Fishl was sitting there in the fully buttoned vest. . . . Intimations, maybe, of a second Fishl." If, at this instant, "the real Kenneth" is perceiving the "real Fishl"—if Ken's "inner spirit" is making contact with Fishl's—then the border between "inner" and "outer" reality has, at least momentarily, been dissolved (186). Under the influence of his uncle, Ken transcends, at least momentarily, the mind-body "split" and penetrates, in Citrine's phrase, "behind the appearances."

The theme of idolatry, although less pronounced in *More Die of Heartbreak* than in *Humboldt's Gift*, permeates the later novel as well. To begin with, Benn's early praise of Matilda's external "perfection"—her "classic face" and "hyacinth hair"—suggests his tendency to idolize her beauty (53, 124). As Ken says, "It wasn't [Matilda's] beauty that I questioned, it was the Edgar Allan Poe stuff [Benn] was giving me about her. . . . Too much of the marble statue in the stained-glass niche" (121). Underscoring the connection, Ken comments on Matilda's silence, "Edgar Allan Poe's Helen standing in her niche had nothing to say. The representative of beauty was dumb, a terrific advantage for a sensitive devotee of classic figures" (139). Like Renata Koffritz's exquisitely preserved beauty, moreover, Matilda Layamon's marble "perfection" is suggestively associated with death. An "extravagant, luxuriant sleeper," Matilda, Benn observes upon marrying her, abandons herself to sleep like "Psyche embracing Eros in a blind darkness" (142). Here, as in the earlier novel, Bellow implies that when Eros is idolized, "the sex embrace was death-flavored" (69).

The gradual "disintegration" of Matilda's image in Benn's eyes—and his attempts, at the same time, to deny his troubling "visions"—ultimately precipitate his "fall" from "whole" vision into "critical consciousness" (265). Benn's "fallen state" is shockingly revealed to the "plant clairvoyant" one night at the Layamons' luxurious duplex. Temporarily staying with his wife at the home of her parents, Benn is awakened by a disturbing telephone call. Too restless, after the call, to return to bed, he wanders about the Layamon residence while the rest of the family are asleep; eventually he enters his mother-in-law's private study, customarily barred to outsiders, in order to "have plant contact" with a beautiful azalea he has admired from afar (299). To his shock and dismay, he finds that this exquisite plant is actually a fake.

Standing in the corner of Mrs. Layamon's study, the red azalea—from whose flowers Benn has, from outside in the hallway, repeatedly drawn inspiration—proves a cunning silk replica wrought by Oriental hands. The "plant clairvoyant" has been duped by a "damn near perfect imitation" that is thoroughly "false." In shock, Benn telephones his nephew in the middle of the night, to report the disastrous news:

> A stooge azalea—a stand-in, a ringer, an impostor, a dummy, a shill! I was drawing support for weeks and weeks from this manufactured product. Every time I needed a fix, a contact, a flow, I turned to it. Me, Kenneth! After all these years of unbroken rapport, to be taken in. . . . The one thing I could always count on. My occupation, my instinct, my connection . . . broken off. (300, latter ellipsis Bellow's)

To Benn this dismal error is much more than a "sign" of professional failure. He blames himself for having severed his "connection" not only to the plant kingdom but to that inner kingdom of his essential self. For betraying his calling—the serious business of "contemplating flowers"—he has, he tells his nephew, been duly "punished": "I've been punished, Kenneth. For all the false things I did, a false object punished me" (300).[3] Gulled by desire, Benn has forfeited "wholeness" for idolatry. Like the "grumpy old man" in Menasha Klinger's story, who takes the mere appearance of a flower for the real thing, Benn has been seduced by "the plastered idols of the Appearances" (HG 487).

When Benn reveals to his nephew the humiliating discovery—that he has "lost the privilege of vision, fallen into the opposite and brutal prevailing outlook"—Ken, registering the impact of that "fall," loses heart (328). "What had happened to [Benn] affected me as well," he says. "I could feel the perturbation widening and widening . . . and became aware that I had come to depend upon his spirit. Without its support, the buoyancy went out of me."

That buoyancy gone, Ken feels more convinced than ever of the "inner poverty" of "modern life," which his new country, America, embodies in the extreme: "Your soul had its work cut out for you in this extraordinary country," he laments. "You got spiritual headaches. . . . There seems to be a huge force that advances, propels, and this propellant increases its power by drawing value away from personal life and fitting us for its colossal purpose. It demands the abolition of such things as love and art . . . of gifts like Uncle's" (301, latter ellipsis Bellow's).

Fortunately, just at the moment Ken begins to formulate a general picture of doom, he recovers, if not his former "buoyancy," a more lucid state of mind:

> Of course, we all have these thoughts today instead of prayers. And we think these thoughts are serious and we take pride in our ability to think, to elaborate ideas, so we go round and round in consciousness like this. However, they don't get us anywhere; our speculations are like a stationary bicycle. And this, too, was dawning on me. These proliferating thoughts have more affinity to insomnia than to mental progress. Oscillations of the mental substance is what they are, ever-increasing jitters. (301)

With this revelation Ken breaks off his formulations, pondering his uncle's parting words. It is "time," Benn tells him before hanging up the telephone, "I took hold" (300). "When you've fallen from grace, what do you take hold of?" Ken wonders (301).

Instead of sinking into misery, however, he recollects a story about "Whistler the painter," told to him by his Aunt Lena, Benn's first wife:

> It was Lena who introduced [Ken] to the valuable idea that modes of seeing were matters of destiny, that what is sent forth by the seer affects what is seen. She liked to give the example of Whistler the painter when he was taken to task by a woman who said [of his art], "I never see trees like that." He told her, "No, ma'am, but don't you wish you could?" This could be a variation on "Ye have eyes and see not." (305)

Whistler's retort offers a challenge to those who, like the woman in Aunt Lena's story, worship "the plastered idols of the Appearances."[4] Thus, Ken recalls the biblical passage, "Ye have eyes and see not," the judgment against idolatry that recurs throughout the Old and New Testaments. Entranced by appearances, Whistler's interlocutor "sees not"; the victim as well as the perpetrator of "inner poverty," she deprives herself of a rich and vital picture of the world.

Resolving to "take hold" of his own life, Ken decides to fly out to Seattle to visit Treckie and his daughter. On his way to the city, however, he experiences another setback. In a fit of vengeful fury that recalls Herzog's abortive plan to murder his rival, Gersbach, Ken imagines beating up Treckie's current lover, a ski instructor, and fighting him to the death. Arriving at Treckie's apartment, he finds that the "ski instructor," whom he has mentally stereotyped as thick and brutal, has "gone to Mass." Venting his jealousy and frustration, Ken heads for the bathroom, proceeding to "wreck it" by smashing everything in sight. But then, as in Herzog's case, "actuality" takes over, demonstrating the futility of his actions. Treckie's "settled intimacy" with another man, he notes, is manifested in every concrete detail—confirmed even by the household odors and mundane arrangement of objects (309–10).

His illusions shattered, Ken realizes that he has been guilty of that same "Edgar Allan Poe stuff" he has scoffed at in Benn (311, 121). Even his admiration for another woman, his friend Dita Schwartz, has not released him from this "ordeal of desire."[5] Now, however, face to face with Treckie, the "child-woman," he perceives not a work of "perfection," not a "marble statue" or idol, but a specific human being—a human being, furthermore, who wants no part of him. Although the revelation is "downright shocking" to his ego, Ken faces the fact that, as he puts it, "I failed to turn *her* on" (312, Bellow's italics). For her part, Treckie calmly accepts Ken's "tantrum," regarding his wreck of the bathroom as a "minor inconvenience" and their "mutual quitclaim" (319).

As Ken and Treckie "conclude the matter" of their failed relationship, Uncle Benn is present both in Ken's thoughts and in his conversation with Treckie. "He's a famous man in his field," Treckie says of Benn, "but he does make an awfully flaky impression when he sounds off." His statement, "quoted in the paper," that "more people died of heartbreak than of radiation poisoning," strikes her as "a crazy remark" (315). Meanwhile Treckie, aware that Ken looks down on her interest in trendy "California-type-stuff" like "applied Zen" and "group psychotherapy," defends her "life-style." As their daughter watches television cartoons in the next room, she tells Ken, "We're a pluralistic society, after all. Multiple acculturation is what it's all about." To Ken, in search of "a desperately needed human turning point," Treckie's relativistic chatter is virtually indistinguishable from the "cartoon sound effects" coming from the television set: "the bangs, whistles, buzzings, blams and tooting" (314–16). He sees, nonetheless, that for Treckie he "didn't even exist. That was nothing to get excited about, as it was one of the commoner human experiences—neither to give a damn nor to be given a damn about. In practice it was accepted as a matter of course, though at heart nobody quite came to terms with it" (319).

What human beings know "at heart," this passage reminds us, is quite different from what they *appear* to accept. This is the meaning suggested by the novel's title, which draws attention to the "hidden design" behind the appearances of modern life. To say, as Benn does, that "more people die of heartbreak" is not to diminish the dangers of radiation or the threat of nuclear disaster. It is to say that other, less obvious but still urgent "matters" also threaten us. On the other hand, Benn's statement may have a still more radical implication for contemporary culture. Bellow may be suggesting that the widespread apprehension of material doom is itself symptomatic of a deeper crisis. In any case, Bellow's narrator reaffirms, in words that articulate the novelist's own search for a way out of the current state of "human impoverishment," his commitment to "Project Turning Point" (330). Ken remains convinced "that, really, conscious existence might be justified only if it was devoted to the quest for a revelation, a massive reversal, an inspired universal change, a new direction, a desperately needed human turning point" (315).

After saying goodbye to Treckie and flying back to the Midwest, Ken receives another telephone call from his uncle, one that signals a "turning point" or "new direction" in Benn's life. Taking hold of his fate in radical fashion, Benn has decided to abandon Matilda, her family and Dr. Layamon's schemes. Calling his nephew from a Miami airport, Benn is on his way to the North Pole, where "an international team of scientists" is conducting "special researches. And I signed on," says Benn, "to check out lichens from both poles . . . and work out certain morphological puzzles." Benn's timely escape from Matilda may indicate that he will never overcome his "confused relations with women"; yet his present determination to save himself is a marked departure from his former "evasive action" (233). In contrast to his tortuous attempts to quell his "visions" and to rationalize his alliance with Matilda, Benn's current decision, he tells his nephew, has been "carefully felt through. Rather than thought out. It's a survival measure" (334).

Like Henderson, who went "beyond geography" to save his soul, Benn must take extreme measures for his own "survival." "We're going to be based in northern Scandinavia," he tells Ken, "at the edge of Finland, actually. And beyond." There, at the edge of the world, "night and ice" will provide a "corrective" to internal disarray: "Ice for the rigor. And also because there'll be no plants to see, except the lichens. Because if there's no rapport," says Benn, "if the rapport is dead, I'm better off in plant-free surroundings" (334). Ken does not condemn his uncle's flight from the Layamons; though "mystified," he gives Benn's "expedition [his] blessing." For what his uncle must accomplish, he knows, even "Novaya Zemlya" may not be "remote enough" (335). In so chaotic a time, "when so many supports and stabilities are removing themselves from [the individual]," one must take radical steps to regain a sense of connection. Clearly, Benn must "remove himself" from the distractions of modern life—from the "magnetic attraction of anarchy" (330).

To the North Pole, where "magnetic attraction" does not exert its customary force, Benn Crader sets out to "preserve himself humanly"—and, if possible, to recover his "gift" of vision. Whether or not he will redeem his "fall from grace," Benn's gift for "contemplating flowers" still offers Ken a model for achieving "perfected insight." Minding Benn's apartment and his plants while his uncle is away, Ken will continue, as he says, to "retrieve from my memory bank those wonderful hours when, under [Benn's] influence, not only my lungs were breathing but my mind breathed too. Some of his powers of seeing *had* been transmitted to me. So I saw" (278, Bellow's italics). Having stilled "the oscillations of consciousness," Ken can "breathe" mentally as well as physically—the expansion of the "chest," Lewis's "seat" of feeling, effecting an expansion of the psyche and its powers.

At the end of *More Die of Heartbreak*, Ken Trachtenberg remains committed to his "Project Turning Point." His author, moreover, appears to be engaged in a similar project: the search for a "turning point," the "quest for a revelation." In the latter stages of this quest, the novels published since *Mr. Sammler's Planet*, Bellow has ventured more and more openly against the grain of contemporary formulations and cultural "orthodoxy." And while he continues to enlist the conventions of the realist novel, the impact or effect of his fiction is to overturn some of realism's time-honored traditions. In most realist fiction from Cervantes to Dreiser to Hemingway, "the conditioning forces" clearly hold sway over the tiny figure of the individual, who is caught in their force-field even as he seeks a "channel" to freedom. Yet the central preoccupation of Bellow's fiction appears to be moving further and further "beyond" that force-field and its "magnetic attraction." In his own rendering of reality the novelist seems headed, like Benn Crader, for "the edge" of the familiarly known world: "And beyond."

True, Bellow still honors the novelist's obligations to the historical moment and the geography of place; and he delights, perhaps more than ever, in rendering the significant details and particular absurdities of the contemporary urban scene. At the same time, however, his handling of these traditional materials tends, like Charlie Citrine's "upside-down" postures, to overturn the realist's ruling premises. What Ken Trachtenberg says of his "Project Turning Point" thus has special relevance for the direction that Bellow's fiction is taking: "The secret of our being still asks to be unfolded. Only now we understand that worrying at it and ragging it is of no use." Instead, the individual "must maneuver [him]self into a position in which metaphysical aid can approach" (330–31). Engaging in his own novelistic "maneuvers," Bellow has been working his way through the local coordinates of history and geography to regions of human experience as remote from Stendahl's "mirror carried along a highway" as "Novaya Zemlya." By effecting this "massive reversal" in the genre's traditional emphases and effects, he may have reached a "turning point" not only in his own career but in the development of the realist novel: a point at which the "primordial person," rather than his alteration by "the conditioning forces," is of crucial interest. In Bellow's own fiction, in any case, it is the "secret" of the human being, his "hidden design," that the novelist's art is increasingly dedicated to unfolding.

Chapter 10

From Head Culture to Lead Culture:
The Dean's December

In "late Bellow" the temperature has plummeted: even the title of *The Dean's December* (1982) draws attention to the stark climatic conditions of his two latest novels. As the frozen North beckons Benn Trachtenberg, promising refuge from distraction, the searing cold of winter behind the Iron Curtain—Albert Corde's December in Rumania—likewise impels contemplation of last things. Bucharest's "funeral weather," thickened by the "cast-iron gloom" of a totalitarian regime, provides a fitting atmosphere for the constrictions in voice, tone and form that Bellow's fiction has undergone in the last decade (208, 233). "In late Bellow," Martin Amis points out, "the vision has widened but also become narrower," subduing both laughter and the narrator's "beguiling switches of register."[1] In search of a "new direction" or "turning point," Bellow devotes more attention than ever to global, even cosmic, conditions. But as Amis suggests, this breadth, or depth, of vision also serves to limit the novel's dramatic range.

Preoccupied by Henderson's "fundamentals" and "ultimates," Bellow's protagonist is more contemplative than ever—less given to confrontation, antic behavior or outbursts of wrath, delight, lamentation. In *The Dean's December*, says Daniel Fuchs, the characters lack "personalist charge"; "event is disproportionately retrospective," the author "dismissive of everyday life." Cancelling both conflict and comedy, the meditative mode is so dominant, Fuchs adds, that "affirmation is itself at a remove . . . barely expresse[d] in reflection, let alone action."[2] Appropriately, it would seem, critical response to *The Dean's December* has been decidedly chilly; readers have been even less inclined to "warm up" to its protagonist, Albert Corde, than to Artur Sammler (208).[3] Drawing a parallel between these two novels of "reclusive" meditation, each with its mood of "leave-taking" and preoccupation with "final lucidities," Amis observes: "*The Dean's December* inaugurates Bellow's 'late period' but *Mr. Sammler's Planet* prefigured it—old Sammler, with his 'farewell detachment,' his 'earth-departure-objectivity': 'the luxury of non-intimidation by doom.' "[4]

At first glance, the protagonist of *The Dean's December* appears even more removed than Sammler from the human activity around him. In Bucharest, the American Corde finds himself physically, socially, professionally and linguistically cut off from his regular life in Chicago. He is, as Sammler has only dreamed of becoming, "a visiting consciousness" in an alien environment. And while Corde shares the elderly Sammler's passion for thinking, the younger man's internal dynamics throw off decidedly less heat. In Corde there operates, if you will, a different thermodynamics of consciousness: less friction is created, less energy wasted. In Corde, less friction occurs because his perceptions, and his psyche, are not as riven as Sammler's. To Corde, abstract formulations carry less weight than the immediate "particulars" and "actualities" of existence (16–17). Thus, he suffers less strain at the top; he is more ready to unseat the rule of "the generality-mind" (266). As the "modern, conflicted self," to recall Clayton's phrase, makes evident progress toward psychic integration in "late Bellow," fewer sparks fly.[5] Yet (to extend the metaphor) by conserving so much heat-energy, Bellow has charged his penultimate novel with an extraordinary degree of light. Rendering with supernal brilliance the author's vision of last things and "final lucidities," *The Dean's December* also exposes, to an unprecedented degree, the "clairvoyant" quality of Bellow's insight and his increasingly radical perception of reality.[6]

The vehicle for Bellow's revelation of "final lucidities," Albert Corde is, like Sammler, called to witness the dire conditions of contemporary civilization. As readers of both novels are sure to recognize, the following description of Corde might easily be appropriated by Sammler himself: "What a man he was for noticing! Continually attentive to his surroundings. As if he had been sent down to *mind* the outer world, on a mission of observation and notation. The object of which was? To link up? To classify? To penetrate?" (210, Bellow's italics). Yet Corde, for all his apparent disengagement, does not share Sammler's longing for "earth-departure-objectivity." Corde *does* share Sammler's "strong preference for disinterested judgments"; but, as he himself is quick to add, "it was nothing like nonattachment, not negative objectivity" (163). Fulfilling his "mission of observation," Sammler requires an entire novel to comprehend the hazards of seeking detachment from earthly matters. Corde, on the other hand, recognizes from the outset the essential need for *connection* to others and to creation itself.

"Although people," Corde reflects, "talked to themselves all the time, never stopped communing with themselves, nobody had a good connection or knew what racket he was in—his *real* racket. . . . For most of his life he [Corde] had had a bad connection himself. There was just a chance, however, that he might, at last, be headed in the right direction" (32, Bellow's italics).

Even Corde's name serves to convey his urgent quest for connection: the "cord" that binds him to all that he sees and the heart—"cor" in Latin—that registers this connection.[7] In the writings of Aquinas, Owen Barfield points out, "*verbum cordis*" signifies the "inner, unspoken word" within each person, which is directly "related to the word (*vox*) that is actually vocalized."[8] It is Corde's own, unspoken sense of connection—the "verbum Cordes," if you will—for which he (and his author behind him) seeks a viable language, or voice.

The need to establish his connection with others appears to have led Corde, several years before the novel's opening, to return to his native Chicago and take up an academic position. As he says, "I had some reading to do, and wanted to find people to talk to. The right people to talk to—that's the hardest part of all" (60). A former newspaper correspondent located in Paris, Corde grew weary of dancing attendance on the ephemeral, of charting the inconclusive ebb and flow of daily events. Renewing his acquaintance with Plato and Aristotle, he took refuge from distraction in the academy. In his current position as Dean of a Chicago college, however, Corde has been caught in the toils of administrative problems and tasks. When, however, his Rumanian mother-in-law suffers a stroke, Corde is temporarily relieved of his professional responsibilities; he accompanies his wife, Minna Raresh, a world-renowned astronomer, home to visit her dying mother. In Bucharest, Corde is largely left to his own devices, unless summoned to aid Minna in her struggles with the Communist bureaucracy. As a defector to the West—shielded by an American passport and husband, and by an international scientific reputation—Minna is hardly in favor with the authorities. Most troublesome of all is a certain Colonel in the secret police. In charge of the hospital where her mother is under intensive care, the Colonel severely restricts Minna's visiting privileges.

Arriving in Bucharest in a state of exhaustion, Corde welcomes his sudden isolation; it gives him the chance to reflect on a recent storm of publicity at home, brought on by a couple of articles on Chicago that he wrote for *Harper's* magazine. Charged with apocalyptic images of decay and disaster, his depiction of his native city has incited just about everyone who is anyone in Chicago, including the Provost of his college. The violence of the "black underclass," Corde wrote, is actually condoned by a social and economic establishment that has failed "to approach"—to seek real contact with—this population. White middle-class society hasn't "even conceived that reaching it may be a problem. So there's nothing but death before it" (207). The communication gap is filled by drugs, crime, sexual assault; they are the means by which a doomed population speeds the tortuously slow process of its own extinction. Adding to the public displeasure with Corde and to his own administrative headaches is a murder trial; two blacks have been accused of killing a white student at his college. The Dean's December in Rumania is complicated, therefore, by transatlantic calls from the Provost and encounters with an old schoolfriend, Dewey Spangler—a celebrated newspaper columnist whose curiosity is provoked by the "visionary" tone of Corde's *Harper's* articles.

As Corde's attention shifts between immediate events in Rumania and troubling developments at home, Bellow juxtaposes the worlds of Bucharest and Chicago, past and present, East and West. The comparisons drawn between these far-flung cities begin with the weather: "No more sun, that was gone, only linty clouds and a low cold horizon. . . . It was like the Chicago winter, which shrank your face and tightened your sphincters" (208). Even when Corde allows for the geographical, historical and political differences between the communist and capitalist cities, he is drawn to contemplate a deeper affinity: "If the cold reminded you of Chicago, the faces [in Bucharest] were from the ancient world. But then in Chicago you had something like a vast international refugee camp, and faces from all over" (209).

Similarly, the "air-sadness" of the Rumanian atmosphere is not simply a climatic condition. "Everywhere in Bucharest, the light was inadequate"; and every day, in "the final stage of dusk," the fall of night brings "a livid death moment" (3). Like the Chicago winter it constantly recalls, December in Bucharest heralds more than the end of a year. More than the old social order is dying. At both ends of the world, Bellow suggests, the values by which humankind has aligned itself with creation are being obliterated. Ethical principles, the distinction between good and evil, have been forsaken; mechanistic concepts and data are the only approved signposts of reality. Machines multiply, the mighty prosper—but the moral center is crumbling. To Corde, contemporary society is a monstrous superstructure precariously erected, like Sammler's "superstructures of explanation," upon a spiritual void: "the slums we carry around inside us. Every man's *inner* inner city" (207, Bellow's italics).

Engraved by modern history, the urban landscape is also inscribed with apocalyptic portents. Chicago's urban blight, like the "cast-iron gloom" of Rumania's totalitarian regime, serves as an emblem for universal deprivation. In a visit to Chicago's derelict South Side, Corde has read the signs of that human impoverishment. Noting the "low sky, wind, weed skeletons, ruin," he "got out of the car feeling the lack of almost everything you needed, humanly. Christ, the human curve had sunk down to base level, had gone beneath it. If there was another world, this was the time for it to show itself. The visible didn't bear looking at" (188–89). To his credit, however, Corde keeps on "looking"—attempting to bear witness to such unbearable conditions.

For Corde, furthermore, bearing witness to human loss and tragedy demands a language of connection. He does not wish to assume the expert's "position of autonomy and detachment, a kind of sovereignty we're all schooled in. The sovereignty of atoms—that is, of human beings who see themselves as atoms of intelligent separateness" (262). In his *Harper's* articles, he had attempted to get beyond the strictures of the analytic view—to close the gap between observer and observed that makes "men and women . . . shadows, and shadows within shadows, to one another." In Corde's view, "these appalling shadows *condemned*," by the spectacle of their reduced humanity, "our habitual manner of interpretation" (32, 78, Bellow's italics). Severed from connection to life and one another by the deadening language of detachment, human beings become mere "shadows" to those who observe them: "sketches, cartoons instead of human beings"—mere "outsides without insides" (204).

Such verbal "sketches" constitute, in Mikhail Bakhtin's formulation, the "sclerotic deposits" of a once vital process of signification. The "linguistic markers" of "professional jargon," he points out in *The Dialogic Imagination*, are "signs left behind on the path of the real living project of an intention. . . . Discourse lives, as it were, beyond itself, in a living impulse [*napravlennost'*] toward the object; if we detach ourselves completely from this impulse all we have left is the naked corpse of the word, from which we can learn nothing at all about the social situation. . . ." By abandoning the "living impulse" to connect with the "objects" of verbal signification, we end up, in Bakhtin's view, with dead signs. Words "grow sickly, lose semantic depth and flexibility," become the rigid "corpse" of a once supple language.[9]

Taking a similar view of the relationship between language and society, but extending its implications, Corde perceives the deadly effect of "sclerotic" language upon Chicago's "black underclass." By employing "professional jargon" to represent this doomed population, the experts unwittingly conspire in the decay of both language and society. The linguistic production of verbal "corpses" does not oppose, but actually abets, the destructive social conditions that spawn real corpses. In the *Harper's* articles, therefore, Corde's "aim" was to find a language of connection rather than detachment—"pictorial" rather than "analytical" in nature (197). "In our flesh and blood existence," he explains, "I think we are pictures of something": "pictures of the soul and spirit" (204).

Having tried, in the *Harper's* articles, to become "the moralist of seeing," Corde discovers that his audience, especially in Chicago, "mostly hated me for it" (123). The journalist is accused of being irresponsible as well as unfair, of introducing "poetry" into the language of fact and thereby embarrassing himself professionally. Rehearsing portions of those articles in his Rumanian solitude, the Dean is himself critical of certain excesses in his style and approach. But what he most deplores in the writing is "the generalizing, philosophizing passages" (159). He is convinced that "the increase of theories" and of abstract "discourse" has contributed to "false consciousness"—to "new strange forms of blindness." The "first act of morality," he avows, is "to disinter the reality, retrieve reality, . . . represent it anew as art would represent it" (123). Conversely, when the strictly analytic methods of the "scientific worldview" are applied to the study of human beings, standards of measurement rather than moral insight obtain.

The stylistic flaws and excesses permeating his *Harper's* articles are, Corde notes, symptomatic of the social awkwardness he feels, seeking a humanly *attached* language in which to articulate contemporary conditions. To appeal to moral imperatives, to the mystery of good and evil and the reality of "the soul," is to sound embarrassingly unscientific. "For science," after all, "there can be no good or evil" (278). Abandoning the safe haven of detached observation, Corde is fearful of lapsing into "beatitude language": "for an American who had been around, a man in his mid-fifties, this beatitude language was unreal. To use it betrayed him as a man wildly disturbed, a somehow crazy man. It was foreign, bookish—it was Dostoevsky stuff, that the vices of Sodom coexisted with the adoration of the Holy Sophia" (130).

Over a decade ago, we recall, Bellow alluded to the "two different speeches" characterizing advanced Western consciousness: the rationalist discourse of "head culture," which has all the public respect; and the private language of "internal beliefs," which remains a well kept "secret" among the ranks of the "educated."[10] Like other Bellow protagonists, Corde, an intellectual and academic dean, does not suffer his education lightly. Despite his search for a language of "connection" he—like Sammler, Herzog, Citrine and their predecessors—is wary of the social and intellectual embarrassment that attends, among the "educated," any hint of "beatitude language." When Corde meets up with Dewey Spangler in Rumania, he tries to shield himself from undue exposure. Aware that he is "serious about matters he couldn't even begin to discuss with Dewey," he tries to keep them "secret": "There was, for instance, the reunion of spirit and nature (divorced by science)"—a pressing concern of Corde's that he must keep to himself. Dewey, he knows, is "rough on writers who talked about 'spirit,' intellectuals in flight from the material realities of the present age" (122).

Still, Corde is convinced that the "superstructures of explanation" offer increasing opportunity for moral evasion rather than understanding. The intellect formulates as a "problem" that "mystery" in which, as Sammler discovers, we all share. Evil does not simply exist on the "outside," but within each human being. "It was not so much the inner city slum that threatened us," he recollects telling Varennes, Chicago's public defender, "as the slum of innermost being, of which the inner city was perhaps a material representation" (201). Contemporary society is in spiritual disarray; human impoverishment begins here, in the denial of moral knowledge, which is "universal, the common property of all human beings" (202). At this point, the Dean recalls, he began to feel embarrassed. "I felt that I looked ailing and sick. A kind of hot haze came over me. I felt my weakness as I approached the business of the soul—its true business in this age. Here a dean (or a writer of magazine articles) came to see a public defender to talk about a limited matter and their discussion became unlimited—their business was not being transacted" (201). How does one "talk straight" about the "business of the soul" (205)? "You learn," Corde tells himself, "to keep your humanity to yourself, the one who appreciates it best" (262). "He was a very nice man," he observes of Varennes. "Almost talkable-to. Those are the worst. For a while you almost feel you're getting somewhere" (207).

Nevertheless, Corde is not dissuaded from the arduous task of making contact, of finding connection. For this reason, he devotes serious attention, during his December in Bucharest, to a prospective project at home. An eminent Chicago scientist, Professor Beech, has read Corde's *Harper's* articles and is convinced that he can provide "the real explanation of what goes on in those slums." The true cause of the human impoverishment and despair described by Corde is, the scientist says, "chronic lead insult." According to Beech, "millions of tons of intractable lead residues [are] poisoning the children of the poor"; it is in "those old slum neighborhoods" that "the concentration is measurably heaviest." Eager to communicate the findings of his research to "the Humanists" as well as to the scientific community, Beech seeks Corde's help in writing up his findings—in hopes of gaining the widest possible audience (136–37).

Poring over the large number of documents, tapes and articles Beech has supplied him, Corde is both impressed and "terribly moved, restless, clawed within," by what he learns. The scientist's description of the "biological dysfunction" caused by "the deadly poisoning of water, vegetation and air" during "three industrial centuries" strikes home. Corde has firsthand knowledge of these symptoms: "This irritability, this combination of inflammation and deadening—by God, I feel it myself!" Still, he is dubious that so simple an explanation for human misery exists. "Once more," he observes, the scientist locates "a direct material cause" for "everything." Of course, Corde acknowledges, "direct material causes" do exist for poverty, crime and human "despair." Who, after all, "could deny them? But what was odd," he notes, "was that no other causes were conceived of" (137–41). Addressing the "mental disturbances" that give rise to "terrorism, barbarism, crime, cultural degradation," Beech has become, "without realizing it," a "burning moral visionary." But to expose "the most potent, i.e., most manifest evils," he lacks an adequate language. "Here science itself . . . experienced a singular failure." Seeking a direct "material cause" for every form of human disorder, the analyst examines data and calculates the "mass situation." In "the current language" of science, unfortunately, "nothing"—nothing touching on the true source of these human "evils"—"could be communicated" (140).

As Corde studies Beech's findings, he is struck by the way the geophysicist "had incorporated the planet itself into his deepest feelings, as if it were a being which had given birth to life. Beech was shocked by *Homo sapiens*

sapiens [*sic.*], by its ingratitude and impiety. *Homo sapiens sapiens* was incapable of hearing earth's own poetry, or, now, its plea" (141). Thus Corde detects, beneath the scientist's formulations, an outcry of spirit against human folly and blindness. Honoring no other language than "the current language" of scientific rationalism, Beech can, however, give only the faintest intimation of his deeper intuitions. "The same methods, the same energies" that the scientist employs in the laboratory "could not be applied to the deeper questions of existence." The inadequacy of scientific formulations is not the only realization at which Corde arrives. "It was conceivable," Corde reflects, "that science had drawn all the capacity for deeper realizations out of the rest of mankind and monopolized it. This left everyone else in a condition of great weakness" (141).

Corde's intuition, that rationalist faith has sapped the human being's capacity for other modes of knowing, and for expressing that knowledge, has the greatest influence upon his own quest for an adequate language of connection: a language in which the *"verbum cordis"*—and not just the formulations of *"Homo sapiens sapiens"*—may be articulated. One of the triumphs of Corde's inner quest is that, in response to Beech's inadequate language, he (and behind him, his author) succeeds in articulating, in the language of metaphor and moral vision, a more penetrating account of the "chronic lead insult" afflicting contemporary humanity. In reviewing his *Harper's* articles and the experience that contributed to their writing, Corde is critical of his previous efforts, but not discouraged. Rather, contemplation of the difficulties involved, even of his failures, provokes thoughts of writing "a new version, wider in perspective, closer to the real facts, taking bigger forces into account" (198). Meanwhile events in Bucharest, particularly the death of Minna's mother, Valeria, strengthen Corde's resolve to bear witness in the language, and from the vantage, of "attachment."

After Valeria Raresh's death and funeral—at the "very instant," in fact, that her body "might be going into the fire" at the crematorium—Corde goes for a walk with one of Professor Beech's colleagues, Vlada Voynich, an old friend of Minna's who has also turned up in Bucharest. Corde is still shaken by his experience at the crematorium—where he was obliged "to identify Valeria" before her body was offered to the fire. Feeling that he is barely hanging on, "crawling between heaven and earth," he has trouble making the transition from the crematorium's death-furnace to Beech's lofty formulations. As Corde ironically observes to Vlada, "I'm strolling in this park with you, I'm a gentleman again, taking the grand survey of man's future and the fate of the earth" (221, 223). For Corde, awareness of last things undermines, to the point of ludicrousness, this "grand" posture—the enlightened observer taking a remote "survey" of man's fate and future as the flames of the crematorium devour flesh and bone.

On his earlier visit to the crematorium, when he first accompanied Minna there to make arrangements for her mother's funeral, Corde was astonished to find himself walking past a row of corpses, neatly "laid out in their best clothes." All at once he had found himself praying: "Lord, I am ignorant and a stranger to my fellow man. I had thought that I understood things pretty well. Not so" (173). What is most remarkable about Corde's direct confrontation with the material "fact" of death, however, is the way that it undermines, rather than reinforces, "rational orthodoxy." Having seen the "roaring furnace" at the crematorium, Corde later pictures to himself the flames—now a Yeatsian "refining fire"—as they attack Valeria's dead body and "consumed the skin, flashed away the fat, blew up the organs, reached the bones, bore down on the skull—that refining fire, a ball of raging gold, a tiny sun, a star" (220). As the flames, in his mind's eye, ravage Valeria's corpse, matter explodes into sheer energy. Thus Corde envisions a "tiny" metaphorical "sun, a star"—a point of light and source of energy—pulsing at the heart of reality. Radiating from the ashes of Valeria's body, this "star" thematically prefigures the novel's conclusion. There, standing in the dome of the Mt. Palomar observatory in California, Corde will gaze at the infinite reaches of "astral space" and discover, paradoxically, the individual's intimate bond with creation: the living connection between the remotest stars "out there" and "the very blood and the crystal forms inside your bones" (311).

Any scientist will acknowledge the material "fact" of this connection: that the earth and its creatures contain within them—down to the "very blood and the crystal forms" inside their bones—atoms bequeathed by the remotest stars. Yet for Corde the tiny "star" radiating from the ashes of Valeria's corpse also brings awareness of a *different* order of fact. Finding that his perceptions are becoming "much more clear" and "much more singular" as he contemplates the "fact" of his mother-in-law's death, Corde reflects:

> Valeria was certainly dead. She had died, and she was dead, and last arrangements were being made. But he couldn't say that she was dead to him. It wouldn't have been an accurate statement. One might call this a comforting illusion, . . . but in fact there was nothing at all comforting about it. . . . Nor was it anything resembling an illusion. It was more like an internal fact of which he became conscious. He hadn't been looking for it. And he was not prompted to find a "rational" cause for this. Rationality of this sort left him cold. It was particularity that interested him. (176)

Convinced that this "internal fact"—his transcendent connection to Valeria, despite her physical obliteration—cannot be attributed to a single " 'rational' cause," Corde is aware of the ready explanations that any analyst or doctor could supply him. Yet such generalities, couched in the language of "rationality," strike him as wholly inadequate; they have no bearing on the particular facts—the "internal facts"—of the case. The only possible language for articulating the "internal fact" of Valeria's unextinguishable life is the language of attachment. Corde's vision of that "tiny sun, a star," radiating from an invisible center—the vanishing point of Valeria Raresh's terrestrial existence—manifests the "internal fact" that, as Corde has earlier said, "in our flesh and blood existence . . . we are pictures of something." And even when these concrete "pictures of the soul and spirit" vanish from view, the "internal fact"—the "something"—persists.

To this "something," "soul" or "spirit" surviving the "raw fact" of extinction, Corde must attribute his abiding connection to Valeria. When, shortly before her death, he visits her in the hospital, he has an inkling of this connection—of the mystery of love and the elusive "something" from which it emanates. In the intensive care ward, hooked up to various machines measuring her heartbeat and her rate of breathing, Valeria appears all but dead. Unable to open her eyes or to move her lips, she reacts with violent intensity, nonetheless, when her son-in-law, in a whisper, delivers his "essential message"—that he loves her: "One of her knees came up, her eyes, very full under the skin of the lids, moved back and forth. She made an effort to force them to open. The monitors jumped simultaneously. All the numbers began to tumble and whirl" (128). Significantly, the machines are unable to register, in their quantitative language, the charge of Valeria's response; the "numbers" only "tumble and whirl."

Corde himself is not certain what to make of his love for Valeria.[11] After various attempts at self-explanation, he breaks off: "Well, never mind the philosophy. But on her deathbed an old woman hears the deep voice of her son-in-law, and it tells her that he loves her. Loves! With what! Nevertheless it *was* true, however queer." Then, underscoring both the strangeness and the strength of his affirmation, Corde recalls the phrase that "an old Englishman" once put to him on a "Channel train": "There *was* nothing too rum to be true." On this truth, he admits, "he depended . . . now" (133, 115, Bellow's italics). Corde knows that he loves Valeria even though he cannot empirically locate the origin or seat of love's power. From time immemorial human beings have, as a matter of convention and convenience, located the source of love in that muscular organ, the human heart. Corde understands, however, that his love for Valeria is really a mystery emanating from an invisible source—that "something," that core of being to which we assign names (the Latin *cor*, for example) but which we cannot objectively locate.

Although the phrasing is distinctly British, the Englishman's colloquial observation—that there is "nothing too rum [i.e., strange, odd or queer] to be true"—may be traced to Pascal. Respectful as Pascal was of the "sovereign rights of reason," he refused to set its law above divine mystery. As the Russian philosopher, Lev Shestov, has pointed out, "Pascal sees in the inexplicable and incomprehensible nature of our surroundings the promise of a better existence, and every effort to simplify or to reduce the unknown to the known seems to him blasphemy."[12] That Corde perceives an analogous connection between the inexplicable—particularly the mystery of love—and the divine mystery of "God" is suggested in various passages linking the Englishman's phrase to its ultimate implication: that "God did exist" (115, 130).

After Valeria's funeral, Corde challenges, in conversation with Vlada Voynich, Professor Beech's assumption that "liberal humanist culture is weak because it lacks scientific knowledge" (222). A misplaced faith in "scientific knowledge," he tells Vlada, may constitute the real source of current social and cultural distress. Reinterpreting the phenomena, looking at them from the inside out, Corde perceives in Beech's "lead insult" the symbol of a deeper spiritual malaise. Speaking to Vlada in the impassioned language of connection, he sketches a "picture" of the internal facts: "Man's great technical works, looming over him, have coated him with deadly metal. We can't carry the weight. The blood is sobbing in us. Our brains grow feebler" (225). To Corde, the statistical proofs for Beech's hypothesis are less important than the telling image of the "lead insult." "Lead communicates something special to us about matter, our existence in matter." It conveys our "sinister" belief in our own "earthenness," which consigns us, along with everything "sclerotic, blind, earthen," to "the general end of everything." Like Charles Citrine, Corde draws a direct parallel between materialist faith and biblical idolatry: with "eyes that see not, ears that hear not," says Corde, we enslave ourselves to matter and perish, finally, from its deadly weight (224).

Although convinced that Professor Beech is "a man of feeling and even a visionary" who "wants to protect and to bless," Corde finds the scientist's language not just inadequate but highly dangerous. The language of detachment and calculation offers the "proposition," unacceptable to Corde, that "human wickedness is absolutely a public health problem, and nothing but. No tragic density, no thickening of the substance of the soul, only chemistry or physiology" (227). Scientific rationalism accords all the "weight," all the significance to matter, while human beings are reduced, once again, to mere "outlines," "sketches, cartoons." Inadvertently, Professor Beech—like the professional analysts devising systematic theories to explain the decay of America's inner cities—contributes to the very conditions he is attempting to rectify.

"Where Beech sees poison lead I see poison thought or poison theory," says Corde. "The view we hold of the material world may put us into a case as heavy as lead" (227). An ultimate connection exists, therefore, between the death-saturated cities of Chicago and Bucharest and "advanced modern consciousness"—which is actually "a reduced consciousness"—"humanly so meager, so abstract," that it proves "basically murderous" (193). "To recover the world that is buried under" the lead weight and "debris" of "false description or nonexperience" is, Corde affirms, the only way we can uncover "the substance of the soul." Heaping up more "abstract, stillborn, dead" concepts only adds to the lead weight of "nonexperience" that seals us off from life (243). It is this vision of his task or calling—to find an appropriate language to register "the facts of experience"—that Corde tries to communicate to his old friend, Dewey Spangler, near the end of the novel. To Dewey, however, Corde's language is hopelessly "cloudy, and even mystical"; and he finds Corde's sense of mission ludicrous—as though "the voice of God [were] saying, 'Write this up, as follows'" (243–44).

Narrowly observing his old friend as they sit talking, over drinks, in Bucharest, Corde begins, in his mind, to caricature Spangler as an aspiring "Walter Lippman" type. But then, catching himself playing the "murderous" game of "false description" that he deplores, he immediately warns himself: "I'm going to miss something about the man while I gratify my taste for wicked comment." What happens next, as Corde takes in his old friend with awakened eyes, is a direct manifestation of the Dean's developing powers of insight:

> Then for some reason, with no feeling of abruptness, he became curiously absorbed in Dewey . . .—the whole human Spangler was delivered to Corde in the glass-warmed winter light with clairvoyant effect. He saw now that Spangler was downslanted in spirit. . . . Seeing him so actual, vanities were dissipated, you were in no position to judge, and there was no need for judging. . . . Maybe on this death day Corde was receiving secret guidance in seeing life. Perhaps at this very moment the flames were finishing Valeria, and therefore it was especially important to think what a human being really was. (244–45)

Like Herzog gazing at Gersbach bathing his daughter, Corde discovers the saving power of the "actual," which liberates him from the "basically murderous" tendencies of leaden abstractions. Dispensing with dangerous formulations, he discovers the power and freedom of attached observation. And like Ken Trachtenberg gazing *into*, not at, "the real Fishl," Corde becomes "absorbed in Dewey," registering what he sees with "clairvoyant effect." Although he takes in the vivid details of Spangler's physical "outsides"— including his "tortoise-shell beard," the "skin scraped and mottled where the beard was trimmed"—it is the "whole human Spangler" that is "delivered" to his insight. Corde plumbs that "something" constituting Dewey's inner life and imbuing the concrete "picture" that Dewey presents to his eye.

In such vivid forms of attachment, Corde knows, his "soul had a lifelong freehold." And even though this "real knowledge" has at times seemed "repugnant" and felt like "captivity," he understands that there is no freedom, no reality without connection. "What you didn't pass through your soul didn't even exist. . . . Reality didn't exist 'out there.' It began to be real only when the soul found its underlying truth. In generalities there was no coherence—none"

(265–66). The highest responsibility is, then, to realize the world, make it *actual*, by actively engaging with its particulars—*connecting* with them, passing them "through your soul." Breaking through the strictures imposed by "the generality-mind," Corde affirms, more directly than any previous Bellow protagonist, the soul's connection to creation. The Cartesian duality, the mind-body split creating so much mental and emotional friction in Sammler and others, is discovered to be a manifestation—indeed a creation—of the "modern, conflicted self." Corde's revelation is not confined to the level of abstract "discourse," however. At the end of the novel, Bellow articulates his character's felt connection to the universe, his bond with all creation; and he does so by creating verbal "pictures" traced in the very language of attachment that Corde has been seeking.

The Dean's December ends with a vivid "picture," or representation, of connection—despite the fact that Corde winds up, as he began, in the cold. Here, in the novel's concluding pages, Corde finds himself in the "clear piercing" air of Mt. Palomar—the California observatory where he has, after Bucharest, accompanied Minna once again. As he enters the "vast, unlighted, icy, scientific Cimmerian gloom" of the observatory, he is aware of penetrating the very temple of "scientific knowledge." The vaulting "hugeness of the dome" both recalls and surpasses in scale any dome housed in the world's greatest "mosques or churches, Saint Paul's, Saint Peter's." Having come for "a look at astral space," Corde registers the "absolute" cold of the atmosphere: "it was appropriate that you should have a taste of the cold *out there*, its power to cancel everything merely human." As though confirming this power to cancel, Corde is reminded, as the lift mounts toward the open dome and "the open, freezing heavens," of the crematorium in Bucharest: "*that* rounded top and its huge circular floor" (309–11, Bellow's italics). There, passing the rows of "stiffs" lined up behind the curtains, Corde had felt himself enacting his own "death rehearsal." Yet afterward, envisioning the flames devouring Valeria's body, the realization of his lasting bond with her took him beyond the consuming fact of death: the image of a tiny gold "sun," radiating light, created a point of contact between Valeria's "real being" and his own.

Now, at Mt. Palomar, gazing at the starry vastness of "the living heavens," Corde does not feel dwarfed, crushed to insignificance, by the infinite reaches of "astral space" and "the cold out there." To the contrary, he experiences the full impact of his earlier revelation: "Reality didn't exist 'out there.' It began to be real only when the soul found its underlying truth." What is "out there" is intimately attached to what is "inside" us; the one is known by and completed in the other. The world of "astral space," with its myriad nebulae and exploding stars, does not "cancel" us but draws us, binds us to it. "Standing in the eye of the giant telescope," says Gloria Cronin, "Corde at last begins to see through his glass brightly."[13] In this temple of scientific observation he discovers, paradoxically, that human beings know more of reality than their senses can apprehend. With the eye one sees, Corde says, "only as much as could be taken in through the distortions of the atmosphere. Through these distortions you saw objects, forms, partial realities. The rest was to be felt" (311).

Such heartfelt vision is not, however, the product of mere sentiment or "comforting illusion." The soul and the world are together so constituted, Bellow appears to suggest, that the one is *drawn* to the other; they are intimately, intersubjectively, related. This "internal fact," accessible only to a knowing subject—not to an objective observer—constitutes Corde's ultimate revelation of his bond with all creation:

> You were drawn to feel and to penetrate further, as if you were being informed that what was spread over you had to do with your existence, down to the very blood and the crystal forms inside your bones. Rocks, trees, animals, men and women, these also drew you to penetrate further, under the distortions (comparable to the atmospheric ones, shadows within shadows) to find their real being with your own. (311)

From this profound experience of attachment Corde receives, paradoxically, a heady sense of freedom. The "claustrophobia" of modern consciousness is here transcended. "Free!" Corde exclaims, "you were free!"—"the grip of every sickness within you disengaged by this pouring out." But Corde's expansive sense of freedom, it may be objected, sounds more like escape than attachment. Doesn't a "pouring out" into the universe signify dissolution rather than binding? One cannot gainsay the note of disengagement, of Sammlerian release from mortal strife, that sounds in Corde's declaration. Yet, I would suggest, the liberation he experiences is not escape from existence but release from "the grip" of materialist perception and the "sickening" claustrophobia it fosters. The process of liberation began in Bucharest, where Valeria's death and funeral paradoxically served to reinforce Corde's understanding of what is "eternal in man" (285). In Chicago, where he and Minna return briefly before setting out for Mt. Palomar, Corde has had further intimations of this freedom.

Seated on the "sixteenth-story porch" of their Chicago lakeside apartment, Corde gazes at the expanse of sky and water, enjoying the unusual warmth of "an afternoon of January thaw." Noting the vertical "bars" of the balcony rail, he both queries and answers himself: "Did the bars remind you of jail? They also kept you from falling to your death" (290). What confines us, he suggests, defines and safeguards our temporal existence—keeps us from losing our balance in the physical world and from cutting short our tenure in it. Both the "porch rail" and the finite boundaries of perception thus appear, in Corde's liberated view, a necessary condition—local rather than absolute. His intimation is not of escape from this mortal condition but of connection to transcendent reality. "It was like being poured out to the horizon, like a great expansion. What if death should be like this, the soul finding an exit. The porch rail was his figure for the hither side. The rest, beyond it, drew you constantly as the completion of your reality" (290). Here, as at Mt. Palomar, the condition of being "drawn to feel and to penetrate further" becomes an "internal fact" signalling the individual's connection to creation. In this way Corde's "soul finds an exit" not from reality but, as Henderson says, from "unreality."

What transcends the "raw fact" of death, then, is the "internal fact" of connection: Buber's intersubjective relationship of "I–Thou" is, to recall Gilson's phrase, evident "to a soul, not to a mind." As King Dahfu has told Henderson, "You are related to all. The very gnats are your cousins. The sky is your thoughts. The leaves are your insurance, and you need no other. There is no interruption all night to the speech of the stars." Although Albert Corde's perspective is as far from Dahfu's as the Dean's sixteenth-floor Chicago apartment is from the tribal chieftain's rustic palace, the two characters appear to speak the same language. Through them both Bellow articulates the processes of intersubjective perception and knowledge, ultimately taking his readers—in every sense including the colloquial—"far out": beyond the familiar coordinates of space-time and the ruling premises of contemporary thought.

That an eminent member of the intellectual establishment, a college dean, arrives at a vision of existence as "far out" as the "daffy" African king's is itself telling. Bellow, having devised Dahfu's colorful speech beneath the protective shade, and within the sheltering obscurity, of a mythical forest, has in subsequent novels brought his "primordial" language to bear directly upon the iron realities of twentieth-century urban life. The difficulties of such a task, itself an arduous effort at connection, may account for the subdued, at times even exhausted, tone of "late Bellow." The affirmation at the end of *The Dean's December* sounds in a distinctly minor key; no thunderous chords provide a coda. The majestic lines of Handel's *Messiah* do not resonate throughout this novel as they do in *Henderson the Rain King*. Nor does Corde possess Henderson's monumental vitality, his strength to leap and cavort in "the gray Arctic silence." Far from cavorting, the Dean of Bellow's penultimate novel is chilled to the bone by the "absolute" cold at Mt. Palomar. Asked, at the end, if he "minded" the cold at the top of the observatory dome, Corde closes the novel by replying: "The cold? Yes. But I almost think I mind coming down more" (312). That "almost" is all that stands between Albert Corde's reluctance and his readiness to resume his role in the clamorous world below. And yet that single word—"almost"—takes on resounding significance when we consider the context in which it is uttered. Against the massive data of global society—all the accumulated evidence of urban decay, totalitarian repression, collective death-wish and grinding despair—that faintly voiced qualifier, "almost," sounds with its own kind of heroic resonance.

Afterword: *A Theft* and Beyond

Having set out, in *More Die of Heartbreak*, for the frozen North "and be-yond," Bellow has lately returned from that distant territory with an unex-pected gem. In his latest work of fiction, the novella *A Theft* (1989), an emerald ring, bearing a stone of piercing clarity, is first stolen and then mysteriously returned to its owner, Clara Velde. A present from Ithiel (Teddy) Regler, the man she has loved for twenty years, the emerald ring represents to Clara the "permanent form" of their attachment:

> She held the ring to her face, felt actually as if she were inhaling the green essence of this ice. . . . In it Ithiel's pledge was frozen. Or else it represented the permanent form of the passion she had had for this man. The hot form would have been red, like a node inside the body, in the sexual parts. That you'd see as ruby. The cool form was this concentrate of clear green. This was not one of her fancies; it was as real as the green of the ocean, as the mountains in whose innards such gems are mined. She thought these locations (the Atlantic, the Andes) as she thought the inside of her own body. In her summary fashion, she said, "Maybe what it comes to is that I am an infant mine." She had three small girls to prove it. (43)

The foregoing passage recapitulates a dominant motif in "late Bellow," but in a tone distinctly less somber. Like Albert Corde, gazing at "astral space" through the dome of Mt. Palomar, Clara Velde can bridge the apparent abyss stretching between inner and outer reality—so that distant "locations," as far off as the Andes or Atlantic, are "thought" by her from "inside."

Clara Velde is no unworldly contemplative, however. Born and raised in Indiana, educated in the East, she is a highly paid executive in a New York publishing firm; and she lives, with her three daughters and indifferent fourth husband, in a "vast Park Avenue co-op apartment" (12). The first female to serve as the protagonist of a Bellow novel, Clara has endured the marital disappointments and failures that befall most of her male predecessors; she is, however, neither bitter nor scornful of the possibilities for love. As restless and troubled (she has twice attempted suicide) as any of Bellow's heroes, she has this singular advantage. Like Henderson's wife Lily, Clara regards love as the fundamental fact of being. "You couldn't," she asserts, "separate love from being" (31). Grounded in this sure sense of *being*—the elusive goal of so many of Bellow's agonized male intellectuals—Clara is not caught in the toils of Herzog's "Prussian delusions" or the "superstructures of explanation." As she tells a friend, "I don't actually take much stock in the collapsing culture bit. I'm beginning to see it as the conduct of life without input from your soul. Essential parts of people getting mislaid or crowded out" (89).

As the central figure and intelligence in *A Theft*, Clara Velde radiates energy and warmth—what Ithiel calls her "solar power" (58). Further contributing to the sanguine atmosphere of Bellow's latest work are the passages of high-spirited comedy, and sexual parody, that recall his earlier fiction. Once more the absurdities of twentieth-century life prove laughable as well as grotesque. Thus Clara describes her visit, with Ithiel in the 1970s, to an Italian "billionaire revolutionist":

> [Giangiacomo] was a kind, pleasant man, good-looking except for his preposterous Fidel Castro getup, like a little kid from Queens in a cowboy suit. He wore a forage cap, and in a corner of his fancy office there was a machine gun on the floor. He invited Ithiel and me to his château. . . . At lunch, the butler was leaning over with truffles from Giangiacomo's own estate to grate over the *crème veloutée*, and he couldn't because Giangiacomo was waving his arms, going on about revolutionary insurgency. (22)

In Italy Clara and Ithiel also meet an oil tycoon named Spontini, who later becomes Clara's third husband. Insisting on driving his visitors back to their Milan hotel, Spontini tries to take advantage of his position: "Clara wasn't about to tell Teddy that in Milan when Mike Spontini had invited her to sit in front with him, she had found the palm of his hand waiting for her on the seat, and she had lifted herself up immediately and given him her evening bag to hold" (25). Adding to the sexual comedy is the fun of watching a clever woman turn the tables on a fumbling male cliché. Even critics who regard Bellow's female characters as distillations of male fantasy rather than reality will concede that Clara provides a striking exception. The most fully rendered figure in her landscape, she is clearly cherished by her author—cherished, it might be said, to a fault. For the loving attention Bellow pays Clara seems at times responsible for the sketchiness with which various minor characters are rendered—from Clara's shadowy confidante, Laura Wong, to the young Haitian who steals her emerald ring. In her review of *A Theft*, Joyce Carol Oates justifiably maintains that although "inspired in passages and over all an intriguing possibility, the novella seems underimagined."[1]

Clara, on the other hand, is richly imagined—and a good deal larger than life. As Bellow's anonymous narrator comments, "Really, everything about her was conspicuous. . . . She must have decided long ago that for the likes of her there could be no cover-up; she couldn't divert energy into disguises. So there she was, a rawboned American woman" (1). It is Clara's extraordinary vitality, her "solar power," that both attracts Ithiel Regler, her onetime lover and longtime soulmate, and possibly keeps him from marrying her. "Looking back" on their affair, which ended years earlier, Clara recalls her "devouring, fervid" passion for Ithiel and wonders whether she had been "carrying too much of an electrical charge" (21). Repelled, perhaps, by the force of that "charge," Ithiel nevertheless remains Clara's most loyal friend and admirer. As he himself admits, "his attachment, his feeling for her was . . . permanent. His continually increasing respect for her came over the horizon like a moon taking decades to rise" (42).

A prominent expert on international relations, sought out by foreign heads-of-state as well as by American presidents, Ithiel places all of his worldly experience at the service of celebrating Clara's rare and generous spirit: "Straight-nosed Ithiel, heading for Washington and the Capitol dome, symbolic of a nation swollen with world significance, set a greater value on Clara than on anything in *this* place or any place." Thus Ithiel avows, "In all the world, now, there wasn't a civilized place left where a woman would say"—as Clara has said to him—"'I love you with my soul.' Only this backcountry girl was that way still. If no more mystical sacredness remained in the world, she hadn't been informed yet." Possessed of what Ithiel calls a "tenth-century soul," Clara believes in the message of "Matthew 16:18: 'the gates of hell shall not prevail against it'—*it* being love, against which no door can be closed" (35, 42, 48, Bellow's italics). To Ithiel, then, the rarest gem is not the emerald he once gave to Clara, although it is worth thousands of dollars, but the clear "green essence" of her love.

To Clara, however, the emerald ring is a symbol of their enduring bond; when this "life support" disappears, "her very grip on existence" is threatened (70). Suspecting (correctly) the Haitian boyfriend of her Austrian au pair girl, Clara orders the young woman, Gina Wegman, to get the ring back—and not to return without it. Later, after Gina leaves and Clara has calmed down, she is furious with herself for turning "like a maniac on this Austrian kid" (71). With the loss of Ithiel's ring, Clara's sense of threatening chaos, internal and external, begins to mount. Fearing the dangerous world into which she has ejected Gina—a "Gogmagogsville" where "all the rules" of decency are fast "crumbling"—she asks herself, "So where did love fit in? Love was down in the catacombs," nowhere to be seen or felt but "in the personal neuroses of women like herself" (65, 73).

Trying to locate Gina and make amends, Clara comes to reflect on the young woman's exceptional qualities—her "great sense of honor" and "responsibility." Thus she tells Ithiel, "I've come to love that girl" (94). Not until months later, however—after the ring mysteriously reappears on her bedroom nightstand—does Clara learn of Gina's special regard for her. When they meet for the last time, just before Gina flies home to Vienna, Clara fails to find out how Gina managed to get the ring back from the Haitian boyfriend, whom she has subsequently abandoned. What Gina does explain, however, is why—despite Clara's furious dismissal of her—she set out to regain the ring. "I decided," she tells Clara, "you were a complete person, and the orders you gave you gave for that reason." Clara objects, "Oh, wait a minute, I don't see any complete persons. In luckier times I'm sure complete persons did exist. But now? . . . You look around for something to take hold of, and where is it?" To which Gina replies, "I see it in you," adding: "With all the disorder, I can't see how you keep track. You do, though. I believe you pretty well know who you are" (108).

At this time Clara also discovers that her daughter Lucy has cooperated with Gina in her efforts to replace the stolen ring. Struck by the extraordinary self-possession of a ten-year-old who could secretly transfer the ring from Gina to her mother's nightstand, Clara tells her former au pair, "I see how you brought it all together through my own child. You gave her something significant to do, and she was equal to it. Most amazing to me is the fact that she didn't talk, she only watched. That level of observation and control in a girl of ten" (107). Of Clara's three daughters, it is Lucy who has most worried her mother. "Patsy and Selma were graceful children, and they made Lucy seem burly, awkward before the awkward age. She would be awkward after it, too, just as her mother had been, and eruptive, defiant and prickly." Now Clara's abiding intuition, that beneath the child's clumsiness there is "something *major* in Lucy," appears confirmed (47, Bellow's italics). She recognizes that her "own child" may "possibly" be one of those rare human beings—a "complete" person—capable of taking hold, as Gina says Clara has done, in a time of disorder. Acknowledging the decisive role that her own love for Lucy has played in her daughter's formation, Clara receives confirmation of her profoundest belief: that love is "as real" as "the mountains in whose innards such gems are mined." Awed by love's energy, and by the mysteries of motherhood, Clara knows herself, once again, to be "an infant mine"—with "three small girls to prove it."

At the end of *A Theft*, Clara says goodbye to Gina Wegman and, weeping from emotion and relief, hurries, "crying, down Madison Avenue, not like a person who belonged there but like one of the homeless, doing grotesque things in public, one of those street people turned loose from an institution" (109). Beneath the flood of Clara's tears, the New York sidewalk surges up, "more a sea than a pavement." Recalling the eloquent closing passage of *Seize the Day*, Clara's tears symbolically dissolve material appearances, washing away the social signposts that separate her from the less fortunate. Like

Wilhelm Adler, who sinks "deeper than sorrow" as he weeps for a dead stranger, she is absorbed by her tears into the community of human suffering. Thus she sees herself not as a fashionably dressed, highly paid executive with a Park Avenue address, but as one of the "homeless," anonymous and destitute, wandering in isolation outside the bastions of the powerful and rich.

As Clara's tears well up, from "the main source," to blur her vision and impede her progress down Madison Avenue, she senses that "she wasn't getting anywhere, she was still in the same place" (109). In the context established by Bellow's previous fiction, her revelation takes on special significance. Caught up, like Wilhelm, in the difficult "business of the soul," Clara appears to recognize her essential "homelessness" in the world of Madison Avenue. As though "turned loose" from the social edifice, she is symbolically divested, in Trilling's phrase, of all those "cultural superstructures" that serve to locate her position in the "material and social establishment." And yet Clara is not frightened by this sense of displacement; to the contrary, she rejoices in knowing, as she tells herself in the novella's closing lines, "who it is that's at the middle of me" (109). Celebrating that original self, or soul, existing prior to its alteration by the conditioning forces of history and culture, Clara Velde takes her place in the long line of her male precursors: all those Bellovian heroes who, "turned loose" from the ruling "institutions" of modern-day culture, affirm their independent connection to creation.

Asked recently whether *A Theft* is a "lighter" piece of fiction than his previous works, Bellow remarked, "I consider it a more straightforward story. I think I've now done all the thinking that I'm going to do. All my life long I have been seriously pondering certain problems and I'll probably continue to do that, but I'm now in a position to use this pondering as a background for the story, and not intrude it so much into the narrative."[2] A definite sense of repose, of having accomplished a long and arduous task, informs Bellow's newly awakened interest in the novella form. By his own testimony, he has already finished a second novella and is "working on a third. There may be," he adds, "a fourth and a fifth."[3] After a lifetime of pondering the major dilemmas of contemporary life, the novelist has apparently worked through, or moved beyond, the agony of unrelenting conflict. The internal division suffered by his characters, if not resolved, has grown more muted and, as the shorter length of the novella testifies, need not take up so much time or energy. Instead of Moses Herzog—struggling through hundreds of pages and countless words to silence the "demon" of "modern ideas" intoning decline and despair—Bellow gives us Clara Velde, who "doesn't take much stock in the collapsing culture bit."

Despite this latest shift in the perspective of Bellow's fiction, the novelist's ongoing commitment remains the same: to create stories that offer, as he says, "an independent view of reality different from the prevailing contemporary view."[4] Older now in years than his own world-weary septuagenarian, Artur Sammler, Bellow shows no sign of surrendering to the ruling "orthodoxies" of our time. At this late hour of twentieth-century life and letters, he is more committed than ever to uncovering "the radiance" of "common life" and to capturing the "silent speech" of the soul in a viable language of connection. Clearly such an enterprise requires courage, and Bellow's literary daring cannot be lightly dismissed. "Few writers today will risk the critical mockery stirred by hints of man's redemptive possibilities," Ben Siegel aptly observes, remarking the rare exception of Bellow's own, "open and challenging" fiction.[5] On a similar note, Cynthia Ozick, herself a contemporary writer, says that Bellow has "risked mentioning—who can admit to this without literary embarrassment?—the Eye of God." To articulate the individual's bond with God and creation is, Ozick knows firsthand, a "shamelessly daring [feat] just now in American imaginative prose."[6]

Exhibiting their author's literary "daring," virtually all of Bellow's novelistic protagonists engage in the search for connection: Corde, Sammler, Citrine, Herzog, Henderson, Ken Trachtenberg, Wilhelm Adler, the list goes on. Having heard from each of these protagonists in turn, as well as from their author, the reader will recognize their kinship with the narrator of "Cousins," one of the stories in Bellow's second collection, *Him with His Foot in His Mouth* (1984). Searching for his "real being under the debris of modern ideas," Cousin Ijah Brodsky discovers a form of enlightenment "altogether different from the lucidity of *approved* types of knowledge." Recalling his Cousin Shana's description of him as a boy-genius—a child, in her phrase, possessing "an open head"—Ijah in retrospect corrects her:

> It wasn't the *head* that was open. It was something else. We enter the world without prior notice, we are manifested before we can be aware of manifestation. An original self exists, or, if you prefer, an original soul. . . . I was invoking my own fundamental perspective, that of a person who takes for granted distortion in the ordinary way of seeing but has never given up the habit of referring all truly important observations to that original self or soul. (267–68, Bellow's italics)

Against the many "approved types of knowledge" disseminated by contemporary culture, the narrator of "Cousins" affirms, even more boldly than Mr. Sammler, the soul's own "natural knowledge."

As the creator of all these seekers after "real being," Bellow still honors the novel's incapacity to deliver "absolutes." Affirmation of the soul's "natural knowledge" is always dramatic and personal, the protagonist (and his author) making no claims for "objective truth." In the earlier novels, especially, Bellow's protagonists scarcely understand their struggle for awareness. And in the later novels—whether the protagonist begins his search, like Sammler, in a state of intense inner conflict or, like Corde, already has an inkling of his tie to creation—the internal harmony he achieves is always precarious, besieged unrelentingly by the chaotic forces of twentieth-century life. As acutely aware as a Corde, a Herzog or a Sammler of the sheer mass of "objective" evidence bearing down, with crushing force, on the fragile "internal facts" of human attachment, Saul Bellow continues, nonetheless, to articulate the "shamelessly daring" language of connection. In each successive novel, and with increasing boldness from *Mr. Sammler's Planet* on, he has pitted the art of his fiction against the grain of contemporary "head culture"—defying the leaden authority of its reigning idols.

Notes

Introduction

1. John Updike, "Toppling Towers Seen by a Whirling Soul," rev. of *The Dean's December*, *New Yorker* 22 Feb. 1982: 127.

2. Charles Newman, *The Post-Modern Aura: The Act of Fiction in an Age of Inflation* (Evanston, IL: Northwestern UP, 1985) 73–74, 70, Newman's italics.

3. M. A. Klug, "Saul Bellow: The Hero in the Middle," *Dalhousie Review* 56 (1976); rpt. *Critical Essays on Saul Bellow*, ed. Stanley Trachtenberg (Boston: G. K. Hall, 1979) 192.

4. Keith Michael Opdahl, *The Novels of Saul Bellow: An Introduction* (University Park: Pennsylvania State UP, 1967) 169, n. 7. In this important early study, Opdahl's primary focus is, as he says, on the "social and psychological" aspects of Bellow's fiction. He emphasizes, however, that "Bellow's imagination" is essentially "metaphysical and religious, passing from the historic fact to the larger universal issue" (6–7). Ten years later, in an essay titled " 'True Impressions': Saul Bellow's Realistic Style," *Saul Bellow and His Work*, ed. Edmond Schraepen (Brussels: Free U of Brussels, 1978) 61–71, Opdahl reiterates the importance of Bellow's "belief in spirit" (69).

5. Saul Bellow, "A World Too Much with Us," *Critical Inquiry* 2, 1 (Autumn 1975): 6. "Our head-culture," Bellow adds, "inordinately respects the collective powers of mind and the technical developments that have produced the most visible achievements of this civilization."

6. Robert Boyers, "Literature and Culture: An Interview with Saul Bellow," *Salmagundi* 30 (Summer 1975): 8.

7. Jo Brans, "Common Needs, Common Preoccupations: An Interview with Saul Bellow," *Southwest Review* 62 (1977), rpt. Trachtenberg, *Critical Essays* 58–59. Bellow's reference to *Humboldt's Gift* appears to be the mnemonic combining of two separate statements in the published novel. Defending the tenets of spiritual philosophy and "religion" to his ex-wife, the novel's protagonist, Charlie Citrine, says, "Test me on the scientific world-view and I'd score high. But it's just head stuff" (227–28). Of his belief in "the soul" Citrine later observes, "Only my head-culture opposes it" (350).

8. William James, *The Varieties of Religious Experience* (1902), The Works of William James (Cambridge, MA: Harvard UP, 1985) 66–67.

9. In his published "Nobel Lecture," *American Scholar* 46 (Summer 1977): 316–25, Bellow, echoing James, observes the tacit silence induced by the educated person's respect for rationalistic procedures. "We are reluctant to talk [about our internal beliefs]," says Bellow, "because there is nothing we can prove, because our language is inadequate, and because few people are willing to risk talking about [these matters]. They would have to say, 'There is a spirit,' and that is taboo. So almost everyone keeps quiet about it" (325).

10. Lionel Trilling, *Sincerity and Authenticity: The Charles Eliot Norton Lectures, 1969–1970* (Cambridge, MA: Harvard UP, 1971) 12, 42.

11. Trilling 41–42, 1.

12. Leon Roth, *Judaism: A Portrait* (London: Faber, 1960) 56–58.

13. James 33–34. James's definition of "personal religion" is also cited by Opdahl, *The Novels of Saul Bellow* 169, n. 6.

14. Jane Howard, "Mr. Bellow Considers His Planet," *Life* 3 April 1970: 59.

15. Sanford Pinsker, "Saul Bellow in the Classroom," *College English* 34, 7 (April 1973): 977.

16. Irvin Stock, "Man in Culture," rev. of *Mr. Sammler's Planet, Commentary* 49 (1970); rpt. Trachtenberg, *Critical Essays* 41.

17. Irvin Stock, "The Novels of Saul Bellow," *Southern Review* 3 (Jan. 1967): 13–42, rpt. Irvin Stock, *Fiction as Wisdom* (University Park: Pennsylvania State UP, 1980) 193.

18. In "Saul Bellow and Norman Mailer: The Secret Sharers," *Saul Bellow: A Collection of Critical Essays*, ed. Earl Rovit (Englewood Cliffs, NJ: Prentice-Hall, 1975) 161–70, Earl Rovit notes the "larger ease and freedom" with which Bellow moves, in his "later novels," through "the bleak foreground of his own world." Especially "apparent in *Mr. Sammler's Planet*," he adds, "is a greater receptivity to the possibilities of religious experience" (167).

19. Pinsker 977.

Chapter 1

1. Robert Boyers, "Literature and Culture: An Interview with Saul Bellow," *Salmagundi* 30 (Summer 1975): 8.

2. Alfred Kazin, *Bright Book of Life: American Novelists and Storytellers from Hemingway to Mailer* (Boston: Little, Brown, 1973) 134, 136–37.

3. John J. Clayton, *Saul Bellow: In Defense of Man*, 2nd ed. (Bloomington: Indiana UP, 1979) 234–36; also see Mark Schechner, "Down in the Mouth with Saul Bellow," *American Review* 23 (1975): 67, 64, cited in Clayton, *Saul Bellow* 235; and David Galloway, "*Mr. Sammler's Planet*: Bellow's Failure of Nerve," *Modern Fiction Studies* 19, 1 (Spring 1973): 23–24. An outstanding exception to this general view is provided in William J. Scheick's essay, "Circle Sailing in Bellow's *Mr. Sammler's Planet*," *Essays in Literature* 5, 1 (Spring 1978): 95–101. Disclosing the "dynamic aesthetic informing the novel," Scheick aptly describes Sammler as "a man in motion, his weary mind . . . moving among a clutter of thought, his fatigued body shuffling back and forth through impinging urban chaos" (97, 100).

4. According to L. H. Goldman, "Saul Bellow and the Philosophy of Judaism," *Studies in the Literary Imagination* (issue on Philosophical Dimensions of Saul Bellow's Fiction, ed. Eugene Hollahan) 17, 2 (Fall 1984): 81–95, there is a link between Meister Eckhart and Jewish thought: "The Bible commentaries of Meister Eckhardt [*sic.*] . . . owe their origins to Eckhardt's contacts with Jewish philosophy, especially Maimonides' *Guide*" (82).

5. Jane Howard, "Mr. Bellow Considers His Planet," *Life* 3 April 1970: 59.

6. See, for example, Malcolm Bradbury, " 'The Nightmare in Which I'm Trying to Get a Good Night's Rest': Saul Bellow and Changing History," *Saul Bellow and His Work*, ed. Edmond Schraepen (Brussels: Free U of Brussels, 1978) 28; also see, in Schraepen, Brigitte Scheer-Schäzler, "Epistemology as Narrative Device in the Work of Saul Bellow" 105, 109 and *passim*; M. Gilbert Porter, "Hitch Your Agony to a Star: Bellow's Transcendent Vision" 80, 87 and *passim*; and Tony Tanner, "Afterword" 132; also see Clayton, *Saul Bellow* 262. In *The Novels of Saul Bellow: An Introduction* (University Park: Pennsylvania State UP, 1967), Keith Opdahl aptly points out that "the conflict which Bellow defines . . . lies not between the self and the world but [between] two attitudes toward the world" (28). Opdahl does not pursue the epistemological dilemma implied by Bellow's "two opposing visions" but focuses, instead, on the conflict between contrary desires, emotions and impulses: "To control or to give, to master or to revere, to survive or to enjoy, to will or to love—the center of Bellow's fiction lies within this general tension" (5).

7. *Pascal's Thoughts*, trans. W. F. Trotter, in Blaise Pascal, *Thoughts, Letters, Minor Works*, ed. Charles W. Eliot, The Harvard Classics 48 (New York: Collier, 1910) 9–10.

8. Discussing the influence of Schopenhauer's thought on Bellow's fiction, Stanley Trachtenberg, "Saul Bellow and the Veil of Maya," *Studies in the Literary Imagination* 17, 2 (1984): 39–57, points out that Schopenhauer similarly validates "knowledge gained not through rational means nor subject to the principle of sufficient reason by which we determine objective relationships." Such "intuitive" knowledge, Trachtenberg adds, is wholly distinct from the "pragmatic method, useful in science" (41).

9. According to Sarah Blacher Cohen, *Saul Bellow's Enigmatic Laughter* (Urbana: U of Illinois P, 1974) 180, Sammler's affirmation of the soul's "natural knowledge" is linked to "the Hasidim, the more mystical sect of Judaism who believe that life, although essentially inscrutable, can in some ways be understood through nonrational means."

10. Robert Boyers, "Nature and Social Reality in Bellow's *Sammler*," *Critical Quarterly* 15 (Autumn 1973): 44.

11. Étienne Gilson, *The Unity of Philosophical Experience* (New York: Scribner's, 1937) 184, 173.

12. Cohen adds, "[Bellow] does not consider man's creatureliness repugnant, nor does he deem it inconsequential and focus exclusively on man's higher faculties. Bellow holds, as did Aristotle before him, that the body is not merely a useless repository for the soul, serving only to obstruct it" (10–11).

13. In *Whence the Power? The Artistry and Humanity of Saul Bellow* (Columbia: U of Missouri P, 1974), M. Gilbert Porter also perceives in Sammler's impaired eyesight an emblem of polarized vision, which he distinguishes as "outward" versus "inward" perception: "His good right eye records characters, actions and events in the world around him. His blind left eye symbolically subjects current events to introspective analysis, to historical and philosophical perspective" (161–62).

14. Clayton, *Saul Bellow* 245, also 249–50, 260; in addition see Bradbury, "The Nightmare" 23; and David Galloway, "Culture-Making: The Recent Works of Saul Bellow," Schraepen 59.

15. Boyers, "Interview with Bellow" 19.

16. Gabriel Marcel, *Metaphysical Journal*, trans. Bernard Wall (Chicago: Henry Regnery, 1952) 160–61.

17. Marcel, *The Mystery of Being* I, trans. G. S. Fraser (Chicago: Henry Regnery, 1950): 211–12. Marcel is quoting himself here; the passage is taken from the English translation of his *Being and Having*.

18. I am indebted to Richmond Hathorn, who discusses Marcel's meditations on evil in his study, *Tragedy, Myth and Mystery* (Bloomington: Indiana UP, 1962) 17.

19. Marcel, *The Mystery of Being* I: 212.

20. Gordon Lloyd Harper, "Saul Bellow: An Interview," *Paris Review* 37 (Winter 1965), rpt. *Saul Bellow: A Collection of Critical Essays*, ed. Earl Rovit (Englewood Cliffs, NJ: Prentice-Hall, 1975) 14.

21. See, for example, the psychoanalytic interpretation in Clayton, *Saul Bellow* 238. In "Saul Bellow and Mr. Sammler: Absurd Seekers of High Qualities," Rovit, *Saul Bellow* 122–34, Ben Siegel finds the "strangest misreading" of the novel to be made by those who view the pickpocket as an expression of the author's " 'hostility' to black skin. This 'racist' view," says Siegel, "requires the reader not only to ignore the impressive black figures in *Henderson the Rain King* but also to scan *Mr. Sammler's Planet* with one eye closed" (132).

22. As Nathan A. Scott, Jr., *Three American Moralists: Mailer, Bellow, Trilling* (Notre Dame, IN: U of Notre Dame P, 1973) perceptively notes, "Sammler cannot help feeling a profound sympathy" for the pickpocket. "He recognizes a certain bond of kinship between himself

and this black thief" (141). In "Culture-Making," on the other hand, Galloway says that Sammler's role as "the thief's protector . . . is an inconsistency which the author never resolves" (55).

23. Søren Kierkegaard, *Concluding Unscientific Postscript*, trans. David F. Swenson and Walter Lowrie (Princeton, NJ: Princeton UP, 1968) 118.

24. Étienne Gilson, *Being and Some Philosophers* (Toronto: Pontifical Institute of Mediaeval Studies, 1949) 143–44.

25. To link Sammler with Kierkegaard is not to deny his or his author's Jewish heritage and past. Other critics have identified Bellow's theme with the Jew's history and experience. As Daniel Walden says in "The Resonance of Twoness: The Urban Vision of Saul Bellow," *Studies in American Jewish Literature* 4, 2 (1978): 9–21, "an instinctive faith in every form of life was part of the [Jew's] equipment of survival. . . . The Jew, in the face of the grimness of the Christian world he inhabited, was conscious of the presence of an ideal world within the everyday world" (12). In *The Sweeter Welcome, Voices for a Vision of Affirmation: Bellow, Malamud and Martin Buber* (Needham Heights, MA: Humanitas Press, 1976), Robert Kegan, although he does not discuss *Mr. Sammler's Planet*, notes the relevance of Martin Buber's comments on Hasidism to Bellow's fiction. In *Mamre: Essays in Religion*, trans. Greta Hort (Melbourne: Melbourne UP, 1946) 78, Buber says that Hasidism teaches "the hallowing of the everyday. The issue is not to attain a new type of acting which . . . would be sacred or mystical; the issue is to do . . . the common obvious tasks of daily life according to their truth and according to their meaning" (Kegan 19).

26. Søren Kierkegaard, "Fear and Trembling: A Dialectical Lyric," trans. Walter Lowrie, *A Kierkegaard Anthology*, ed. Robert Bretall (Princeton, NJ: Princeton UP, 1947) 123.

27. Edward Alexander, "Imagining the Holocaust: *Mr. Sammler's Planet*, and Others," *Judaism* 22, 3 (Summer 1973), rpt. as "Saul Bellow: A Jewish Farewell to the Enlightenment," *Saul Bellow: A Symposium on the Jewish Heritage*, eds. Shiv Kumar and Vinoda (Hyderabad, India: Nachson Books, 1973) 19.

28. See, for example, Clayton, *Saul Bellow* 246; Cohen 193; and Porter, *Whence the Power?* 180.

29. Kazin 137.

Chapter 2

1. Ernst Cassirer, *An Essay on Man: An Introduction to a Philosophy of Human Culture* (New Haven, CT: Yale UP, 1944) 16.

2. M. Gilbert Porter, *Whence the Power? The Artistry and Humanity of Saul Bellow* (Columbia: U of Missouri P, 1974) 19–20.

3. Daniel Fuchs, *Saul Bellow: Vision and Revision* (Durham, NC: Duke UP, 1984) 41.

4. Fuchs, *Saul Bellow* 32.

5. Ernst Cassirer, *The Philosophy of the Enlightenment*, trans. Fritz C. Koelln and James P. Pettegrove (1932; Boston: Beacon Press, 1955) 39–40.

6. Porter, *Whence the Power?* 6.

7. Fuchs, *Saul Bellow* 42.

8. As Cassirer observes in *An Essay on Man*, "the only purity that has a religious significance and dignity is purity of the heart," which he identifies as the shared goal of all great religions (107).

9. Along with other critics, Malcolm Bradbury, in *The Modern American Novel* (Oxford: Oxford UP, 1983), views the novel's ending as "ambiguous": it "can be read as a stoical movement toward engagement with community" or "as a dangerous compromise between a broken liberalism and modern force" (135). While decidedly inconclusive, the ending is hardly ambiguous; the radical alternation in Joseph's viewpoint, evinced by the last two entries of his journal, continues to manifest the divided consciousness that characterizes him throughout.

10. Tony Tanner, *Saul Bellow* (New York: Barnes and Noble, 1965) 19.

Chapter 3

1. In addition to the passages just cited, Leventhal's impassivity, indifference, studied casualness, and/or inexpressiveness are noted or described on the following pages of the novel: 5, 7, 27, 44, 59, 71, 98, 100, 141, 171, 203, 247, 266, 283, 290. Passages describing his dread and fear occur almost as frequently, usually in conjunction with descriptions of his impassivity, etc.; see pages 9, 25, 31, 59, 88, 91, 120, 136, 177, 234, 265, 277, 290.

2. As a result of this repression, notes Andrew Gordon, " 'Pushy Jew': Leventhal in *The Victim*," *Modern Fiction Studies*, 25, 1 (Spring 1979): 129–38, "Leventhal alternates between depression and sudden rage, much like Joseph, the hero of *Dangling Man*" (130).

3. Stanley Trachtenberg, "Saul Bellow's *Luftmenschen*: The Compromise with Reality," *Critique* 9, 3 (1967): 42.

4. Sarah Blacher Cohen, *Saul Bellow's Enigmatic Laughter* (Urbana: U of Illinois P, 1974) 60. Schlossberg possesses, Cohen adds, "what Martin Buber calls 'joy in the world as it is.' "

5. Schlossberg's speech, Andrew Gordon points out, is itself "a performance": "Schlossberg illustrates good acting and good behavior through his persuasive rhetoric and convincing delivery. He defends the higher qualities by portraying them," "Acting and Authenticity in the Novels of Saul Bellow" (paper delivered at Saul Bellow International Conference, University of Haifa, Israel, April 29, 1987). Quoted by permission of the author.

6. "Schlossberg's speech," M. Gilbert Porter observes, "ties together a number of related threads having to do with tickets, acting, and the theater, providing what is at last a unifying metaphor in the novel" (*Whence the Power? The Artistry and Humanity of Saul Bellow* [Columbia: U of Missouri P, 1974] 43).

7. See Maxwell Geismar, "Saul Bellow: Novelist of the Intellectuals," *American Moderns: From Rebellion to Conformity* (Hill and Wang, 1958), rpt. *Saul Bellow and the Critics*, ed. Irving Malin (New York: New York UP, 1967) 13. John Clayton, in his chapter on *The Victim*, discusses some of the similarities and differences between the American novel and its Russian model (*Saul Bellow: In Defense of Man*, 2nd ed. [Bloomington: Indiana UP, 1979] 141–44, 151, 157). Daniel Fuchs further notes that Dostoevsky's *The Double* "is the precursor of both" *The Eternal Husband* and *The Victim* (*Saul Bellow: Vision and Revision* [Durham, NC: Duke UP, 1984] 43).

8. The "double" theme has been noted by many critics, most of whom interpret it psychoanalytically. Discussing Allbee's violation of Leventhal's bed, Gordon cites Jonathan Baumbach's remarks, in *The Landscape of Nightmare: Studies in the Contemporary American Novel* (New York: New York UP, 1965) 43: "In finding Allbee in his bed with a woman who resembles the landlady Mrs. Nunez, whom Leventhal has covertly desired," says Baumbach, "Leventhal is momentarily horrified, as if Allbee has in some way cuckolded him." Gordon adds, "The oedipal tensions of this primal scene—finding another man in your bed with the 'landlady' you secretly covet—seem unmistakable" ("Pushy Jew" 134). Clayton similarly believes that Leventhal is "seeing a projection of his own unconscious desires—seeing the scene he wanted to act out" (*Saul Bellow* 151).

9. Stanley Trachtenberg perceives in Leventhal's revelation another instance of Schopenhauer's influence on Bellow. The philosopher's positive concept of "the neutralization of the will through knowledge" is, according to Trachtenberg, here being expressed: "The individual abandons the claim of uniqueness in order to establish . . . universal connections, and so in concert with others he restores the ambition of a meaningful destiny he has had to surrender on his own" ("Saul Bellow and the Veil of Maya," *Studies in the Literary Imagination* 17, 2 [1984]: 45–46).

Chapter 4

1. According to Irving Howe, this theme is central to the tradition of Yiddish literature, which celebrates the "virtue of powerlessness, the power of helplessness, the company of the

dispossessed, the sanctity of the insulted and injured," Introduction to *A Treasury of Yiddish Stories*, ed. Irving Howe and Eliezer Greenberg (New York: Viking, 1954) 51, cited in Daniel Walden, "The Resonance of Twoness," *Studies in American Jewish Literature* 4, 2 (1978): 18. Not only has Bellow translated several works of Yiddish literature into English but, as Walden reminds us, the novelist "spoke Yiddish before he spoke English or French."

2. Matthew C. Roudané, "An Interview with Saul Bellow," *Contemporary Literature* 25, 3 (Fall 1984): 276.

3. Saul Bellow, "A World Too Much with Us," *Critical Inquiry* 2, 1 (Autumn 1975): 9.

4. In "Recent American Fiction," a lecture delivered at the Library of Congress and subsequently published in *Encounter* 21 (November 1963): 29, Bellow says: "Modern writers sin when they suppose that they *know*, as they conceive that physics *knows* or that history *knows*. The subject of the novelist is not knowable in any such way. The mystery increases, it does not grow less as types of literature wear out" (Bellow's italics).

5. In *The Added Dimension: The Art and Mind of Flannery O'Connor*, ed. Melvin J. Friedman and Lewis A. Lawson, rev. ed. (1966; New York: Fordham UP, 1977), see Louis D. Rubin, Jr., "Flannery O'Connor and the Bible Belt" 68; Frederick J. Hoffman, "The Search for Redemption: Flannery O'Connor's Fiction" 42; and P. Albert Duhamel, "The Novelist as Prophet" 97.

6. *Pascal's Thoughts*, trans. W. F. Trotter, in Blaise Pascal, *Thoughts, Letters, Minor Works*, ed. Charles W. Eliot, The Harvard Classics 48 (New York: Collier, 1910): 99–100.

7. Bellow's affinity with the Romantics has been discussed by several critics. In *The Novels of Saul Bellow: An Introduction* (University Park: Pennsylvania State UP, 1967), Keith Opdahl cites Bellow's belief in "the superiority of the concrete to the abstract, the importance of subjectivity, and the rejection of reason for intuition." He specifically links Bellow with "Emerson, Wordsworth, Whitman and Thoreau," who "reject orthodox dogma to base their faith on what is perhaps the source of all religious belief—man's infrequent but persistent intuition of a spiritual reality" (24). In "Bellow and English Romanticism," *Studies in the Literary Imagination*, 17, 2 (Fall 1984): 7–18, Allan Chavkin cites four critics who examine the influence of Romanticism on specific novels (7); he then offers a detailed discussion of the Romantic influence throughout Bellow's canon. In Chavkin's view, Bellow is a "twentieth-century romantic" who expresses "a qualified hope that man will redeem himself and his world by the powers of the imagination" (7, 18).

8. In "Brueghel and *Augie March*," *American Literature* 49 (1977): 83–88, rpt. *Critical Essays on Saul Bellow*, ed. Stanley Trachtenberg (Boston: G. K. Hall, 1979) 83–100, Jeffrey Meyers offers a detailed discussion of Brueghel's painting, *The Misanthrope* (1568), as "a symbolic center" that expresses "some of [the novel's] dominant meanings" (83).

9. Noting "the dissatisfaction many feel with the Mexican episode," Opdahl attributes negative critical reaction to the "shift" at this point in the novel "from Augie's early joy to his later disillusionment and from the Machiavellians as a center of attention to Augie himself" (*The Novels of Saul Bellow* 87). Yet despite the structural and thematic problems arising from this shift, Augie's adventures with Thea's "birds and worms"—her bald eagle and deadly snakes—ring some profound changes on the theme of earthly power.

10. Lev Shestov, *In Job's Balances: On the Sources of the Eternal Truths* (1929), trans. Camilla Coventry and C. A. Macartney (Athens, OH: Ohio UP, 1975) 70.

11. This passage echoes William James, who says in *The Varieties of Religious Experience* (1902), The Works of William James (Cambridge, MA: Harvard UP, 1985): "The early Greeks are continually held up to us in literary works as models of the healthy-minded joyousness which the religion of nature may engender. . . . But . . . the moment the Greeks grew systematically pensive and thought of ultimates, they became unmitigated pessimists. The jealousy of the gods, . . . the all-encompassing death, fate's dark opacity, the ultimate and unintelligible cruelty, were the fixed

background of their imagination. The beautiful joyousness of their polytheism is only a poetic modern fiction" (120–21).

12. Passage cited in Shestov, *In Job's Balances* 318.

Chapter 5

1. Eusebio Rodrigues, "Reichianism in *Seize the Day*," *Critical Essays on Saul Bellow*, ed. Stanley Trachtenberg (Boston: G. K. Hall, 1979) 89. In "Saul Bellow and the Concept of the Survivor," *Saul Bellow and His Work*, ed. Edmond Schraepen (Brussels: Free U of Brussels, 1978) 89–101, Earl Rovit shrewdly hints at another explanation for the reader's "ambiguous responses" to the protagonist: "Struggling to survive in a world which ignores or feels contempt for the values he can scarcely articulate, [Wilhelm] exercises the same fascination on the reader who is simultaneously beguiled and repelled by him. He is an undesirable witness who forces us to regard what we are usually careful to be blind to" (98).

2. John Clayton, *Saul Bellow: In Defense of Man*, 2nd ed. (Bloomington: Indiana UP, 1979) 70–72. Also see Daniel Weiss's study of Wilhelm's masochism, "Caliban on Prospero: A Psychoanalytic Study on the Novel *Seize the Day*, by Saul Bellow," *The American Imago* 19 (Fall 1962), rpt. *Saul Bellow and the Critics*, ed. Irving Malin (New York: New York UP, 1967) 114–40; and Irving Malin, *Saul Bellow's Fiction* (Carbondale: Southern Illinois UP, 1969) 25, 68. Clayton not only diagnoses Wilhelm's masochism but also extends the label to all of Bellow's protagonists as well as to their author. These "pathological social masochists" or "depressive, masochistic characters," says Clayton, betray—even beneath the comic bravado of an Augie or a Henderson—Bellow's underlying sense of "alienation, masochism, despair" (*Saul Bellow* 53, 74, 76).

3. To approach *Seize the Day* psychoanalytically, as a study in masochism, is to dismiss from the outset, of course, the spiritual or religious significance of Wilhelm's suffering. Not only did Freud regard religion as obsolete in the scientific era, he viewed all religion, even when vital to a culture, as a "shared neurosis"—a collectively held "delusion" or set of fantasies tending to enslave people's minds and inhibit their mental development. In Freud's view, as Philip Rieff points out in *Freud: The Mind of the Moralist* (1959; New York: Doubleday, 1961), it is only by analyzing "the human weakness" for religion that it may be "rationally understood" and overcome (316–18).

4. See, for example, Clinton Trowbridge, "Water Imagery in *Seize the Day*," *Critique* 9, 3 (1967): 62–73; Opdahl, *The Novels of Saul Bellow: An Introduction* (University Park: Pennsylvania State UP, 1967) 96–98, 110–15; and M. Gilbert Porter, "The Scene as Image: A Reading of *Seize the Day*," *Saul Bellow: A Collection of Critical Essays*, ed. Earl Rovit (Englewood Cliffs, NJ: Prentice-Hall, 1975) 52–71. Paying close attention to the novel's imagery leads, significantly, to a much more affirmative reading of the novel and of Wilhelm's character. All three critics recognize the ambiguous or paradoxical nature of Wilhelm's drowning—which is, as Porter says, "also a baptism, a rebirth" ("The Scene as Image" 70).

5. In "Water Imagery in *Seize the Day*," Clinton Trowbridge similarly perceives "the saving end of what more often appears to [Wilhelm] as a destructive element—his own intensely emotional nature. He continually blames his failures on his strong and often uncontrollable emotions; yet we are finally made aware that it is just this capacity to feel . . . that makes possible the birth of Wilhelm's soul at the end of the novel" (64).

6. Rodrigues, "Reichianism in *Seize the Day*" 94.

7. C. S. Lewis, *The Abolition of Man* (1947; New York: Macmillan, 1978) 34.

8. See, for example, Weiss, "Caliban on Prospero: A Psychoanalytic Study" 120–21; and Clayton, *Saul Bellow* 70. In "Reichianism in *Seize the Day*," Rodrigues, on the other hand, regards Wilhelm's gleaning of the real "business of his life" as a sign of his potential to break through the "armoring that constitutes the masochistic character." According to Rodrigues's

account of Reichian theory, these "mysterious promptings" arise from the "core layer" of Wilhelm's vital being and signal "the presence of orgone energy" (90–91).

9. Earl Rovit identifies Wilhelm, on the other hand, as "the Bellow survivor." A modern-day Wandering Jew, the burdened "survivor" bears mankind's history "on his stooped shoulders," painfully serving as "the world's conscience and memory" ("Saul Bellow and the Concept of the Survivor" 96–97).

10. Clayton, *Saul Bellow* 72.

11. In "The Art of Dr. Tamkin," *Modern Fiction Studies* 1, 25 (Spring 1979), rpt. *Saul Bellow*, ed. Harold Bloom, Modern Critical Views (New York: Chelsea House, 1986) 147–159, Gilead Morahg goes so far as to identify Tamkin as Bellow's representative of the "literary artist" and "man of vision"—"the estimation of whose work is to be completely disassociated from any moral judgment concerning his personality and conduct" (158–59). Even if we dismiss as irrelevant Tamkin's shady "personality and conduct," the hilarious crudity of his poem, with its baffling syntax and jumbled rhythms, radically undermines Morahg's argument.

12. Matthew Roudané, "An Interview with Saul Bellow," *Contemporary Literature* 25, 3 (Fall 1984): 279.

13. In his study of Bellow's manuscript revisions, Daniel Fuchs painstakingly demonstrates how Bellow makes "the paradox of transfiguration through suffering" clearer in each succeeding draft of the novel. In a penultimate draft of *Seize the Day*, Fuchs points out, Bellow actually spells out the value of Wilhelm's suffering in a phrase that is deleted from the final version: "He sank deeper than sorrow, and by the way that can only be found through sorrow." The meaning of the novel's ending, Fuchs comments, "is clear enough without" this explanatory phrase. "Maybe life's most important work *was* being done in suffering, as Wilhelm once thought," he adds. "This is further evidence that Bellow does not simply regard his protagonist as a moral masochist" (*Saul Bellow: Vision and Revision* [Durham, NC: Duke UP, 1984] 96–97, Fuchs's italics).

Chapter 6

1. Sarah Cohen, *Saul Bellow's Enigmatic Laughter* (Urbana: U of Illinois P, 1974) 119, 142. In "Jewish Humor and the Domestication of Myth," *Veins of Humor*, Harvard English Studies 3, ed. Harry Levin (Cambridge, MA: Harvard UP, 1972), rpt. Robert Alter, *Defenses of the Imagination: Jewish Writers and Modern Historical Crisis* (Philadelphia: Jewish Publication Society of America, 1977) 155–67, Robert Alter notes that Henderson follows "parodistically on the trail of Conrad's Marlow, Lawrence's Kate Leslie, and other modern questers into dark regions" (158). In "Reality and the Hero: *Lolita* and *Henderson the Rain King*," *Modern Fiction Studies* 6 (Winter 1960–61), rpt. *Saul Bellow and the Critics*, ed. Irving Malin (New York: New York UP, 1967) 69–91, Daniel Hughes points out that both Nabokov's "*Lolita* and *Henderson the Rain King* begin with a version of reality that is parodic and farcical and end with a vision of parody overcome and farce turned to real anguish and real discovery" (70–71).

2. Gabriel Marcel, *The Mystery of Being* II, trans. René Hague (Chicago: Henry Regnery, 1951): 153. As Marcel points out, "what we loosely call [the] 'beyond' " has no geographical location; rather, it is the "unknown dimensions or perspectives within a universe of which we apprehend only the one aspect in tune with our own organo-psychic structure" (157–58).

3. Martin Buber, *I and Thou*, trans. Walter Kaufmann (New York: Scribner's, 1970) 66. "Feelings," Buber adds, "accompany the metaphysical and metapsychical fact of love, but they do not constitute it. . . . Feelings one 'has'; love occurs. Feelings dwell in man, but man dwells in his love. This is no metaphor but actuality; love does not cling to an I, as if the You were merely its 'content' or object; it is between I and You. Whoever does not know this, know this with his being, does not know love, even if he should ascribe to it the feelings that he lives through, experiences, enjoys and expresses. Love is a cosmic force [*ein welthaftes Wirken*]."

4. Marcel, *The Mystery of Being* II: 153–54, his italics.

5. Marcel, *The Mystery of Being* II: 152. "In a world in which the arid influence of technique seems to prepare the radical disappearance of intersubjective relations," Marcel observes, "death would no longer be a mystery, it would become a raw fact like the dislocation of some piece of mechanism." He adds, "this world deserted by love . . . is not yet our world; and it depends on us whether it will ever be so" (151–52).

6. Deemed unconvincing and "unearned" by a number of critics, the novel's concluding section is often assumed to have been tacked on by Bellow in a last-ditch effort to end the novel affirmatively. In his careful examination of Bellow's manuscript revisions, Daniel Fuchs finds that the opposite is true: "The ending of [*Henderson the Rain King*], then, is not a case of Bellow writing himself out of dramatic difficulties but a stroke of boisterous lyricism that is part of the fabric of this essentially lyrical creation. The last section of the book (chapters twenty to twenty-two) . . . is the one for which there is the least manuscript material" (*Saul Bellow: Vision and Revision* [Durham, NC: Duke UP, 1984] 119).

7. In one of his many references to the "spirit's sleep," Henderson says, "It's too bad, but suffering is about the only reliable burster of the spirit's sleep. There's a rumor of long standing that love also does it" (78). At the outset of his quest, Henderson knows far more of suffering than of love, regarding only the former as authentic. By the end of his journey, however, he can validate the reality of love—which he knows through experience rather than "rumor."

8. Voicing the conflict between "mind" and "flesh," Paul declares, "O wretched man that I am! who shall deliver me from the body of this death? I thank God through Jesus Christ our Lord" (Romans 7:24–25).

9. Duane Edwards, "The Quest for Reality in *Henderson the Rain King*," *Dalhousie Review* 53 (1965): 248. Like Mr. Sammler, Willatale possesses one "good eye" and a blind "mother-of-pearl eye." Similarly, it is the "closed white shutter" of Willatale's blind eye that, as in Sammler's case, "signifie[s] her inwardness" (HRK 79, 82).

10. According to Duane Edwards, "The Quest for Reality," the Arnewi help Henderson to arrive at "a new level of emotional experience" but do not possess the intellectual capacity to teach him "the next task: learning discipline." Henderson must learn "from the Wariri (and especially Dahfu)" that "the mind [must] govern the passions," that sense must temper "send-sation" (249–50, 255). Edwards grants that the "relationship of mind and body" is "not very simple"; the conventional distinctions he makes, however, spring from the same Cartesian duality that has fostered Henderson's crisis.

11. Henderson's false worship, or idolatry, becomes even more evident in the light of Yehezkel Kaufmann's remarks on the Hebrew prophet Isaiah's denunciation of idol-worship. In *Great Ages and Ideas of the Jewish People* (New York, 1969) 70, cited in Shiv Kumar, "The Hero: A Study of Bellow's Fiction," *Saul Bellow: A Symposium on the jewish Heritage*, eds. Shiv Kumar and Vinoda (Hyderabad, India: Nachson Books, 1973) 140, Kaufmann says that Isaiah spoke against many forms of idolatry including "man's self-deification, man's trust in his own handiwork (i.e., in his technological 'know-how'), . . . his avarice, his violent impulses, his lust to dominate." As should be obvious, Kaufmann's remarks offer a remarkably close commentary on Henderson's traits as a protagonist.

12. Marcel, *The Mystery of Being* II: 180.

13. In "Finding Before Seeking: Theme in *Henderson the Rain King* and *Humboldt's Gift*," *Modern Fiction Studies* 25 (Spring 1979): 93–101, David Dougherty observes that in contrast to the Arnewi, "who fulfill Henderson's expectations and . . . can teach him nothing," the Wariri, "who defy Henderson's expectations and shock his sensibility," can "teach him what he needs to know" (96).

14. John Clayton states the connection between Dahfu's name and his "daffy" qualities, *Saul Bellow: In Defense of Man*, 2nd ed. (Bloomington: Indiana UP, 1979) 168. In "Finding Before Seeking," Dougherty, in essential agreement with Clayton, points out, however, that "it is consistent with Bellow's use of irony for comic purposes that Dahfu is both a crackpot and

someone who can transmit important values to Henderson—precisely because the 'useful' values Dahfu transmits are not contained in what he says, but in the pragmatic consequences of embodying those concepts in action" (97, n. 5). Dahfu is, significantly, the first to recognize Henderson's need not for reasonable instruction but for immediate action and experience. Bellow, furthermore, has Henderson consider the possibility that Dahfu "has lost his head" only to reject the conventional implications of the term: "And when I say that he lost his head, what I mean is not that his judgment abandoned him but that his enthusiasms and visions swept him far out" (235).

15. Wilhelm Reich's psychological theories have been regarded, by most critics, as the model for King Dahfu's "therapeutic" treatment of Henderson. See, for example, Eusebio Rodrigues, "Reichianism in *Henderson the Rain King*," *Criticism* 15 (1972): 212–33. In a later article, "Beyond All Philosophies: The Dynamic Vision of Saul Bellow," *Studies in the Literary Imagination* 17, 2 (1984): 97–110, Rodrigues qualifies his earlier assessment of the nature and extent of these Reichian patterns. As Daniel Fuchs has recently pointed out, the novel's manuscripts reveal that not Reich but Paul Schilder, a neurophysiologist, "was the greater influence" (*Saul Bellow* 111–115). Yet as Fuchs observes, Schilder's ideas, set forth in *The Image and Appearance of the Human Body* (New York: International Universities Press, 1950), have been dramatically transformed by Bellow in the novel. In Matthew Roudané, "An Interview with Saul Bellow," *Contemporary Literature* 25, 3 (Fall 1984), Bellow incorrectly recalls the work's title and author, citing "a book by Professor Schindler, a neurophysiologist, *The Image and Idea of the Human Body*" (269–70).

16. Psalm 19 opens: "The heavens declare the glory of God;/And the firmament sheweth his handywork./Day unto day uttereth speech,/And night unto night sheweth knowledge,/There is no speech or language,/Where their voice is not heard."

17. Discussing Rodrigues's article, "Reichianism in *Henderson the Rain King*," Fuchs aptly points out the limitations of reading any Bellow novel as though it were "there for the sake of Reichian (or Schilderian) ideas; Bellow's character . . . is much more important to him than the theoreticians he learns from" (*Saul Bellow* 115).

Chapter 7

1. Giles Gunn, *The Culture of Criticism and the Criticism of Culture* (New York: Oxford UP, 1987) 61.

2. Matthew Roudané, "An Interview with Saul Bellow," *Contemporary Literature* 25, 3 (Fall 1984): 276.

3. Paul Tillich, *The Courage To Be* (New Haven, CT: Yale UP, 1952) 40.

4. Tillich, *The Courage To Be* 42, 87.

5. Roudané, "An Interview with Saul Bellow" 269.

6. Daniel Fuchs, *Saul Bellow: Vision and Revision* (Durham, NC: Duke UP, 1984) 158.

7. Paul Tillich, *Theology of Culture*, ed. Robert C. Kimball (New York: Oxford UP, 1959) 22–26.

8. For a detailed discussion of Herzog's struggle to free himself of the deterministic fetters of historicism on the one hand and Freudian psychoanalysis on the other, see Judie Newman, "*Herzog*: History as Neurosis," *Saul Bellow and History* (London: Macmillan, 1984) 95–132. In an essay on "Bellow and Freud," *Studies in the Literary Imagination* 17, 2 (1984): 59–80, Daniel Fuchs points out that Herzog, in a preliminary draft of the novel, writes a letter to Spinoza that "undermines Freud's foundation of the unconscious by dismissing" his "biological determinism" and "the programme of the pleasure principle" (63). A summary of the numerous drafts of *Herzog* is provided by Fuchs, *Saul Bellow* 121–22.

9. Tillich, *Theology of Culture* 54–55.

10. Roudané, "An Interview with Saul Bellow" 268.

11. In "Urbanism and the Artist: Saul Bellow and the Age of Technology," *Saul Bellow Journal* 2, 2 (1983): 1–14, Daniel Walden observes, "Herzog, who had accepted reason as his

bulwark of reality, was shaken only when he saw human dignity destroyed by reason—that is, empiricism and technology." He comes to realize, Walden adds, "that modern rationalism . . . represent[s] a form of reality opposing the law of the heart, ['] alien necessity gruesomely crushing individuality[']" (2, 6).

12. Søren Kierkegaard, *Concluding Unscientific Postscript*, trans. David F. Swenson and Walter Lowrie (Princeton, NJ: Princeton UP, 1968) 99–108.

13. The relevance of Herzog's conflict to the situation of the other characters in the novel, and to that of contemporary culture in general, is ignored to a surprising degree by a recent critic. In *On Bellow's Planet: Readings from the Dark Side* (Rutherford, NJ: Fairleigh Dickinson UP, 1985), Jonathan Wilson condemns Bellow as a "solipsistic writer whose novels," having become "increasingly autobiographical," "finally reveal far more to us about their author than they do about the country in which he lives" (26).

14. Fuchs, *Saul Bellow* 130.

15. Keith Opdahl cites some of the early reviewers who "recognize that Herzog finds peace at the end, but reject it as insignificant or unconvincing" (*The Novels of Saul Bellow: An Introduction* [University Park: Pennsylvania State UP, 1967] 143, 179, n. 4). Overlooking Herzog's efforts to discard intellectual formulations, John W. Aldridge, in "The Complacency of *Herzog*," *Time to Murder and Create* (New York, 1966), rpt. *Saul Bellow and the Critics*, ed. Irving Malin (New York: New York UP, 1967) 207–10, mistakes the protagonist's affirmation of being for intellectual self-satisfaction: "At the end the novel heaves a fatty sigh of middle-class intellectual contentment. . . Herzog is finally as arrogantly complacent in his new-found affirmative position, [as] stuck with his loving and erudite self, as Bellow dares to allow him to be" (210). In *Saul Bellow* (New York: Barnes and Noble, 1965), Tony Tanner adopts a more measured tone; he finds Herzog's alleged closeness, at the end of the novel, "to some vague beneficent 'God' " a compensation for social isolation (109). In "The Hero as Jew: Reflections on 'Herzog,' " *Judaism* 17, 1 (Winter 1968), rpt. *Saul Bellow: A Symposium on the Jewish Heritage*, eds. Shiv Kumar and Vinoda (Hyderabad, India: Nachson Books, 1973) 23–37, Harold Fisch similarly observes: "The intensity that [Herzog] discovers in himself at the end [of the novel] does not bring his fundamental isolation to an end." His "affirmation," Fisch therefore concludes, is only "a private, empty gesture" (36).

16. Tillich, *The Courage To Be* 66–67, his italics. "In the neurotic state self-affirmation is not lacking," Tillich further states. "But the self which is affirmed is a reduced one." The neurotic "affirms something which is less than his essential or potential being. He surrenders a part of his potentialities in order to save what is left."

17. Victoria Sullivan, "The Battle of the Sexes in Three Bellow Novels," *Saul Bellow: A Collection of Critical Essays*, ed. Earl Rovit (Englewood Cliffs, NJ: Prentice-Hall, 1975) 101.

18. In "The Battle of the Sexes," Sullivan contends that although Herzog's decision about the flowers "may look like a sign of health," it is not. By assuring himself that the flowers "couldn't be turned against him," Herzog is, she says, "once more sinking into the trap of strategy and tactics" that characterizes the ongoing battle of the sexes (111). On the other hand, I would point out, Herzog resolves to keep the flowers for the dinner table; and this expression of confidence is underscored by his new assertiveness as Ramona's host.

19. Tillich, *Theology of Culture* 124, 142–43.

Chapter 8

1. Demonstrating how "*Humboldt* and *Sammler* are tied together," Daniel Fuchs points to various characters from *Mr. Sammler's Planet*—including Angela Gruner and a man named Pawlyk, "one of Sammler's manuscript names"—who appear in early manuscripts of *Humboldt's Gift*. Bellow, says Fuchs, put aside his "already substantial novel about Humboldt to work on *Mr. Sammler's Planet*," which he completed before returning to work on *Humboldt's Gift* (*Saul Bellow: Vision and Revision* [Durham, NC: Duke UP, 1984] 269–70).

2. See Ben Siegel, "Artists and Opportunists in Saul Bellow's *Humboldt's Gift*," *Contemporary Literature* 19, 2 (Spring 1978), rpt. *Critical Essays on Saul Bellow*, ed. Stanley Trachtenberg (Boston: G. K. Hall, 1979) 169. "Lawyer, literary scholar, anthroposophist, and Fellow of the Royal Society of Literature, Owen Barfield (b. 1898)," says Siegel, "has published [many] wide-ranging studies" (174, n. 24). The author of several books on English Romantic poetry as well as studies of language and poetic diction, Barfield has also written extensively on the philosophy of Rudolf Steiner, whose works are explicitly treated in *Humboldt's Gift*. In a discussion of the influence of literary romanticism on Bellow's novel, "Who Would Not Sing for Humboldt," *English Literary History* 48 (Winter 1981): 935–51, Michael G. Yetman identifies Barfield as "Steiner's most respected apologist in this century and a man whom Bellow interviewed while writing *Humboldt's Gift*" (943). When recently queried about this, however, Bellow said that he did not interview Barfield but only "met with him several times" (Bellow's statement to author, April 21, 1988, at 7th Annual Writer's Conference, Trenton State College, New Jersey).

3. Owen Barfield, *Saving the Appearances: A Study in Idolatry* (1957; New York: Harcourt, Brace, 1965) 62. "*Alpha-thinking*," Barfield explains, is "a thinking *about*." Here "we remain unconscious of the intimate relation which [representations] in fact have, as representations, with our own organisms and minds." The process of "*beta-thinking*" occurs, on the other hand, when "we think about the *nature* of collective representations as such, and therefore about their relation to our own minds." Through beta-thinking, adds Barfield, we remind ourselves "that we do, in fact, still participate in the phenomena." But we "forget it again as soon as we leave off [beta-thinking]" (24–25, 34–35, Barfield's italics).

4. Barfield, *Saving the Appearances* 17. Taking the simple example of a tree, Barfield points out that the tree he sees is "the outcome of the [unrepresented] particles and my vision and my other sense-perceptions. Whatever the particles themselves may be thought to be, the tree, as such, is a representation." The point is, he adds, that "whatever may be thought about the 'unrepresented' background of our perceptions, the *familiar* world which we see and know around us"—e. g., "the blue sky," the "shapes of flowers and their scent," the "faces of our friends"—is "a system of collective representations. The time comes when one must either accept this as the truth about the world or reject the theories of physics as an elaborate delusion" (16–18, Barfield's italics). Thus Barfield employs the theories of modern physics to challenge the positivistic faith— the belief in tangible, visible matter as the objective and ultimate indices of reality—that arose as a result of the scientific revolution.

5. Jeanne Braham, *A Sort of Columbus: The American Voyages of Saul Bellow's Fiction* (Athens, GA: U of Georgia P, 1984) 34, 116.

6. In *Romanticism Comes of Age* (1944; Middletown, CT: Wesleyan UP, 1967), Owen Barfield characterizes the "puzzling" denigration of Steiner on the part of "the educated public" as the "combination of a refusal to investigate with a readiness to dismiss." He adds, "I have sometimes tried to attribute the boycott to Steiner's occasional use of the detested word 'occult' . . . [although] an hour or two's receptive reading would be enough to reveal that, in the context, the word signifies no more than what a more conventionally phrased cosmogony would determine as 'non-phenomenal,' 'noumenal,' 'transcendental.' " While Steiner, Barfield says, employs the term to "signify 'concealed' (from the senses, because by definition not accessible to the senses . . .)," to the educated public "it will still signify 'secret' (because witchery)! And it is the same with the vocabulary of [Steiner's] spiritual science as a whole, which is commonly taken 'literally' even by those well-equipped to know better" (17–19).

7. Joseph Epstein, "A Talk with Saul Bellow," *NY Times Book Review*, 5 Dec. 1976: 93, cited in Siegel, "Artists and Opportunists" 169. Siegel also cites remarks Bellow made in an interview with Walter Clemons and Jack Kroll, "America's Master Novelist," *Newsweek*, 1 Sept. 1975: 39. "Both Steiner and Barfield" convinced him, Bellow says, "that there were forms of understanding, discredited now, which had long been the agreed basis of human knowledge" (Siegel 169).

8. Fuchs, *Saul Bellow* 279.

9. M. M. Bakhtin, *The Dialogic Imagination*, ed. Michael Holquist, trans. Caryl Emerson and Michael Holquist (Austin: U of Texas P, 1981) 264, 286, 366–67. In Valery's criticism Bakhtin might well have detected the objections of a poet-monologist to the dialogic spirit and structure of the novel.

10. Bakhtin, *The Dialogic Imagination* 332.

11. Fuchs, *Saul Bellow* 276–77.

12. In " 'Humboldt's Gift,' " *The Imaginary Library: An Essay on Literature and Society* (Princeton, NJ: Princeton UP, 1982), rpt. *Saul Bellow*, ed. Harold Bloom, Modern Critical Views (New York: Chelsea House, 1986) 179–193, Alvin B. Kernan analyzes the effect of this phrase in another passage from the novel. "Citrine has continually pondered the question of why the gifts of the artist seem never to achieve their promised end in America: 'I meant to interpret the good and evil of Humboldt, understand his ruin, translate the sadness of his life, find out why such gifts produced negligible results, and so forth.' The overhasty 'and so forth,' " says Kernan, "suggests Citrine's lack of desire or inability to get to the bottom of Humboldt's failure" (191).

13. As most readers know, the fictional Humboldt's self-destructive life is based on that of Bellow's own dead friend, the writer Delmore Schwartz. For details on the parallel lives of the real and fictional writers, see David Kerner, "The Incomplete Dialectic of 'Humboldt's Gift,' " *Dalhousie Review* 62 (Spring 1982), rpt. Bloom 165–67; and Kernan, " 'Humboldt's Gift' " 179–181.

14. Citrine is not the first of Bellow's protagonists to be interested in Goethe. Early in *Dangling Man*, we recall, Joseph cites Goethe on the "mainsprings of our earthly life"; characteristically, however, Joseph soon despairs of realizing the German poet's envisioned "connection with the universe" (DM 18, 78). In "*Humboldt's Gift* and Rudolf Steiner," *Centennial Review* 22, 4 (1978): 479–89, Herbert J. Smith draws a further connection between Bellow and Goethe, one that leads to Rudolf Steiner. "Transcendentalism," says Smith, is "a major philosophical source for both Steiner and Bellow," a fact that "best explains Bellow's fascination with Steiner's philosophy." For Steiner the source is German transcendentalism, especially "Goethe's World-Conception"; for Bellow it is American Transcendentalism, "especially the works of Emerson and Whitman." Steiner's view of a "comprehensive soul world," Smith adds, is very "similar to Emerson's concept of the Over-Soul" (481, 487).

15. Cited in Paul Marshall Allen, Foreword to Rudolf Steiner, *The Philosophy of Spiritual Activity: Fundamentals of a Modern View of the World*, trans. Rita Stebbing (New York: Rudolf Steiner Publications, 1963) 7. According to Allen, when the first English translation of Steiner's *Die Philosophie der Freiheit* was being prepared, the author suggested that the title not be literally translated as *The Philosophy of Freedom*. "Spiritual activity" would, Steiner believed, more accurately characterize the book's theme in English (9–10).

16. Barfield, *Saving the Appearances* 140.

17. Hugo Berman, Introduction to Steiner, *The Philosophy of Spiritual Activity* 14–15, his italics.

18. Barfield, *Romanticism Comes of Age* 250. According to Barfield, Steiner's work, *Truth and Science*, "showed that, if we analyse it, the sense-experience from which we take our start [in building up a picture of the world], discloses itself to be no such ultimate element. It may be a 'public,' but it is nevertheless a highly subjective, picture of the world and one which is 'overcome' in the process of knowledge itself. Positivism (and—in so far as it is based on an uncritical acceptance of positivist doctrine—this is true of modern science also) treats this initial experience . . . as constituting also the *ultimately* given starting-point for all reliable knowledge. This was where Steiner differed from them [positivism and modern science] both" (250–51, Barfield's italics).

19. Herbert Smith notes "the high value [Steiner] assigns to thinking" but does not venture further (480).

20. Steiner, *The Philosophy of Spiritual Activity* 79, his italics.

21. In "The Role of Rudolph [*sic.*] Steiner in the Dreams in *Humboldt's Gift,*" *Ball State University Forum* 24, 1 (1983): 27–29, Frederica K. Bartz says, "Citrine is studying [Steiner] to relieve his anxiety over death" (27). Smith less narrowly observes that Steiner's works assist "Citrine's quest for higher knowledge and his attempts to come to a more complete understanding of death" (479).

22. While Bellow demonstrates how reductive is this equation of the heart with a thing or machine, *Humboldt's Gift* testifies to the practical benefits, such as medical technology, that have accrued to humanity because of this view. In *Saving the Appearances*, Barfield also discusses the benefits, "so often and so fully emphasized by others," to which current forms of "idolatry" have given rise. "Surgery, as an example, presupposes an acquaintance with the human anatomy exact in the same mode that our knowledge of a machine is exact" (142–43).

23. David Kerner identifies Renata, "whose name may be taken as an anagram for 'nature,' " with one pole of Bellow's soul-body dialectic. Reminding us of the limitations imposed on human life by biology and mortality, she "remains Renata despite the [romantic] enchantment in Charlie's head, [and] twice she marries death" (163).

24. Fuchs, *Saul Bellow* 334, n. 14. By associating Renata with Ahriman, Citrine registers her intrinsic opposition to his search for higher "wisdom." In *An Outline of Occult Science,* 4th ed. (New York: Rand McNally, 1914), Rudolf Steiner says, "The power of Ahriman in earthly life tends to make the physical sense-existence appear to be the only one, and thus to bar the way to any vista of a spiritual world" (286).

25. Barfield, *Saving the Appearances* 177–78, his italics. Echoing this passage, Jesus, at the end of the parable of the sower, similarly connects the condition of spiritual emptiness with the deafness of both idol and idol-worshipper: "Who hath ears to hear, let him hear." When his disciples ask him why he speaks in parables, Jesus cites the "prophecy of Esaias [Isaiah 6]," suggesting that those who "have ears to hear"—those, in other words, who are not idolaters—will understand him (Matthew 13). "The parable," says Barfield, "was about the sowing of the word, the Logos, in earthly soil. It was an attempt to awaken his hearers to the realization that this seed was within their own hearts and minds, and no longer in nature or anywhere without. . . . Henceforth the life of the image is to be drawn from within. The life of the image is to be none other than the life of imagination" (178–79). Bellow suggests a similar relationship between imagination's iconoclastic power to shatter "the plastered idols" and the ability to hear the divine Word planted within. Near the end of the novel, Citrine says to Humboldt's widow, "Now we must listen in secret to the sound of the truth that God puts into us" (477).

26. Kernan 184–85.

27. Kernan 191.

28. Kernan 192–93.

29. In "*Humboldt's Gift*: Transcendence and the Flight from Death," *Saul Bellow and His Work*, ed. Edmond Schraepen (Brussels: Free U of Brussels, 1978) 31–48, John Clayton finds the "immortality" theme not only unconvincing but deliberately so. Bellow creates this effect, Clayton maintains, in order to show that Charlie's "newfound faith" is only a symptom of "*denial*, defense against anxiety" (35, Clayton's italics).

30. The crocuses may also qualify Citrine's earlier lament: "Ah, poor . . . Humboldt. His flowers were aborted in the bulb. The colors never came into the light" (462). Braham observes, "Citrine's discovery of crocuses at [Humboldt's] grave suggests another flowering of his spirit" (110).

Chapter 9

1. In *Knowledge of the Higher Worlds and Its Attainment*, trans. George Metaxa (Spring Valley, NY: Anthroposophic Press, 1947), Rudolf Steiner instructs a student of his philosophy "to

place before himself the small seed of a plant" and to contemplate both its visible and "*invisible*" reality by picturing the "*plant of complex structure*" that will "*later be enticed from the seed by the forces of earth and light*" (60, Steiner's italics). In *An Outline of Occult Science*, Steiner elucidates the relationship between the "force" of "light" and the human capacity to see: "There lies hidden in what is perceived by an organ the force by which that same organ was formed. The eye perceives light; but without light there would be no eye. Creatures spending their lives in darkness do not develop organs of sight" (86). Echoing Steiner's thought, Ken Trachtenberg says, "The light pries these organs out of us creatures for purposes of its own" (14).

2. While reviewers of *Herzog* tended, to Bellow's dismay, to overlook the novel's "comic portrait of the enfeeblement of the educated man" (Roudané, "An Interview with Saul Bellow," *Contemporary Literature* 25, 3 [Fall 1984]: 268–69), reviewers of *More Die of Heartbreak* were more alert. Even though Terrence Rafferty, "Hearts and Minds," *New Yorker*, 20 July 1987: 89–91, found the novel "phenomenally dull," he noted the "comedy" created when the 'characters' high-powered cerebral equipment . . . gets tangled up in the works" of everyday life. More favorably disposed toward the novel, Paul Gray, "Victims of Contemporary Life," *Time*, 15 June 1987: 71, deemed *More Die of Heartbreak* "a consistently funny variation on the theme of intellectual haplessness."

3. Earlier in the novel, Benn is described as perceiving, beneath the plastic dusting on a Christmas tree, that the tree, contrary to all appearances, is *real*. "You couldn't fool Uncle about a tree," Ken confidently asserts (127). Now that statement must be retracted; having "deviated" from his "original, given nature," Benn is duped by a fake. Here too Steiner's influence seems to be operating. In *Knowledge of the Higher Worlds and Its Attainment*, Steiner distinguishes between a real plant seed and its "*artificial imitation*, which does not contain "*secretly enfolded within it*" the "*force of the whole plant. . . . And yet both [the real and the imitation seeds] appear alike to my eyes. The real seed, therefore, contains something invisible which is not present in the imitation*" (60–61, Steiner's italics). It is this "invisible something" or "hidden design" that Benn has lost the power to detect.

4. The incident concerning Whistler is also described by Owen Barfield in his study of idolatry, *Saving the Appearances: A Study in Idolatry* (1957; New York: Harcourt, Brace, 1965): "When a lady complained to Whistler that she did not see the world he painted, he is said to have replied: 'No, ma'am, but don't you wish you could?' " Both Whistler and the lady, Barfield points out, are referring to the activity—"which in Whistler's case was intenser than the lady's"—of "*figuration*": the process by which each individual perceives and represents to himself the phenomenal world. This activity consists, Barfield adds, of "two operations": "First, the sense-organs must be related to the particles [of light, waves, quanta, etc.] in such a way as to give rise to sensations; and secondly, those mere sensations must be combined and constructed by the perci-pient mind into the recognizable and nameable objects we call 'things' " (24, Barfield's italics). Barfield's account of "figuration" articulates in more philosophical terms Ken Trachtenberg's assertion about "modes of seeing": "that what is sent forth by the seer affects what is seen."

5. Though highly attractive in her own right, Dita Schwartz does not produce the illusion of "perfection." She has been marked, and marred, by existence. Her "scarred" face, the result of "an adolescent case of acne," takes on emblematic significance in the novel. In contrast to Treckie's smooth and "pink face," as well as Matilda's "classic face," Dita's blemished skin, though it causes her anguish, bespeaks her honest and straightforward nature (205, 189).

Chapter 10

1. Martin Amis, *The Moronic Inferno: And Other Visits to America* (London: Jonathan Cape, 1986) 2.

2. Daniel Fuchs, *Saul Bellow: Vision and Revision* (Durham, NC: Duke UP, 1984) 306, 308–09.

3. In her review of the novel, "Saul Bellow's Winter of Discontent," *Commentary*, April 1982: 71, Ruth R. Wisse describes *The Dean's December* as "the coldest of Bellow's novels." Identifying that coldness with the novel's protagonist, Dean Flower, "Fiction Chronicle," *Hudson Review* 35, 2 (1982): 283–85, finds Corde "a wintry-cold saint of composure," a "withdrawn protagonist" who handles his "betrayal" with "almost condescending ease." Identifying Corde's propensity for reflection with Sammler's, Hugh Kenner believes that the Dean's "drear December has left his creator bereft of occasion for the sort of comic epiphany that can salvage all" for the reader, "From Lower Bellowvia," *Harper's*, Feb. 1982: 63, 65. Similar comments on Corde's and the novel's bleakness appear in reviews by James Wolcott, "Dissecting Our Decline," *Esquire*, March 1982: 134–36; Jack Beatty, "A Novel of East and West," *The New Republic* 3 Feb. 1982: 38–40; and James Atlas, "Interpreting the World," *Atlantic*, Feb. 1982: 78–80, 82.

4. Amis, *Moronic Inferno* 8, 202.

5. Although John Updike's review of the novel is full of penetrating insights, he notes only the negative effects of Corde's lack of conflict: "all conflict in 'The Dean's December' is frittered away, consigned to retrospect, allowed to pass" ("Toppling Towers Seen by a Whirling Soul," *New Yorker* 22 Feb. 1982: 123). In "The Graying of Saul Bellow," *Saturday Review*, January 1982: 17, Helen Dudar implicitly notes the relationship between Corde's lack of conflict, or internal friction, and the sacrifice of narrative "sparks." Comparing *The Dean's December*, a "bleached autumnal work," unfavorably with *The Adventures of Augie March*, she says that in the earlier novel "Bellow found a personal voice that struck sparks on the page" and "energized his narrative."

6. In Jo Brans's interview with Bellow, "Common Needs, Common Preoccupations," *Southwest Review* 62 (1977), rpt. *Critical Essays on Saul Bellow*, ed. Stanley Trachtenberg (Boston: G. K. Hall, 1979), the novelist admits to having discovered "some 'clairvoyant powers' " of his own. "I have trained myself in an attitude of mind," says Bellow, "which provides" the "material" of other people's "unexpressed thoughts and feelings." He adds, "It may not be clairvoyance, but I have sometimes definitely sensed that it's a little more than a natural process. Something beyond positivistic, rationalistic common sense, or the clear light of day." To Brans's comment, "That seems a curious thing for you to say, when your books are so full of ideas," Bellow replies: "Well, not all ideas are clear and rational. And not all ideas belong to the modern idea of scientific provability" (57–58).

Although Bellow's experience of being a conduit for other people's "unexpressed thoughts and feelings" is shared by many writers, his linking of this process with "clairvoyance"—with "ideas" and processes inaccessible to "the canon of head culture"—is more unusual. Unlike most contemporary writers, he refuses to attribute these "deeper motives" or "powers" to "the unconscious, because," he says, "that's a term preempted by psychoanalysis," whose "analytic explanation of [the] deeper motives" he rejects. For Bellow, it seems, the "enterprise" of writing is itself a "spiritual activity." While thought, imagination, memory obviously play their part in this "activity," its wellspring appears to be "the soul" itself (Brans 59).

7. In *On Bellow's Planet: Readings from the Dark Side* (Rutherford, NJ: Fairleigh Dickinson UP, 1985), Jonathan Wilson says, on the other hand, that Corde's name signifies his role as yet another Bellovian "dangling man"—"caught between a need for order in his life and a propensity to create chaos" (31–32).

8. Owen Barfield, *Saving the Appearances: A Study in Idolatry* (1957; New York: Harcourt, Brace, 1965) 154.

9. M. M. Bakhtin, *The Dialogic Imagination*, ed. Michael Holquist, trans. Caryl Emerson and Michael Holquist (Austin: U of Texas P, 1981) 292, 353–54.

10. Robert Boyers, "Literature and Culture: An Interview with Saul Bellow," *Salmagundi* 30 (Summer 1975): 8.

11. In "A *Cri De Coeur*: The Inner Reality of Saul Bellow's *The Dean's December*," *Studies in the Humanities* 11, 2 (1984): 5–17, Matthew C. Roudané also finds "Corde's relation-

ship with Valeria . . . thematically central to the novel," which "suggests something of the unifying force of love." Revealing "the depth of Corde's capacity to love," his attachment to Valeria validates the human "possibility of communicating [with] and loving the other" (10, 15).

12. Lev Shestov, *In Job's Balances: On the Sources of the Eternal Truths* (1929), trans. Camilla Coventry and C. A. Macartney (Athens, OH: Ohio UP, 1975) 282, 317.

13. Gloria L. Cronin, "Through a Glass Brightly: Escape from History in *The Dean's December*," *Saul Bellow Journal* 5, 1 (1986): 32.

Afterword

1. Joyce Carol Oates, "Clara's Gift," *NY Times Book Review* 5 March 1989: 3.

2. Sybil Steinberg, "A Conversation with Saul Bellow," *Publishers Weekly* 3 March 1989: 60.

3. Steinberg, "A Conversation with Saul Bellow" 59.

4. Steinberg 59.

5. Ben Siegel, "Artists and Opportunists in Saul Bellow's *Humboldt's Gift*," *Contemporary Literature* 19, 2 (Spring 1978), rpt. *Critical Essays on Saul Bellow*, ed. Stanley Trachtenberg (Boston: G. K. Hall, 1979) 172.

6. Cynthia Ozick, "Farcical Combat in a Busy World," *NY Times Book Review* 20 May 1984, rpt. *Saul Bellow*, ed. Harold Bloom, Modern Critical Views (New York: Chelsea House, 1986) 240.

Index